Advanced Data Processing
in the
University Library

by

Louis A. Schultheiss
Don S. Culbertson
Edward M. Heiliger

The Scarecrow Press, Inc.

New York   1962

PREFACE

The authors asked us to contribute this preface to present the objectives and the methodology followed by General Electric Company personnel in performing its contract on the Illinois Project.

For many years we have been convinced that the larger libraries and specialized information centers must employ new intellectual disciplines to keep pace with the rapidly developing intellectual revolution, and that they must adopt and adapt modern technology to serve the population which creates this revolution and lives in its environment.

Consequently we welcomed the opportunity to participate with Mr. Edward Heiliger, Librarian, Chicago Undergraduate Division, University of Illinois, and his staff in the development of the project as described in Chapter I of this book. At that time our association with General Electric personnel on information handling problems of intelligence agencies and on brief surveys of libraries had shown us the value of the systems approach to library problems. It was also becoming clear that computerized information storage and retrieval operations, while glamorous, were expensive and underused, and that other library operations of greater volume could probably be performed with electronic systems at potentially lower cost and with greater immediate utility.

We subscribed wholeheartedly to the objectives stated in the application for the grant (see Chapter I) and to the idea that this pioneering effort should be fully documented and published for the critical consideration of the library profession. At the same time we recognized that there was a significant challenge to a corporation in undertaking such a project on a small contract.

We proceeded from the view that libraries are institutions in which the public has not yet invested any significant amount of capital funds for research and development, in comparison with the private, corporate and governmental funds which have been expended for many years in research and development efforts in agriculture, chemistry, engineering, defense and medicine, for example.

The first problem we faced was to allocate the project's resources effectively under the terms of the contract. The basic alternatives were to design and implement a particular subsystem, such as circulation, or to spend time in analyzing the major flows of information within the Library. The latter course was chosen because it afforded the potentially greater gain and because little analysis had been undertaken in this area.

After some preliminary analysis, the major emphasis of the project was applied to information flows in two work areas which are familiar to librarians as the technical services and the reference services. Results of the study of the first area showed that high costs were generated in the materials processing activity due largely to disparate, unequal rates of information flow; that is, books, periodicals, catalog cards, and financial records flow through the processing system by separate routes at dissimilar rates. This particular observation was exploited in the basic report.[1] Reference services were given serious consideration and several ideas were developed but these were eliminated from the final report because of their conjectural nature.

Further analysis indicated to us that the circulation function was more closely related to the other technical processes than we had supposed previously.

Recognizing that any preliminary design produced for the report could influence the new system whenever it became operational, we kept two questions always uppermost in our considerations during the study; these questions are fundamental in systems design:

1. Will the system be manageable and economically practical if implemented?

2. Will the system provide the information needed by patrons and staff?

The basic design ideas developed in the report have been applied to other design problems and the available evidence foretold an affirmative answer to the first question. The answer to the second question could only be conjectured. If the answer proved to be "Yes," or "More satisfactory than before," then the Library's data might prove useful for testing of recent work on abstract file structure; if the answer were "No," we hoped that enough information would be obtained to provide a deeper insight into the structure of information flows.

Our effort was limited to a preliminary survey of the Library and to a modest approach to the application of an electronic information system in the Library. The report is concentrated on improving information flow to users and the Library staff members, and the emphasis is placed on frequent throwaway listings of current periodicals received, of new acquisitions received, and of materials circulated; and of annual lists of monographic and serial holdings, with the suggestion that the subject approach be provided by computer permuted subject headings.

Because time and resources did not permit attention to certain important phases of the systems approach to information handling, it was not possible to produce a full preliminary design; and the stages of final design, equipment selection, equipment installation, personnel training and pilot operation were excluded from consideration. Because these phases were omitted from the report, we wish to emphasize the fact that many disciplines are required in information systems engineering. They cannot be provided by an individual engineer or librarian, but require a team effort.

The authors have incorporated the ideas, concepts, tables, charts, figures and much of the text of General Electric's report so satisfactorily in their volume that librarians will rarely need to refer to the General Electric report, and they have added the interpretation and understanding which all librarians will need to venture into this exciting new aspect of librarianship.

We found that the staff of the Library welcomed new ideas and were creative, responsive, and hardworking in their contributions to the Project. Mr. Heiliger and Dr. Robert B. Downs, Director of Libraries, University of Illinois, were steadfast in their support of the purpose of the project. We venture to predict that the stereotype of librarians as conservatives opposed to technological change will vanish whenever librarians are faced with real opportunities to introduce sound technological improvements.

Mr. Gregory P. Williams was designated the project leader and developed the plan for the study and carried it out. He spent many hours discussing the plan, his ideas, and preliminary findings with Mr. Gull, consultant to the project, who influenced the discussions towards the needs of the Undergraduate Division Library as he understood them. In pointing out that information flows in this Library can and should be redirected, Mr. Williams conveyed the results of logical analysis and operations research to both the Illinois and the General Electric project staffs. He was regularly assisted in data gathering and analysis by Mr. Myron Phillips.

Dr. Laurence B. Heilprin of the Council on Library Resources contributed the important suggestion that the Undergraduate Division Library assign some of its own staff full-time to this project, and the adoption of this suggestion made it possible for Messrs. Schultheiss and Culbertson to work several weeks with General Electric personnel in the

Bethesda offices, as well as for General Electric personnel to benefit from their undivided time during visits to Chicago.

During the Project's life, another General Electric team was preparing a successful proposal for another library, and we had valuable communication and correlation with that team headed by Mr. Richard F. Garrard.

During the last month of the project, the draft report was subjected to a thorough review by the Section's technical management, with special attention to completeness, rationale, feasibility and effectiveness; and the portions requiring further attention were redrafted before the report was submitted to the University of Illinois library administration. At all times we had the valuable assistance, criticism and support of our Manager, Mr. Wayne D. Bartlett.

C. D. Gull and G. P. Williams
General Electric Co.
Bethesda 14, Maryland

(1) General Electric Company, Defense Systems Department, Information Systems Operation, Washington, D.C. A Final Report on Improving Information Flow in a University Library, Prepared under contract with the University of Illinois, Chicago Undergraduate Division. Washington, General Electric Company, July 1961. 81 (34) p. Out of print.

CONTENTS

ACKNOWLEDGEMENTS

This book is the final report of the University Library Information Systems Project of The University of Illinois, at Congress Circle, Chicago.

The purpose of the project, funded by the Council on Library Resources, Inc. and the University of Illinois Research Board, was to investigate the possibilities of a total system of mechanization of routines in a university library. This is a paper system and is not in operation, although it is the intention to begin an implementation program as rapidly as possible.

The authors wish to thank all who gave of their time and effort and without whom the project could never have been completed. Thanks are due especially to the staff members of the UIC Library, Miss Marie Rapp, Circulation Librarian, and her chief clerk, Mrs. Phedorah Prescott; Mr. Giles B. Robertson, Head Reference Librarian, the assistant Reference Librarians, Miss Marjorie Bengtson and Mr. Robert Adelsperger, and the Reference Clerk, Miss Geraldine Glover; Mr. Carl Frommherz and Miss Martha Kester, Head and Assistant Cataloger respectively; Fine Arts Librarian, Lloyd Engelbrecht; all for collecting statistics, filling out forms, drawing flow charts, and cooperating, "above and beyond the call of duty."

Thanks too are due the Serials and Acquisitions Department staff, Mrs. Gladys Spargo, Mrs. Mary Lou DeMar, and Mrs. Mary Morris, who valiantly held the fort while both their boss and his assistant spent full time on this project. Miss Frances Stiritz, the Librarian's secretary, and her assistants, Mrs. Kira Gale and Miss Bonnie Snow, should be commended for the typing, filing, record keeping, etc. they performed for the project staff, usually with no notice whatsoever.

We also wish to thank the many librarians from Maine to California who answered our letters and commented on the GE Report so that this book could answer more questions than it might have.

A note of appreciation is due the following publishers for permission to use quotations from their publications: American Library Association, Association of College and Research Libraries; Automation Management, Inc.; Columbia University Press; and the G. & C. Merriam Company.

Louis A. Schultheiss
Don S. Culbertson
Edward M. Heiliger

May 1962
Chicago, Illinois

PART ONE

THE REPORT

CHAPTER 1

Nearly every technological advance in the past eighty-six years has excited the imagination of one librarian or another, and many of them have led to eventual applications by libraries. One example of this is the typewriter. The Sholes and Glidden machine, which used the type-bar principle still in use today, was patented in 1868. By 1873 it was on the market as the Remington.[1] It was not until 1877, during the Conference of Librarians at New York, that the typewriter was mentioned as a possible tool for cataloging.[2] In 1885 the typewriter was discussed at the Conference of Librarians at Lake George.[3] Some of the librarians present had been trying different makes and models and were, at least partially, convinced that catalog cards made with a typewriter were more legible than those made by hand. However, there was still some question about the permanency of the ink.

The first article to appear in the literature explaining an application of Hollerith punched cards, which had been first used in the census of 1890 (and are now produced by the IBM Corporation), was by Ralph Parker,[4] who was at the

3

time Loan Librarian at the University of Texas. His first
experiment, a circulation system, had been installed in February 1936. In 1941, the circulation system at the Montclair,
New Jersey, Public Library was changed to a punched card
machine installation.[5] During this same period the University of Florida Library staff[6] wrote about their experiences
with a mechanized circulation system. The Universities of
Georgia and Virginia had experimented in circulation systems, too. Detailed study of an IBM circulation system for
the Brooklyn College Library was written by Henry Birnbaum
and published by IBM in 1960.[7]

All of these applications were limited to circulation systems, although Margery Quigley, at the Montclair Public Library, originally intended that other phases of library work
were to be included. The only extensive application of
punched card equipment to non-circulation routines in a university library was again by Ralph Parker, this time at the
University of Missouri. Order routines went into operation
in the summer of 1957; the same equipment is now used for
circulation, periodical renewal routines, and the preparation
of statistics.

The problems involved in printing a book catalog from
punched cards have been approached by an entirely different
group of librarians. The first successful effort was the

King County (Washington) Public Library catalog, which was first distributed in 1951.[8] In 1956, two other catalogs were published, the most ambitious of which was that of the Los Angeles County Public Library.[9] The other, from the New York State Library, is well discussed , as are other punched card generated catalogs, by Harry T. Dewey in Punched Card Catalogs--Theory and Technique.[10] This field has not, however, been reserved for public libraries alone, as some special libraries also have been active in this area. Charles A. Vertanes, former librarian of the Long Island Lighting Company, has written of the printed catalog LILCO produced using punched cards and an IBM 407 tabulating machine.[11]

There have been several interesting applications of automation in governmental libraries. One outstanding job of indexing and publishing should be mentioned at this point: punched cards, Friden Justowriters, and the Kodak Listomatic Camera are all being used by the National Library of Medicine in publishing the new Index Medicus. A report on that project appeared in the Bulletin of the national Medical Library Association.[12]

Although there were no plans for implementation, the library staff at the University of Illinois at Congress Circle was aware of the potential of automation from the very beginning of the library. In his first annual report, 1947, the librarian stated:

> Thought has also been given to the possibility of mak-
> ing use of the undergraduate division's extensive in-
> stallation of IBM punched card equipment in the book
> order procedures and it is not at all unlikely that
> some application of this sort will eventually be under-
> taken.

It was not until 1953 that the subject of automation was

mentioned again in an annual report, and then only briefly:

> ...Plans to investigate various types of mechanical
> charging systems, so that the library's present Key-
> sort 'book card' system can be suitably replaced when
> (and if) conditions warrant.

Again, in the annual report of 1958-59, the librarian

states:

> The use of printed catalogs in libraries has usually
> been considered too expensive and too slow. Now,
> with IBM equipment available, these objections are
> not valid. Because the University has such equipment
> available in Chicago, we propose to compare costs
> and consider the possibility of having an IBM printed
> catalog.

The planning, which eventually led to a study of library

automation possibilities, had its beginnings in a library sur-

vey, which was conducted at the request of the librarian. It

was made in 1955 by Raynard C. Swank and was limited to

a survey of the technical processes area. The basic purpose

of this survey was to clear up some inconsistencies in tech-

nical process systems and to bring the UIC procedures more

into line with those in Urbana. In the main, the Swank re-

port recommended changes in paper handling--discarding the

order copy file, use of pre-printed forms, more emphasis on a central serial record, etc. -- and made one observation concerning the "tampering" with the Dewey classification schedules. In his letter of February 24, 1955, Mr. Swank commented:

> First, every modification of an established classification schedule means additional work for the catalogers in the future, since these modifications prevent the department from taking full advantage of centralized cataloging at the Library of Congress. Second, as the library grows, simplifications adopted now might have to be undone and the books redistributed among the original or other similar schedules. By and large, I doubt that any tampering with the Dewey schedule is worthwhile. I have never worked in a library that has not regretted, sooner or later, departures from the standard schedules of classification.

This criticism has serious implications for any library intending to apply any kind of automated system, as one major source of savings in system applications comes through standardization and the elimination of exceptions.

The first step toward automation came in July 1959, when Mr. C. Dake Gull of the General Electric Company met with a group of Chicago librarians, including two from UIC, to discuss the application of computers to library catalogs and routines. This meeting had been set up following the ALA Convention in Washington, D.C., in June, when the UIC Librarian, Mr. Edward Heiliger, and Mr. Gull first met and discussed the possibilities of total mechanization of the

library. Because Mr. Gull is both a librarian and a systems analyst, he was in a unique position to appreciate the
problems of the librarian and to know the value of systems
study and applications to the solution of those problems.
The total systems approach was emphasized at this meeting.

On November 30, 1959, Mr. Gull came to Chicago again.
This time he met with the staff of the UIC library and members of ALA's Library Technology Project. He re-empha-
sized the total systems approach and discussed tape-punch-
ing and tape-driven typewriters; MICR (Magnetic Ink Character Recognition) as printed on bank checks; specific kinds
of computers which would be available to do library work
(the GE 250, which was to be installed at Western Reserve
University in February 1960, and the GE 704, which was
then in production); the possibility of library tools being
available on tape as well as in bound volumes; and cost
problems in each of these.

The second step toward automation came a few weeks
later when the General Electric Company, through Mr. Gull,
offered to supervise the flow charting of the UIC Library's
existing systems. A three-day meeting to explain flow
charting techniques and offer preliminary guidance was arranged for March, 1960.

In accepting this offer, the library committed itself to

spending a great deal of staff time and effort in the analysis of routines. After the three-day training session with Mr. Gull, work was started on the actual flow charting by the members of the department under the supervision of each department head, with frequent staff meetings to discuss problems met in flow charting. In addition, general sessions were conducted on machine nomenclature and technique, and the implications of machines on general library philosophy.

This training of the staff was essential. The importance of flow charting present systems as a first phase of automation (or of good business practice) can hardly be over-emphasized. Improvements can often be made as soon as the current system is accurately defined. To quote from business literature:[13]

> We would like to emphasize that in our experience the successful resolution of any data processing problem depends first on a careful definition of the problem and then upon the most rigid treatment of detail that management can effect. Although today's computers can make comparisons and elect alternative paths on the basis of the comparison, they cannot exercise discretion. Consequently, each possible circumstance must be foreseen and provided for.
>
> This detailed treatment is equally required if simple data processing equipment is to be operated at maximum output. It is therefore hardly surprising that the costs of computer applications studies are recovered many times without acquiring a computer.

Many of the library staff developed a great enthusiasm for the project during the process of flow charting existing processes. Some put in many overtime hours. Articles and books dealing with the subject were read and passed from person to person. This momentum was so great that magazine articles and newspaper clippings on the problems of automation and its application were still being brought to the attention of the project staff nearly eighteen months after this phase was completed.

The basic flow charting was finished by April, and the charts were sent to General Electric's Computer Department in Phoenix, Arizona, for evaluation. All of the charts were accepted after minor changes except those of the cataloging department, which were rejected partially because there had been no attempt to standardize symbols and format at the beginning. Mr. Gull brought the cataloging charts back to Chicago and, with his help, the catalog department recast its charts in a more acceptable form.

At this stage a proposal was drawn up and submitted to the Council on Library Resources on October 5, 1960. There were many reasons for applying for a grant to enable the UIC staff to continue with this work. To quote from the application itself:

The unprecedented growth in libraries over the country
coincides with a serious shortage of professionally trained library personnel. The time is now ripe to adapt
the genius of American industry to the library field.
It is felt that modern mechanical and electronic equipment and systems will be of great service at this
critical period in library development.

This library will grow 1000% in size in less than ten
years. New campus planning calls for 20,000 students
by 1969, with a library building of more than a half,
million square feet (gross). We recognize that such
growth with present methods would require a prohibitive increase in staff members and leave the library
in 1969 at a critical size of 1,000,000 volumes with
no improvement in its operations and capabilities, but
successful implementation of this proposal should put
the library on an entirely new level...

The principles, devices, and combinations developed
will assist this library, as well as all others, to accomplish many of our present functions, meet our expansion of resources, and accomplish functions which
are not yet foreseen. Possibly this will mean fewer
personnel, but certainly more thorough and quicker
service for the clientele. It can possibly mean a re-
direction of our efforts. Many library systems have
grown up over the years without much question of
functions and procedures. The adoption of equipment
and the design of a system require a fresh look at
the library's whole operation.

On December 19, 1960, Mr. Clapp notified the UIC li-

brarian that a grant of $50,000.00 had been made by the

Council on Library Resources.

The library also made application to the University of

Illinois Research Board for additional funds, and was grant-

ed $2442.00, which was to be spent for research materials,

an electric calculator, and to help pay the costs of publica-

tion if they exceeded the original estimates.

The final budget and expenditures are shown in the follow-

ing table:

FIGURE 1

	Estimated Expenditure	Actual Expenditure
Personnel		
Outside consulting	$30,000.00	$30,000.00
1-1/2 man yr. of lib.	13,500.00	12,499.94
Facilities and Equipment		
Automatic calculator	* 985.00	787.50
Electric typewriter	320.00	323.00
Typewriter stand	20.00	22.17
Telephone extension, long distance calls, etc.	566.00	610.00**
Materials and Supplies		
Office supplies, stationery, postage, etc.	None	185.00**
Travel		
Visit contractor, other machine installations, attend professional meetings	1,058.00	1,700.00
Other expenses		
Research materials	750.00	*910.00
Publication costs	1,000.00	† 1,474.39**
Retirement	1,742.00	1,700.00**
Workman's compensation	180.00	170.00
Overhead	2,000.00	2,000.00
		$52,442.00

  * Taken from Research Board Grant
  † Partially taken from Research Board Grant
** Final Bill not in. This expenditure was for the preliminary draft, not for this book, which is published at no
   cost to the project.

REFERENCES

1. Encyclopedia Americana. c1961. v27. p238.

2. Proceedings. The Conference of Librarians at New York. in Library Journal, 2:34, September, 1877.

3. Proceedings. The Conference of Librarians at Lake George. in Library Journal, 10:320-1, September-October, 1885.

4. Parker, Ralph H. The punched card method in circulation work. in Library Journal, 61:903-5, December 1, 1936.

5. Quigley, Margery. Automatic book charging. in Library Journal, 66:803, September 15, 1941.

6. Pratt, E. Carl. International Business Machines' use in circulation department, University of Florida Library. in Library Journal, 67:302-3, April 1, 1942.

7. Birnbaum, Henry. General information manual: IBM circulation control at Brooklyn College Library. White Plains, New York. IBM Corporation. 1960. 32p.

8. Alvord, D. King County Public Library does it with IBM. in PNLA Quarterly, 16:123-32, April 1952.

9. MacQuarrie, Mrs. C. O. IBM book catalog. in Library Journal, 82:630-4, March 1, 1957.

10. Dewey, Harry T. Punched card catalogs--theory and technique. in American Documentation, 10:36-50, January 1959.

11. Vertanes, Charles A. Automation raps at the door of the library catalog. in Special Libraries, 52:237-42, May-June 1961.

12. The National Library of Medicine Index mechanization project. in Bulletin of the Medical Library Association 49:1-96, January 1961. (Part 2 of 2 parts)

13. Eustis, William. A primer to the automatic office. Westboro, Mass., Automation Management, Inc., c1956. p8-9.

CHAPTER 2

One of the most important aims of the Project was to develop new concepts of university library service which would take into account the improved methods of handling and disseminating information made possible by the application of data processing to library operations. It was felt that the university library (and perhaps all libraries) could profit by such advances in a variety of ways. New techniques should not only provide established services more completely and rapidly than ever before, but might provide useful new services that could not previously be offered due to limitations of time and staff. To quote from the original application for the grant, the aim was:

> To develop a philosophy which would be practical for use in college and university libraries. By its very nature the investigation would also indicate what could not be expected at this time and indicate to some degree the aspects which would be useful in given situations.

It is important to point out that such a philosophy is a philosophy of service, not of purpose. The essential purpose of the university library is not changed by the acceptance or rejection of machine methods of operation. The purpose of the library is to support the functions of the

university.   Wilson and Tauber have defined them as "(1)
conservation of knowledge and ideas, (2) teaching, (3) research, (4) publication, (5) extension and service and (6)
interpretation."[1]

The function of the library within the university is affected
by the functions of the university and by the types of students
and faculty members who come to the institution.   Each library gives service on several levels of difficulty at the
same time, with these levels occurring within predictable
upper and lower limits.   As an example of these limits, a
junior college offering largely terminal courses would probably serve a majority of its students on a comparatively
elementary level.   Faculty research would be limited and
service to faculty would probably be at the instructional
materials level.   In such a case, it could be said that the
users would have a low "bibliographical quotient."

A four-year undergraduate college would have freshmen
and sophomores who would make greater demands upon the
library than their junior college equivalents.   The library
would also have to serve the juniors and seniors in addition
to a faculty which would have more research in progress
than their junior college colleagues.   The members of this
group would have higher bibliographical quotients than the
junior college groups, and the library would have to offer a

wider range of services. A large university library has to give service on a still higher level to graduate students and research staff, while continuing services on the undergraduate levels.

The university library, therefore, augments the functions of the university as a whole, and is a service agency which must be designed to give service on the levels at which the users themselves operate. This is a key point in any practical philosophy of library service.

Webster's Third International Dictionary defines a library as a

> collection of books, manuscripts, or other literary materials kept (as in a library) for study or reading or a collection of paintings, musical scores, musical recordings, photographs, maps, or films kept for convenient use, study, or enjoyment.

Few librarians would agree that this definition is complete. In addition to collections of materials, the modern library consists of collections of control documents created to control the flow of library materials and to enable the user and the librarian to get needed material as quickly and as conveniently as possible. These include card catalogs, bibliographies, circulation records, and acquisition and financial records. Without the order, accessibility, and system imposed by these control documents, the collections of materials themselves would be essentially useless.

A library may also be defined as a message center, containing the messages that authors throughout human civilization have written to unknown readers of the future. The primary duty of the librarian, and especially of the cataloger, is to describe and very succinctly abstract these messages in such a way that readers can find them when they are needed, and to arrange them in an orderly fashion so that the message-bearing documents can be found upon demand. The message or information contained within a document is usually more important than the document itself.

A library, therefore, is considerably more than a collection of books, or even the information contained in the books. And it has more permanency than Mr. Hardin[2] indicated when he said:

> We must conceive of the library as a dynamic circulatory system, a channel through which books pass on their way from the publisher to the incinerator.

The service a library can provide to its users at any level, regardless of the excellence of its collections, is only as good as the combination of collections, library staff, and control documents. This is a third key point in any practical philosophy of library service.

There are a number of trends in contemporary librarianship which challenge established concepts of service. There is an ever-increasing volume of publication, especially in the form of journals, and an ever-increasing number of library users. Modern scholarship has become more and more inter-disciplinary in nature, with the result that purely department-al libraries are either increasingly inadequate or overlap in areas of subject interest and require the duplication of mate-rials to an ever increasing extent. There is a continuing shortage of professional librarians for service and supervis-ory duties, and increasing difficulty in competing with other organizations for competent clerical staff. Increases in costs, due partly to higher book prices and salary levels and partly to the increasing complexity of incorporating new materials into larger and larger collections, threaten to cur-tail some traditional library services.

None of these factors is enough in itself to force a change in the pattern or concept of library service, but this combin-ation of factors may well prove to be irresistible. Many library systems simply cannot expect to meet the pressures of increased enrollment, higher academic standards, and an increased volume of acquisition without making drastic chang-es in the established methods of doing things, making budget demands that few university administrations will be prepared to meet, or lowering their standards of library service.

With the exception of the increased volume of publication, all of the pressure factors discussed above are upon the operational, rather than the intellectual, aspects of the library: i.e., upon the staff and control documents sectors. These sectors are similar to the personnel and control sectors of any business firm. In the case of the business firm, of course, the need to provide for adequate control mechanisms, information flow, personnel and equipment, is based on a desire for maximum profit. In the case of the library, these same needs exist, but for a different reason: the library strives for maximum acquisitions and maximum service on a given budget. It is difficult to justify doing anything in the library that does not materially contribute to the acquisition, maintenance, or ease in use of the collections.

In spite of the differences in ultimate purpose, most of the organizational and administrative techniques of libraries and business firms are remarkably similar. Therefore, it seems reasonable to assume that some of the new methods adopted by the business world in the past fifteen years may solve library problems as well.

One of the most important of the new business tools is the electronic computer as a data processing device. The speed of computers and the wide range of routines that they can handle offer possibilities for alleviating the pressures of personnel shortages and turnover, of increased volumes of inventory and user activity, and of demands for more up-to-date records.

Data processing methods offer many advantages over conventional hand methods, but they also impose restrictions
and limitations that are not imposed by hand methods. Machine systems and the routines for their use are not easily
set up, nor are they easily changed. It is true that the
numbers of some kinds of personnel can be reduced. Super-
visory and training duties can be reduced and many records
can be mechanically produced as by-products of an earlier
operation without the need for professional editing each time
the data appears in a different form. However, data processing systems are relatively expensive and do not lend
themselves to small operations that can not keep equipment
busy on a full-time basis. They require a much higher degree of standardization, centralization, and uniformity than
is the case with manual systems, and may require more
rigidly controlled work schedules. Some functions, such as
the machine retrieval of information, may not be possible in
a manner acceptable to the patron unless expensive equipment is available for use on demand. Machines may break
down and paralyze an entire system until they can be repair-
ed. Some operations cannot be carried out by machine because machines capable of carrying them out satisfactorily
have not yet been developed. In spite of these limitations,

machine techniques have been applied successfully to a number of data handling and service problems that appear similar to those found in libraries, and it seems worth while to
study the potential of routines that may suitably be applied to
libraries.

It should be very clearly understood, however, that the
application of machines to library processes will not eliminate professional librarians. It is true that machine applications may reduce the amount of professional time spent in
training clerks and student assistants, and in supervising
and revising their work. But the work for which machines
are most useful is that of carrying out the essentially routine, mechanical operations that should not be carried out by
professional staff in any event. Indeed, the shortage of staff,
both professional and clerical, is one of the compelling reasons for adapting machine methods to library needs.

If machine applications are to be successful, however,
the library intending to adopt them will have to be much
more precise in its planning than has usually been the case
in the past. It will have to develop very clear policies as
to the variety, quantity, and comprehensiveness of the services it intends to provide. Automation cannot operate under
sloppy thinking. Large amounts of money have been wasted
by organizations that leaped into automation without sufficient

forethought, investigation, or analysis. To quote an author-

ity on one phase of this problem:

> The electronic digital computer field has done much,
> in my opinion, to contribute to the furor over auto-
> mation. I do not believe that there has ever been a
> field in which so many amateur publicists and practi-
> tioners plunged in with so resounding a splash--unless
> maybe it was in witchcraft and the psychology of sex.[3]

Any new philosophy of library service incorporating the

automation of processes will have to take into account a

number of factors besides the capabilities and limitations of

data processing equipment if service is to be significantly

improved over that now offered by conventional systems.

These include the growing volume of publication, rising

costs of materials, increased competition for competent staff

(with resultant increases in staff and processing costs), high-

er academic standards, the increasingly inter-disciplinary

nature of contemporary scholarship, the steady trend towards

greater standardization and increasing availability of biblio-

graphic data and services on a national level, and advances

in modern communications.

All of these academic and administrative factors, togeth-

er with the demands imposed by machine methods, indicate

service and organizational parameters somewhat different

than those imposed by conventional methods. Basing its

philosophy of service upon these factors plus the require-

ments of a small urban campus (not to exceed 106 acres),
UIC decided that any automated library suitable for its needs
would have to meet the following service and organizational
requirements:

1. Any new system must be capable of providing the
    patron and the librarian with all of the information
    now available through conventional systems: the loca-
    tion of cataloged materials by author, title, and sub-
    ject; the location of materials not on the shelves or
    in temporary use, the date due, and (for the librar-
    ian, at least) the identity of the borrower; lists of
    books charged to individual faculty members; titles
    on order or in processing; financial data; locations
    and holdings of serial titles, with indication of miss-
    ing issues, latest receipts, bound and unbound issues
    and volumes; as well as workload and use statistics.

2. The new system should provide faculty and students
    with regular information as to the arrival of new ma-
    terials within their fields of interest.

3. Bibliographic input and coding should allow the me-
    chanical compilation of bibliographies and reading lists
    based upon combinations of subject and descriptive
    factors already provided by standard catalog entries:
    (e.g., all of the books in this library which deal with

the American-Mexican War, were published in Great
Britain between 1846 and 1854, and have illustrations).

4. The university library should provide subject indexing
   to the level now provided by the Library of Congress
   and the standard indexing services, but need not go
   beyond that level for the general collections.

5. The university library should not attempt the mechanical retrieval of information in lieu of conventional
   cataloging of publications for the general collections,
   although there may be need for coordinate indexing
   and machine retrieval in specialized research collections.

6. It is likely that the Library of Congress cataloging
   already available in printed form will eventually become available in machine readable form as well.
   This will eliminate the need for cataloging or the
   generation of catalog copy for many titles at the local
   level. Large university libraries should conform to
   Library of Congress standards with as few variations
   as possible. This principle is mandatory if the full
   advantages of automated processes are to be achieved.

7. There should be no departmental libraries. Library
   service should be offered at not less than the divisional level, and every possible means should be taken to

prevent the unnecessary duplication of personnel,
materials, or services.

8. Divisional libraries should be housed in the main
building if at all possible, and information should be
disseminated to faculty in other buildings by means of
printed catalogs and periodical lists, messenger service, telephone and closed-circuit television networks,
liaison staff, or any other practicable means of providing rapid and efficient service.

To recapitulate, the eight-point philosophy of service just
enumerated is based upon a five-point philosophy of purpose:

1. The university library augments the functions of the
university as a whole, and is a service agency which
must be designed to give service on the levels at
which the users themselves operate.

2. The service a library can provide to its users at any
level, regardless of the excellence of its collections,
is only as good as the combination of collections, library staff, and control documents.

3. Except in very specialized situations, the information
contained within a document is more important than
the document itself.

4. It is difficult to justify doing anything in the library
that does not materially contribute to the acquisition,

maintenance, or ease of use of the collections.

5. The application of machines to library processes will not eliminate professional library staff.

It is understandable that some of these purposes may be questioned by other libraries, and that such differences in purpose, together with differences in philosophy of service, will make the machine system based upon these assumptions unsuitable for some libraries. But insofar as others are willing to accept the service parameters set down in this report, the system should be applicable, either wholly or in part, to other college and university libraries.

REFERENCES

1. Wilson, Louis Round and Maurice F. Tauber. The university library. 2d ed. New York, Columbia University Press, 1956. p15.

2. Hardin, Garrett. The doctrine of sufferance in the library. in College and Research Libraries, 8:120-4, April 1947. p122.

3. Myers, James E. Automation. What it is and what it is not. in Special Libraries, 46:308-13, September 1955. p310.

CHAPTER 3

As soon as the library received the grant from the Council, the project staff began to build a collection of back-
ground material for reference use. A systematic program
of reading had already been under way since September 1960,
and an annotated bibliography had been prepared.

Possibly the most important phase of staff orientation was
a series of staff meetings held by the librarian with all the
professional staff of the library to discuss the problems and
opportunities inherent in library automation. These meetings
were continued throughout the study in order to keep the
staff fully informed of the topics currently under consideration by the project staff, and to stimulate staff thinking in
relation to new proposals for the project.

It was evident at the beginning that nearly every staff
member had a different idea as to the goals of the project
and the means necessary to reach them. To help clarify
thinking, each staff member was asked to write an essay of
100 - 300 words on the topic "What I expect the University
Library Information Systems Project to accomplish." These
revealed why some arguments and points of view were being

presented.   To quote from a few of these essays:

> The UIC Library cannot expect to present the library
> world with a fait accompli machine operation, as a
> result of this project, but it can hope to point the way
> through revised routines, revitalized thinking and a
> semantic reevaluation of traditional methods, tools,
> and service to the final future culmination--a success-
> ful machine operation.
>
> > - R. J. Adelsperger

> ...I would like to hope that ways and means of im-
> proving the library image, especially in terms of
> achievement possibilities, can be developed. Perhaps
> release from clerical functions will enable the academ-
> ic library staff to give more consideration to those
> elements necessary to create the proper image.
> More participation in faculty affairs and better train-
> ing in public relations are part of this.
>
> > - E. H. Heiliger

> The decisions which are made with regard to this
> library will, of course, have significance for other
> libraries, even those of different size and type, but
> I do not believe that these broader implications will
> have great importance until any system of mechaniza-
> tion proves itself definitely advantageous in actual
> operation in a specific library situation.
>
> > - M. Kester

> ...It should assist us in improving the fulfillment of
> university and library functions. The accomplishments
> of the project should indicate means of making fuller
> use of library resources at a reasonable cost. It
> should help us to improve our methods--we would hope
> in all departments. It should assist us in raising our
> standards of service, improving our controls, and
> making the best use of our physical lay-out. It should
> make coordination of all library and university services
> easier and better.
>
> > - G. B. Robertson

Although many specific differences as to the goals of the

project existed in the minds of the library staff, it was ob-

vious that one unifying thought underlay these essays: the
project will be considered a success if it helps librarians do
a better job with the resources they have available and that
can be made available to them in the future.

The contractor wished to know staff ideas on fundamental
matters of librarianship. They were interested in knowing if
justification could be made for the very existence of the library and/or its component parts. Therefore, they submitted
a list of debate questions which were to be chosen by staff
members who would present all of the arguments they could
find for their side of the question in a written paper. It was
obvious, of course, that in using this technique some points
would be nearly indefensible and that some essayists would
have to defend propositions in which they did not believe, and
which they knew would be unpopular with other librarians. As
a result of this, the arguments for several points were based
more on emotion than on logic, and other arguments broke
down under the most casual inspection.

Each staff member wrote on three questions and took his
selection from the ones remaining as the list was passed a-
round. In some cases, more than one person wrote on a
topic. The questions, not in the order of their importance
were:

1. Resolved: Each faculty department needs a catalog.

2. Resolved: We should stop binding secondary journals.

3. Resolved: We should stop checking in secondary jour-
    nals.

4. Resolved: We should do away with the library alto-
    gether.

5. Resolved: We should buy cataloging and processing
    from Bro-Dart (Alanar) whenever possible.

6. Resolved: It is more important to serve the faculty
    well than it is to serve the students well.

7. Resolved: The library should buy extra copies of
    journals to put in departmental offices and discard
    them after use.

8. Resolved: The cycle time for a book order should not
    exceed two weeks from receipt until the book goes
    on the shelf.

9. Resolved: We do not check the prices of books before
    ordering unless the acquisitions department thinks it
    might be very high.

10. Resolved: A circulation system should be designed
    which will permit a patron to charge and discharge
    his own books.

11. Resolved: We should do away with all fines.

12. Resolved: The library should be responsible for maintaining a permutation-index skills profile of faculty members for faculty use.

13. Resolved: All acquisitions control should be in the hands of the faculty.

14. Resolved: We need to supply the patron with the location of material in circulation.

15. Resolved: We should charge a fee for bibliographic work done for business and government.

16. Resolved: We will use Library of Congress cataloging as it stands.

17. Resolved: There should be a series of motion picture films and a projection booth, which could be operated by the patron, to give the patron a basic education in the use of library tools.

It is apparent that some of these questions have little real significance for all libraries, while others are germane to the entire library movement.

Between February 10th and 24th, the library's project staff met in Washington, D.C., with the General Electric staff members assigned to the project. During this period several important decisions were made which decided the scope of the project and affected several basic philosophical points.

The most important of the scope limitations was the de-

cision to drop all consideration of reference problems as related to information retrieval. It had been originally thought
that some attention should be given to information searching
and retrieval, but examination of the problem convinced the
project group that the amount of money available made such
consideration impractical. Also a number of organizations
are already attacking the information retrieval problem with
varying degrees of success.

One facet of the retrieval investigation was the analysis of
a sample of reference questions from the UIC library. It was
found that most of the reference questions asked by typical
undergraduate students were vague, couched in incorrect
terms, or were factual questions. Some examples are: "Do
you have any materials on anthropology or civilization?",
"Where can I find a copy of the Congressional Review (Digest)?", "Where is Books in Print?" Supplying answers to
questions such as these would, in the first case, give the
patron such a vast general list that it would be useless, and
in the second case require intuition in order to give a correct
answer. The last question would be so much simpler to answer by conventional methods that it would be absurd to program a machine to answer it.

Another basic decision made at this time was that it
would be desirable to use an electronic computer to manipu-

late bibliographic materials and generate the documents and records necessary for the smooth operation of a library. A comparative chart (Figure 2) was made to show present library systems as compared to both proposed and existing semi-automatic systems and to a completely automated system. It should be noted that manual and semi-automatic systems are centered on the system medium, and vary only in speed and amount of human effort involved. The fully automated system is based on different parameters and is equipment centered. For this reason, it was felt that a project which limited itself to consideration of only semi-automatic systems would find that it was limited to the same parameters that have been the foundation of American libraries since 1876.

The problem of reproducing the card catalog was given much consideration early in the series of meetings. Because the prohibitive cost of reproducing cards and then filing them into another series of catalog trays had already been calculated and discussed in the literature, primary thought was given to using new techniques with present records.

Two methods of dealing with this problem were suggested, explored, and rejected. One of them was a multiple copy microfilm catalog, the other a look-up table to be used in conjunction with the Library of Congress printed catalogs.

FIGURE 2

Operations	Conventional Systems Current Practice	Non-conventional Systems Semi-Automatic	Automatic
Putting information into a system.			
Acquisitions	People	Punched cards	Tape or cards plus Retrieval Function
Identification ⎫ Subject Analysis ⎬	Typewriter Pen and Ink Pencil	Updated punched cards	Telegraphic abstr. & auto-indexing
Input	Paper	cards	Punched cards and punched tape to computer
Arranging	Hand filing	Sorter and Collator	
Storage	Card Catalogs Books	Card Catalogs Books and Punched card files	Magnetic Tape Thermoplastic Film Random access memories
Taking Information out of a system.			
Request Formulation	Patron	Punched Cards	Linguistics
Retrieval	Patron	Collation	Internal Match
Output	Written out	Tabulator Print-out	Computer Print-out
Circulation	Manual	Tab Card Control	Automatic Patron Operated

Both of these methods are discussed at length in the appendix.

The decision not to consider information retrieval as a part of the project has already been mentioned. At the same time the project staff decided that university (and other general) libraries could not afford to catalog to a depth greater than that of the Library of Congress. However, they felt that libraries could make much greater use of the cataloging depth already available to them.

One method made possible by use of a computer is the permutation of significant words. This technique has already been applied to significant title words by Kennedy and Lowry of Bell Laboratories in their index of technical reports. It has been used in the American Chemical Society's new Chemical Titles also. It stems from the KWIC (Key-Word in Context) Index developed by H. P. Luhn[1] of IBM, and uses the significant words in a title or abstract statement, printing the title or statement in an alphabetical listing under each significant word. Each time the entry is printed, the rest of the words in the title which normally precede or follow the word being alphabetized are in their regular place, i.e., in context.

The possibility of using titles to provide additional indexing for the general library was discussed at length, but it was decided that too many general titles have nothing in common with the contents of the book to which they are attached. The problems surrounding the use of subject headings in this manner, however, did not appear insuperable. The first, and virtually only, problem was the difference between the words of a title, abstract, or Uniterm entry which have approximately the same rank, and those in a subject heading which is hierarchical in nature. It was finally decided to treat the hierarchical subject headings as if the words, or groups of words, were of equal rank. In this manner the two or three subject headings normally assigned to each title could be expanded to nine or ten entries in a set of permuted headings created without additional cataloging effort. To get into the spirit of creating catchy names for new systems, the designation POSH (Permutation On Subject Headings) was coined to describe the process.

Several sample pages were drawn up to test the thesis that a POSH Index would be usable in a library. These samples are included as Figures 3 - 8. They include different bibliographical information and different arrangements of the permutation. Entries were taken randomly from BPR (American Book Publishing Record) for January - June 1960. In all, 54 sample entries were chosen. In designing the sample pages, it was assumed that the entire entry would have to be

FIGURE 3

Call No.		Year	Author		Subject
804	T	1959	TATE, ALLEN	AMERICAN LITERATURE -	ADDRESSES, ESSAYS, LECTURES
804	T	1959	TATE, ALLEN	ENGLISH LITERATURE -	ADDRESSES, ESSAYS, LECTURES
204	L	1960	LEWIS, OLIVE STAPLES	CHRISTIANITY -	ADDRESSES, ESSAYS, LECTURES
804	T	1960	TATE, ALLEN	LITERATURE -	ADDRESSES, ESSAYS, LECTURES
350	S	1959	SISSON, CHARLES HUBERT	PUBLIC	ADMINISTRATION
340.094	G	1959	GSOVSKI, VLADIMIR, ED.	TERN JUSTICE -	ADMINISTRATION OF EUROPE, EAS
340.094	G	1959	GSOVSKI, VLADIMIR, ED.	JUSTICE -	ADMINISTRATION OF RUSSIA
804	T	1959	TATE, ALLEN	, ESSAYS, LECTURES	AMERICAN LITERATURE-ADDRESSES
111.1	B	1960	BERGMANN, GUSTAV	PHILOSOPHICAL	ANALYSIS
517	J	1960	JOHNSON, RICHARD E	GEOMETRY,	ANALYTIC
599.744	A	1960	ADAMSON, JOY	OF	ANIMALS, HABITS AND BEHAVIOR
706.994	B	1960	BREMOND, D'ARS, YVONNE DE		ART DEALERS
703	E	1959	ENCYCLOPEDIA OF WORLD ART		ART DICTIONARIES
706.994	B	1960	BREMOND, D'ARS, YVONNE DE LLECTING		ART OBJECTS-COLLECTORS AND CO
704.942	F	1959	FINK, FRANCES SHARF		ART-U.S.-CATALOGS
599.744	A	1960	ADAMSON, JOY	ANIMALS, HABITS AND	BEHAVIOR OF
220.6	D	1960	DAVIDSON, ROBERT		BIBLE-THEOLOGY
016.537	M	1960	MARYLAND. LIB. ENGIN/	CONTROLLED FUSION -	BIBLIOGRAPHY
016.537	M	1960	MARYLAND. LIB. ENGIN/	MAGNETOHYDRODYNAMICS	BIBLIOGRAPHY
016.537	M	1960	MARYLAND. LIB. ENGIN/	LASMA (IONIZED GASES)	BIBLIOGRAPHY P
010	P	1960	POWELL, LAWRENCE CLARK		BIBLIOMANIA
704.942	F	1959	FINK, FRANCES SHARF	GREAT BRITAIN-	BIOGRAPHY-PORTRAITS-CATALOGS
704.942	F	1959	FINK, FRANCES SHARF	PORTRAITS,	BRITISH-CATALOGS
517	J	1960	JOHNSON, RICHARD E		CALCULUS
610.88	B	1960	BREGER, DAVID	MEDICINE -	CARICATURES AND CARTOONS
610.88	B	1960	BREGER, DAVID	ICINE-CARICATURES AND	CARTOONS MED
704.942	F	1959	FINK, FRANCES SHARF	ART-U.S.-	CATALOGS
704.942	F	1959	FINK, FRANCES SHARF	-BIOGRAPHY-PORTRAITS-	CATALOGS GREAT BRITAIN

FIGURE 4

39

610.7	H	1959	TEACHING COMPREHENSIVE MEDICAL CARE	AL MEDICAL CLINIC	COLORADO.UNIV.GENER
706.994	B	1960	IN THE HEART OF PARIS; THE ADVENTURES O/	CTING ART OBJECTS-	COLLECTORS AND COLLE
808	M	1959	PERCEPTIVE WRITER, READER AND SPEAKER		COMMUNICATION
060.58	I	1960	INTERNAT'L. CONGRESS CALENDAR 1960-19/	TIONS-DIRECTORIES	CONGRESSES AND CONVEN
060.58	I	1960	INTERNAT'L. CONGRESS CALENDAR 1960-19/	ES CONGRESSES AND	CONVENTIONS-DIRECTORI
016.532	M	1960	BIBLIOGRAPHY ON PLASMA PHYSICS AND MA/	LIOGRAPHY	CONTROLLED FUSION-BIB
808.06	G	1960	CRIME IN GOOD COMPANY; ESSAYS ON CRIMIN/		CRIME AND CRIMINALS
808.06	G	1960	CRIME IN GOOD COMPANY; ESSAYS ON CRIMIN/	CRIME AND	CRIMINALS
706.994	B	1960	IN THE HEART OF PARIS; THE ADVENTURES O/	ART	DEALERS
128.5	F	1959	MEANING OF DEATH		DEATH
301.152	E	1959	HOW TO HELP GROUPS MAKE DECISIONS		DECISION-MAKING
808.06	G	1960	CRIME IN GOOD COMPANY; ESSAYS ON CRIMIN/	STORIES-TECHNIQUE	DETECTIVE AND MYSTERY
123	F	1960	FREEDOM OF THE WILL	FREE WILL AND	DETERMINISM
703	E	1959	ENCYCLOPEDIA OF WORLD ART 1959-	ART-	DICTIONARIES
463.2	C	1960	CASSELL'S SPANISH DICTIONARY SPANISH-EN/	SPANISH LANGUAGE -	DICTIONARIES-ENGLISH
463.2	C	1960	CASSELL'S SPANISH DICTIONARY SPANISH-EN/	ENGLISH LANGUAGE-	DICTIONARIES-SPANISH
060.58	I	1960	INTERNAT'L. CONGRESS CALENDAR 1960-19/	ES AND CONVENTIONS-	DIRECTORIES CONGRESS
741.29	C	1960	HOW TO CUT DRAWING ON SCRATCHBOARD	SCRATCHBOARD	DRAWING
340.094	G	1959	GOVERNMENT, LAW AND COURTS IN THE SOV/	LAW-EUROPE,	EASTERN
340.094	G	1959	GOVERNMENT, LAW AND COURTS IN THE SOV/	INISTRATION OF-EUR/	EASTERN EASTERN, ADM
340.094	G	1959	GOVERNMENT, LAW AND COURTS IN THE SOV/	EUROPE,	EASTERN-POLITICS
861.2	A	1960	JUAN DEL ENCINA: PROMETHEUS IN SEARCH/	1529?	ENCINA, JUAN DEL, 1468-
660.28	C	1960	CHEMICAL ENGINEERING PRACTICE, V. 11,/	CHEMICAL	ENGINEERING
463.2	C	1960	CASSELL'S SPANISH DICTIONARY SPANISH-EN/	GUAGE-DICTIONARIES	ENGLISH SPANISH LAN
463.2	C	1960	CASSELL'S SPANISH DICTIONARY SPANISH-EN/	TIONARIES-SPANISH	ENGLISH LANGUAGE-DIC
425	S	1959	HANDY GRAMMAR REFERENCE	MMAR-1870	ENGLISH LANGUAGE-GRA
808	M	1959	PERCEPTIVE WRITER, READER AND SPEAKER	ETORIC	ENGLISH LANGUAGE-RH
804	T	1959	COLLECTED ESSAYS	DDRESSES, ESSAYS, L/	ENGLISH LITERATURE-A

FIGURE 5

Call No.	Code	Year	Author	Title	Subject Heading
123	F	1960	FARRER, A	FREEDOM OF THE WILL	FREE WILL AND DETERM / INISM
016.532	M	1960	MARYLAND, U.	BIBLIOGRAPHY ON PLASM/	FUSION-BIBLIOGRAPHY
016.532	M	1960	MARYLAND, U.	BIBLIOGRAPHY ON PLASM/	GASES)-BIBLIOGRAPHY / CONTROLLED PLASMA (IONIZED)
517	J	1960	JOHNSON, R	CALCULUS, WITH ANALYT/	GEOMETRY, ANALYTIC
704.942	F	1959	FINK, F	HEADS ACROSS THE SEA;/	GREAT BRITAIN-BIOGRAP / HY-PORTRAITS-CATA/
350	S	1959	SISSON, C	SPIRIT OF BRITISH ADMIN/	GREAT BRITAIN-POLITICS / GOVERNMENT-1945
340.095	G	1959	GSOVSKI, V	GOVERNMENT, LAW AND	GOVERNMENT-1917 / RUSSIA-POLITICS AND
350	S	1959	SISSON, C	SPIRIT OF BRITISH ADMIN/	GOVERNMENT-1945 GREA / T BRITAIN-POLITICS/
495.918	A	1960	ALLISON, G	MODERN THAI; WITH EXE/	GRAMMAR / SIAMESE LANGUAGE -
425	S	1959	SHURTER, R	HANDY GRAMMAR REFER/	GRAMMAR-1870- / ENGLISH LANGUAGE -
301.152	E	1959	ELLIOTT, G	HOW TO HELP GROUPS M/	GROUPS / SOCIAL -
599.744	A	1960	ADAMSON, J	BORN FREE, A LIONESS OF/	HABITS AND BEHAVIOR OF / ANIMALS -
962.05	W	1960	WHEELOCK, K	NASSER'S NEW EGYPT; A/	HISTORY-1952- / EGYPT -
144	H	1960	HADAS, M	HUMANISM: THE GREEK ID/	HUMANISM
082.2	D	1960	DAVIDSON, R	HUMANITIES IN CONTEMP/	HUMANITIES
500	B	1960	BRANDWEIN, P	YOU AND YOUR WORLD; SC/	HYGIENE
299.7	L	1959	LABARRE, W	PEYOTE CULTURE	INDIANS OF N. AM.-RELI / GION AND MYTHOLOG/
299.7	L	1959	LABARRE, W	PEYOTE CULTURE	INDIANS OF N. AM.-RITES / AND CEREMONIES
607.2	Q	1959	QUINN, J	EVALUATING RESEARCH/	INDUSTRIAL
016.532	M	1960	MARYLAND, U.	BIBLIOGRAPHY ON PLASM/	(IONIZED GASES)-BIBLIO / GRAPHY PLASMA
340.094	G	1959	GSOVSKI, V	GOVERNMENT, LAW AND/	JUSTICE, ADMIN. OF / EUROPE, EASTERN
340.094	G	1959	GSOVSKI, V	GOVERNMENT, LAW AND/	JUSTICE, ADMIN. OF / RUSSIA
463.2	C	1960		CASSELL'S SPANISH DICT/	LANGUAGE-DICTIONARIES / -ENGLISH SPANISH
463.2	C	1960		CASSELL'S SPANISH DICT/	LANGUAGE-DICTIONARIES / -SPANISH ENGLISH
425	S	1959	SHURTER, R	HANDY GRAMMAR REFER/	LANGUAGE-GRAMMAR-18 / 70 SIAMESE
495.918	A	1960	ALLISON, G	MODERN THAI; WITH EXE/	LANGUAGE-GRAMMAR / ENGLISH
808	M	1959	MACRORIE	PERCEPTIVE WRITER, RE/	LANGUAGE-RHETORIC
340.094	G	1959	GSOVSKI, V	GOVERNMENT, LAW AND/	LAW-EUROPE, EASTERN / ENGLISH

FIGURE 6

Subject	Call No.	Author		Year	Title
MACHINE TRANSLATING	410.28	BROWN, A	B	1959	MANUAL FOR A "SIMULATED L/
MAGNETOHYDRODYNAMICS-BIBLIOGRAPHY	016.532	MARYLAND U/	M	1960	BIBLIOGRAPHY ON PLASMA PH/
MEDICAL CARE	610.7	HAMMOND, K	H	1959	TEACHING COMPREHENSIVE M/
MEDICAL CLINIC COLORADO. UNIV. GENER/	610.7	HAMMOND, K	H	1959	TEACHING COMPREHENSIVE M/
MEDICINE-CARICATURES AND CARTOONS	610.88	BREGER, D	B	1960	OH, DOCTOR, PLEASE!
MEDICINE-STUDY AND TEACHING	610.7	HAMMOND, K	H	1959	TEACHING COMPREHENSIVE M/
MEDITATIONS	242	MIDDLETON, R	M	1960	MY CUP RUNNETH OVER
MYSTERY STORIES-TECHNIQUE DETECTIVE/	808.06	GILBERT, M	G	1960	CRIME IN GOD COMPANY, ESS/
MYTHOLOGY INDIANS OF N.AM.-RELIGION AND	299.7	LABARRE, W	L	1959	PEYOTE CULT
NEWSPAPERS-STATISTICS	050.83	UNITED NATIO/	U	1959	STATISTICS OF NEWSPAPERS A/
19TH CENTURY THEOLOGY-COLLECTED W/	210.81	TOLSTOI, L	T	1960	LIFT UP YOUR EYES
NORTH AMERICA-RELIGION AND MYTHOLOGY	299.7	LABARRE, W	L	1959	PEYOTE CULT
N.AM.-RITES AND CEREMONIES INDIANS AND	299.7	LABARRE, W	L	1959	PEYOTE CULT
NUTRITION	641	OERKE, B	O	1960	MEALTIME
OBJECTS-COLLECTORS AND COLLECTING ART	706.994	BREMOND, D	B	1960	IN THE HEART OF PARIS; THE/
OPERATIONS (1941-1945) LEND-LEASE	940.573	DAWSON, R	D	1959	DECISION TO AID RUSSIA
OUTLINES CHILDREN'S SERMONS-	251.027	BRYANT, A	B	1960	SERMON OUTLINES FOR MESSAG/
PERIODICALS-STATISTICS	050.83	UNITED NATIO/	U	1959	STATISTICS OF NEWSPAPERS A/
PEYOTE	299.7	LABARRE, W	L	1959	PEYOTE CULT
PHILOSOPHICAL ANALYSIS	111.1	BERGMANN, G	B	1960	MEANING AND EXISTENCE
PHILOSOPHY CIVILIZATION-	901.9	WEAVER, R	W	1948	IDEAS HAVE CONSEQUENCES
PHILOSOPHY SCIENCE-	501	MADDEN, E	M	1960	STRUCTURE OF SCIENTIFIC TH/
PHYSIOLOGY	500	BRANDWEIN, P	B	1960	YOU AND YOUR WORLD; SCIENC/
PLASMA (IONIZED GASES)-BIBLIOGRAPHY	016.532	MARYLAND U/	M	1960	BIBLIOGRAPHY ON PLASMA PH/
POLITICS EUROPE, EASTERN-	340.094	GSOVSKI, V	G	1959	GOVERNMENT, LAW AND THE/
POLITICS AND GOVERNMENT-1917- RUSSIA-	340.094	GSOVSKI, V	G	1959	GOVERNMENT, LAW AND THE/
POLITICS AND GOVERNMENT-1945- GR.BRIT.-	350	SISSON, C	S	1959	SPIRIT OF BRITISH ADMINISTRA/
PORTRAITS-BRITISH-CATALOGS	704.942	FINK, F	F	1959	HEADS ACROSS THE SEA; AN A/

42

FIGURE 7

ADDRESSES   ESSAYS LECTURES AMERICAN LITERATURE /TATE, A/*COLLECTED ESSAYS* 804 T123C 1959
ADDRESSES   ESSAYS LECTURES ENGLISH LITERATURE /TATE, A/*COLLECTED ESSAYS* 804 T123C 1959
ADDRESSES   ESSAYS LECTURES CHRISTIANITY /LEWIS, C/*WORLD'S LAST NIGHT AND OTHER ESSAYS* 204 L234W/
ADDRESSES   ESSAYS LECTURES LITERATURE /TATE, A/*COLLECTED ESSAYS* 804 T123C 1959
ADMIN. PUBLIC /SISSON, C/*SPIRIT OF BRIT. ADMIN. AND SOME EUROPEAN COMPAR* 350 S345S 1959
ADMIN. OF EUROPE EAST.JUSTICE /GSOVSKI, V/*GOVERNMENT, LAW AND COURTS IN THE SOV* 340.094 G456G '59
ADMIN. OF RUSSIA JUSTICE /GSOVSKI, V/*GOVERNMENT, LAW AND COURTS IN THE SOV. UN.* 340.094 G456G 1959
AMERICAN LITERATURE ADDRESSES ESSAYS LECTURES /TATE, A/*COLLECTED ESSAYS* 804 T123C 1959
ANALYSIS PHILOSOPHICAL /BERGMANN, G/*MEANING AND EXISTENCE* 111.1 B567M 1960
ANALYTIC GEOMETRY /JOHNSON, R/*CALCULUS, WITH ANALYTIC GEOMETRY* 517 J678C 1960
ANIMALS HABITS AND BEHAVIOR OF /ADAMSON, J/*BORN FREE, A LIONESS OF TWO WORLDS* 599.744 A789B 1960
ART DEALERS /BREMOND, D/*IN THE HEART OF PARIS; THE ADVENTURES OF AN ANTIQUE DEALER* 706.994 B890/
ART DICTIONARIES *ENCYCLOPEDIA OF WORLD ART* 703 E901E 1959
ART OBJECTS COLLECTORS AND COLLECTING /BREMOND, D/*IN THE HEART OF PARIS; THE AD/* 706.994 B012I/
BEHAVIOR OF ANIMALS HABITS OF /ADAMSON, J/*BORN FREE, A LIONESS OF TWO WORLDS* 599.744 A123B 1960
BIBLE THEOLOGY /DAVIDSON, R/*THE BIBLE SPEAKS* 220.6 D234T 1960
BIBLIOGRAPHY MAGNETOHYDRODYNAMICS /MARYLAND UNIV. ENGINEERING AND PHYSICAL SCIENCES LIBRARY/
BIBLIOGRAPHY CONTROLLED FUSION /MARYLAND UNIV. ENGINEERING AND PHYSICAL SCIENCES LIBRARY/
BIBLIOGRAPHY PLASMA (IONIZED GASES) /MARYLAND UNIV. ENGINEERING AND PHYSICAL SCIENCES LIBRARY/
BIBLIOMANIA /POWELL, L/*BOOKS IN MY BAGGAGE* 010 P345B 1960
BIOGRAPHY PORTRAITS CATALOGS GREAT BRIT./FINK, F/*HEADS ACROSS THE SEA; AN ALBUM/* 704.942 F456H/
BRITISH CATALOGS PORTRAITS /FINK, F/*HEADS ACROSS THE SEA; AN ALBUM OF/* 704.942 F456H 1959
CALCULUS /JOHNSON, R/*CALCULUS, WITH ANALYTIC GEOMETRY* 517 J567C 1960
CARICATURES AND CARTOONS MEDICINE /BREGER, D/*OH, DOCTOR, PLEASE!* 610.88 B6780 1960
CARTOONS MEDICINE CARICATURES AND /BREGER, D/*OH, DOCTOR, PLEASE!* 610.88 B6780 1960
CATALOGS ART U.S. /FINK, F/*HEADS ACROSS THE SEA; AN ALBUM OF/* 704.942 F456H 1960
CATALOGS GREAT BRIT.BIOGRAPHY PORTRAITS /FINK, F/*HEADS ACROSS THE SEA; AN ALBUM/* 704.942 F456H/
CEREMONIES INDIANS OF N.AM. RITES AND /LABARRE, W/*PEYOTE CULT* 299.7 L789P 1959

FIGURE 8

Subject	Title line	Work	Author	Dewey	Cutter	Year
ADDRESSES	ESSAYS LECTURES AM. LIT.	COLLECTED ESSAYS	TATE, A	804	T012C	1959
ADDRESSES	ESSAYS LECTURES ENG. LIT.	COLLECTED ESSAYS	TATE, A	804	T012C	1959
ADDRESSES	ESSAYS LECTURES CHRISTIANITY	WORLD'S LAST NIGHT AND/	LEWIS, C	204	L123W	1960
ADDRESSES	ESSAYS LECTURES LITERATURE	COLLECTED ESSAYS	TATE, A	804	T012C	1959
ADMINISTRATION	PUBLIC	SPIRIT OF BRIT.ADM.	SISSON, C	350	S234S	1959
ADMINISTRATION	OF EUROPE EASTERN JUSTICE	GOVT, LAW AND COURTS	GSOVSKI, V	340.094	G345G	1959
ADMINISTRATION	OF RUSSIA JUSTICE	GOVT, LAW AND COURTS	GSOVSKI, V	340.094	G345G	1959
AMERICAN	LIT. ADDRESSES ESSAYS LECTURES	COLLECTED ESSAYS	TATE, A	804	T012C	1959
ANALYSIS	PHILOSOPHICAL	MEANING AND EXISTENCE/	BERGMANN	111.1	B456M	1960
ANALYTIC	GEOMETRY	CALCULUS, WITH ANALY	JOHNSON, R	517	J567C	1960
ANIMALS	HABITS AND BEHAVIOR OF	BORN FREE, A LIONESS/	ADAMSON, J	599.744	A678B	1960
ART	DEALERS	IN THE HEART OF PARIS;	BREMOND, D	706.994	B789I	1960
ART	DICTIONARIES	ENCYCLOPEDIA OF WORL		703	E890E	1959
ART	OBJECTS COLLECTORS AND COLLECTING	IN THE HEART OF PARIS;	BREMOND, D	706.994	B789I	1960
BEHAVIOR	OF ANIMALS HABITS AND	BORN FREE, A LIONESS	ADAMSON, J	599.744	A890B	1960
BIBLE	THEOLOGY	THE BIBLE SPEAKS	DAVIDSON, R	220.6	D901B	1960
BIBLIOGRAPHY	MAGNETOHYDRODYNAMICS	BIBLIOGRAPHY ON PLAS/	MARYLAND U.	016.532	M012B	1960
BIBLIOGRAPHY	CONTROLLED FUSION	BIBLIOGRAPHY ON PLAS/	MARYLAND U.	016.532	M012B	1960
BIBLIOGRAPHY	PLASMA (IONIZED GASES)	BIBLIOGRAPHY ON PLAS/	MARYLAND U.	016.532	M012B	1960
BIBLIOMANIA		BOOKS IN MY BAGGAGE	POWELL, L	010	P123B	1960
BIOGRAPHY	PORTRAITS CATALOGS GR. BRITAIN	HEADS ACROSS THE SEA.;	FINK, F	704.942	F234H	1959
BRITISH	CATALOGS PORTRAITS	HEADS ACROSS THE SEA.;	FINK, F	704.942	F234H	1959
CALCULUS		CALCULUS, WITH ANALY	JOHNSON, R	517	J345C	1960
CARICATURES	AND CARTOONS MEDICINE	OH, DOCTOR, PLEASE!	BREGER, D	610.88	B456O	1960
CARTOONS	MEDICINE CARICATURES AND	OH, DOCTOR, PLEASE!	BREGER, D	610.88	B456O	1960
CATALOGS	ART U.S.	HEADS ACROSS THE SEA.;	FINK, F	704.942	F567H	1960
CATALOGS	GR. BRIT. BIOGRAPHY PORTRAITS	HEADS ACROSS THE SEA.;	FINK, F	704.942	F567H	1960
CATALOGS	PORTRAITS BRITISH	HEADS ACROSS THE SEA.;	FINK, F	704.942	F567H	1960

printed on one line for ease of use, and that line length would be limited to 120 spaces, the length limit for most data processing printers and printing tabulators.

The first sample page was made, as were all of the others, on a special sheet mimeographed for the purpose. The sheet has 120 numbered spaces across the top and vertical lines showing the beginning and end of the 120 space line. Figure 3 was organized like the traditional catalog card. The call number is first. The class number was alloted nine spaces, although none of the BPR sample entries had more than seven. Such spacing allows for five figures beyond the decimal point; class numbers going beyond five spaces are limited to four, plus a symbol in the fifth space to show that part of the number is omitted. For example, the class number 371.425747 would be printed 371.4157/, the / indicating that part of the number had been omitted; a number exactly filling the field, such as 711.09773 would be printed in its entirety. With such an arrangement, the dropping of digits would occur only in the permutation index.

The Cutter, or book, number was allowed the same amount of space as the class number. This allows for the initial letter, the digits from a three-place Cutter-Sanborn table, and a five letter work mark. A work mark of that size should be large enough for any library, as this would

allow nearly 12, 000, 000 titles to fall into each Cutter number (26^5 = 11, 881, 376), although certain letter series would
be eliminated due to previous coding: e.g., "Y" following
the Cutter number to denote criticism, etc.

Four spaces are allotted to the date of publication. This
arrangement is preferred to the number of the edition because the date has a predictable number of spaces. The
author's name was given thirty-eight spaces and the balance
was kept for the permutation. No space is left for title, although there were blank spaces left between different classes
of information to increase general readability. Following the
practice of earlier permuted indexes, the alphabetized row is
in the center of the permutation, although this is not really
necessary because the permutation will "wrap around" to
avoid loss of significant words.

The sample page in Figure 4 is exactly like the one in
Figure 3, with one substitution: the title is used instead of
the name of the author. Both of these samples were judged
to be inadequate because both author and title seemed to be
needed. The sample page in Figure 5 gives both author and
title, in the same number of spaces formerly alloted to one.
In Figure 6 the permutation shifts to the left side of the page
and places the alphabetized word in the left margin. The
page in Figure 7 was an exercise to see how much space

could be saved if all blank spaces were eliminated; authors were bracketed with /'s and titles with *'s. Less than ten spaces were saved on any one line, and the copy is very difficult to read.

Figure 8 gives the permutation in its final form. Note both the change in order, the title follows the permutation as an additional aid in subject identification, and the fact that the Cutter numbers have been supplied. The call number is the last item on the line. It was felt that this type of permutation of Library of Congress subject headings would be useful in extending the coverage of subject headings for bibliographies in special areas. The project group does not contemplate using this as a complete subject index to a total collection.

During this study, a brief check was made to determine the frequency with which a subject heading would appear in a special bibliography. The first twenty cards were analyzed in each of the 973.1 and 629.1303 Dewey classes of the UIC shelflist. Specific subject headings appeared an average of 1.95 times in the first group and 1.45 times in the second group. Although this is too small a sample to permit firm conclusions, it can be surmised that the same subject heading would not describe many titles. The greatest frequency any group appeared was six times. The subject headings in the 973.1 class had an average of 2.48 significant words per subject heading, while the 629.1303 class had an average of 2.25 significant words per heading. Permutation of subject headings in those subject areas would not create such long lists as to lose the patron in a maze of paper.

In addition to considering the permutation index as a means of getting more subject approaches for a given amount of subject cataloging, the project group also considered two methods of getting more cataloging done for a given amount of money. The first of these is the method of purchasing books that have already been cataloged and are supplied to the purchasing library complete with card, pocket, due slip, bookplate, catalog cards, and marking. Such a service is now available from Alanar Book Processing, Inc., a subsidiary of Bro-Dart Industries. The second method is that of accepting Library of Congress cataloging and classification without exceptions. Of these two methods, the use of a cataloging service such as Alanar appears more interesting, in that it tends to eliminate the clerical duties of physical preparation (labeling, typing and pasting card and pocket, pasting due slip, and putting on mylar covers) and it provides catalog copy with the book itself. Moreover, there is no physical preparation of cards because they come to the user with call numbers and added entries already typed. In order to test this kind of service, the UIC library agreed to purchase its current American imprints from Alanar on a one-year trial basis. Because the first order was not placed until August 1961, there has not been adequate time or quantity of materials to adequately evaluate the service. However, a few general conclusions can be drawn: one is that it is impossible to avoid some re-cuttering and re-marking unless the cataloging service has a copy of the shelf list and can avoid assigning duplicate call numbers. Another is that unless the cataloging service has an official catalog for each customer (or unless it started the cataloging in the very beginning, and can use its own official catalog), the customer will still have to search all entries against its own records, to be sure that cross references are made, series entries are made, analytics are made, etc., and that the form of author's name does not deviate from earlier entries.

The use of Library of Congress cataloging as a basis for local operations requires more clerical work than the Alanar system (all typing, carding, pocketing, marking, etc. must be done at the local level), but it does offer one advantage over contractual cataloging. This is based on the fact that Library of Congress cataloging is available to the local library before the book is purchased, and that the catalogers can be checking entries and cross references while the acquisitions librarians are waiting for the book to arrive.

Another idea that received a great deal of discussion was that of using liaison librarians to act as go-between from the library to the faculty of the various academic divisions on the campus. Specific duties would include: (1) acquisitions advice in the assigned discipline, assuring close cooperation between the academic departments and the library. Since the book selection by faculty members varies from close, careful control by knowledgeable scholars to practically no interest at all, the duty of the liaison librarian in the first case would be to advise and in the latter case to select all materials to be purchased; (2) to prepare bibliographies for use by faculty members in teaching; (3) to maintain acquisitions desiderata files for their subject area; (4) to assist in the dissemination of information concerning items to be considered for purchase, arrival of new materials, pertinent journal literature, and library policy. This last item is very important, as it is possible to foster good will for the library by introducing policy changes in the proper manner; it would also help to explain current library policy to the faculty.

Wayne State University, at Detroit, is investigating the results of library liaison with its faculty, although their

Monteith Library Project[2] places its emphasis on curriculum

and lesson planning with the aid of project librarians and

bibliographic assistants, who are graduate and upper division

students working under the guidance of project personnel.

Their functions are limited to the preparation of bibliograph-

ies, checking entries, etc. For the purposes of this study,

the function of the liaison librarians would be somewhat dif-

ferent than in the Monteith Project in that emphasis would be

on public relations, and on bibliographic and acquisitions aid.

It was realized that the project's primary concern was

with the analysis and development of systems to help librar-

ians find the right answers by providing them with adequate

control information, and that staff interest in the ideas of

liaison librarians and in-service training should be secondary

interests. Accordingly neither of these ideas was developed

in detail. However, the staff felt that service attitudes

should be mentioned because they can help a library carry

out its service philosophy or make it fail miserably. No

matter how good its basic systems, the raison d'etre of a

college library is diminished every time a student or faculty

member fails to come back for a second book or a second

answer.

Another non-systems factor that might have a bearing on

the effectiveness of present and future library service is

that of speed reading. Special schools have sprung up all over the country, offering to increase reading speed to heights undreamed of a few years ago. The method developed by Evelyn Neilsen Wood claims results ranging up to 15,000 words per minute. Colleges and high schools have shifted the reading course emphasis from remedial reading for the slower students to courses intended to speed up the reading of all students, and these courses are filled to capacity.

The project staff came to the conclusion that libraries are really not faced with the prospects of being overwhelmed by patrons making impossible demands upon the book collections and the circulation system. The type of material that university students are required to use ordinarily requires more than just reading through. If a speed reading course raises a student's speed from 200 to 500 words per minute and his comprehension from 65 to 95 percent, the result may well be a better student who spends less time on his lessons. It seems probable that the majority of reading course students will advance in reading speed, but not to a point that will significantly affect circulation figures.

REFERENCES

1. Luhn, H. P.   Keyword-in-context index for technical
    literature.   Yorktown Heights, New York, International
    Business Machines Corporation, 1959.

2. Knapp, Patricia B.   The Monteith library project: an
    experiment in library-college relationship. in College
    and Research Libraries, 22:256-63†, July 1961.

CHAPTER 4

One of the most important and time consuming jobs of the systems project staff was that of gathering data. These data were divided into two groups: 1) statistical, which included frequency counts for both circulation and cataloging, cost information for all departmental operations, and figures taken from past reports, and 2) organizational data, which includes reference and other service questions, library organization, and statements on operations taken from past reports.

Current statistics from both the circulation and cataloging departments were needed in order to calculate personnel work loads and the unit costs of specific operations. In order to collect these statistics, tally sheets had to be supplied for departmental workers to fill out as they finished various tasks. Proposed tally sheets were designed by the project staff and submitted to the department head for review. This process was repeated until both the project and the department agreed that all pertinent information was included.

The circulation department tally sheets were designed by interviewing all members of the circulation staff and making a list of all of the operations they performed. These were

then listed under broad headings with a column for each day
of the working week and one for totals. All circulation operations were included on this list, regardless of whether or
not they were performed at the main circulation desk. At
first there was serious consideration given to designing a
separate form for each position in the circulation area, but
the final form contained the total list and a separate set was
given to each staff member for the daily recording of those
operations he performed. Figures 9 and 9A show the final
circulation tally sheets. At the end of each week all individual sets of charts were totaled and entered on a weekly master chart and the daily charts were discarded. The fine arts
reading room used the same sheets as the main circulation
department, and the headings unique to fine arts were included in the list.

The tally sheets for the cataloging department were pat-
terned after the action boxes on its flow charts. These
sheets were complicated by the fact that the work flow in
the catalog department consists of three separate kinds of
materials: books, work slips, and catalog cards. In order
to keep these three flows separated (in spite of the fact that
they were all shown on the same set of flow charts), it was
decided to enter the flow of work slips on a separate sheet.
Figure 10 is the sheet for tallying the operations dealing with

decks of manifold slips as they arrive from the acquisitions department. The original plan was to tally manifold sets in units of 100 sets until 1,000 sets were included.

The book flow on the cataloging flow charts was split into two parts: gift monographs and purchased monographs. The steps for handling the books were put on the tally sheets in the order in which the catalog department performed them. The numerical arrangement of the flow chart boxes was ignored, as they had originally been numbered purely for convenience rather than to correspond with work flow. In the two tally columns to the right of the sheet (Figure 10A) blanks were supplied only where applicable. At this point, the steps for ordering and handling catalog cards were included in the tally sheets for both manifold sets and books. It was assumed at this time that the catalogers could make a tally mark each time they acted on a particular book in a group, but they soon found that the books in each group of 100 became so scattered, due to the great number of actions taken on each item by different members of the catalog department staff, that the lists could not be kept together.

The catalogers then suggested that two different sheets be designed, one for the gift monographs and another for the purchased monographs (which are distinguished by the number of slips accompanying the monograph to the catalog de-

FIGURE 9

UNIVERSITY OF ILLINOIS
CHICAGO UNDERGRADUATE DIVISION   Week of _____

CIRCULATION DEPARTMENT
STATISTICAL WORK SHEET

	Mon.	Tues.	Wed.	Thurs.	Fri.	Total
BINDERY						
Sent from Circulation						
CHARGES						
Chess sets						
General books--						
Faculty						
Students						
Language tapes--						
Students listening						
Number played						
Maps						
Newspapers						
Pamphlets						
Paperbacks						
Periodicals						
Phonodiscs played						
Reserve, overnight						

FIGURE 9 (cont.)

	Mon.	Tues.	Wed.	Thurs.	Fri.	Total
Reserve, room use						
Art reproductions						
Earphones used						
Phonodiscs played						
Scores						
CIRCULATION RECORDS						
Time spent--						
Plugging holes						
Sorting cards						
Counting cards						
Filing cards						
EXTENSION COURSES						
Number of exams						
FACULTY LOANS						
Number called in						
FINES						
Cards sent to office						
HOLD CARDS						
Number received						
Number sent						

FIGURE 9A

CIRCULATION DEPARTMENT
STATISTICAL WORK SHEET   Week of _____

	Mon.	Tues.	Wed.	Thurs.	Fri.	Total
INTERLIBRARY LOANS						
Requested						
Sent						
Requests						
Requests granted						
Received						
LOST BOOKS						
Number lost and paid						
OVERDUES						
Number of books						
Cards typed						
First notices sent						
Second notices sent						
Third notices sent						
Time spent						
Letters sent (end of semester)						

FIGURE 9A (cont.)

	Mon.	Tues.	Wed.	Thurs.	Fri.	Total
QUESTIONS ANSWERED						
Directional information						
Reference information						
Refer to Ref. Dept.						
Fine Arts reference						
Refer to Fine Arts						
Circulation questions						
Catalog questions						
RESERVE BOOKS-- PLACING ON RESERVE						
Number of lists received						
Number of books placed on reserve						
Time spent						
SEARCHES, CIRCU- LATION FILE						
Number of books reported on on shelves						
Renewals						

FIGURE 9A (cont.)

	Mon.	Tues.	Wed.	Thurs.	Fri.	Total
Number of tag holds						
STACK SEARCHES						
Number of books searched						
STUDENT WITH-DRAWALS						

FIGURE 10

OUT OF GROUPS OF 100 FIVE-SLIP MANIFOLD DECKS
(LINE I), HOW MANY:

TOTAL COUNT _____

76 Unit card main entry in catalog?)
                                     (
26 Discard one slip to surplus   )   _____

77 Purchase order record here?)
)
27 Stamp one slip "on order"   (
)
 5 File into main catalog   )   _____

78 Order LC cards?)
                   (
45 Start LC deal   )   _____

47 Discard one slip to surplus   _____

79 Cutter?   )
                          (
28 Cutter on one slip)   _____

48 File (ITEM 50: Hold file)   _____

 8 LC reply to order for cards   _____

86 Cards with LC deal?   )
                                           (
52 Search entries, record on top card)   _____

53 Check hold shelf   _____

85 Book with slips found?   )
)
56 Add LC deal to book & slips   (_____
)
75 Forward book, slips and LC)
      deal to cataloger   )

57 Check hold slips file   _____

FIGURE 10 (cont.)

87 Remaining 3 slips found?
   (ITEM 50: Hold file)
                            _____

88 Only one slip found?   )
                                 (
59 Hold LC deal; re-check daily)   _____

89 Book order cancelled?   )
                                 (
60 Destroy slip & LC deal; out)   _____

FIGURE 10A

OUT OF GROUPS OF 100 BOOKS (LINES II & III),
HOW MANY:

TOTAL COUNT _____

	LINE II	LINE III
76 Unit card main entry in catalog?	_____	_____
26 Discard one slip to surplus	_____	
25 Stamp one slip "catalog")		
5 File into main catalog)	_____	
78 Order LC cards?)		
45 Start LC deal)	_____	
47 Discard one slip to surplus?	_____	
79 Cutter?)		
28 Cutter on one slip)	_____	
80 Book here	_____	_____
81 Remaining 3 slips in book?	_____	
84 Order LC cards?	_____	
46 Pull one slip from surplus		_____
45 Start LC deal	_____	_____
82 LC cards on order?		_____
57 Check hold slips file		_____
87 Remaining 3 slips found?		_____
88 Only one slip found?		_____
58 Hold books; recheck daily		_____
51 Add slips to book and/or LC		_____
83 Rush books?		_____
54 Shelve on hold shelf	_____	_____
8 LC replies to order	_____	_____
86 Cards with LC deal?	_____	_____
52 Search entries; record on top card	_____	_____
53 Check hold shelf	_____	_____
85 Book with slip found?	_____	_____
56 Add LC deal to book & slips	_____	_____
75 Forward book, etc. to cataloger	_____	_____
91 Rush book?	_____	_____
92 Completely new title?	_____	_____
29 Pull kindred slip, etc.	_____	_____
99 Unit entry identical?	_____	_____
100 Added part or volume?	_____	_____
93 Exact copy with book?	_____	_____
30 Begin copy search	_____	_____

FIGURE 10A (cont.)

	LINE II	LINE III
94 Exact copy found?	_____	_____
96 LC card (copy) found?	_____	_____
95 Kindred copy found?	_____	_____
31 Prepare copy?	_____	_____
97 Order LC card?	_____	_____
32 Transcribe copy	_____	_____
34 Pull tracing record, all cards	_____	_____
35 Suggest changes on work slip	_____	_____
98 All entries verified?	_____	_____
33 Search all entries	_____	_____
101 Tentative call no. available?	_____	_____
36 Classify, using DC tables)		
37 Add tent. call no. to slip)	_____	_____
102 Tent. call no. accepted?	_____	_____
38 Search & refine call no.	_____	_____
39 Assign definitive call no.)		
40 Record in book & on slips)		
41 Count for book statistics)		
103 Book for reference?	_____	_____
42 Pull blanks from stock)	_____	_____
43 Type card and pocket)		
44 Paste pocket & date due slip)		
69 Label spine	_____	_____
104 Book preparation correct?	_____	_____
70 Correct errors	_____	_____
73 Send book and faculty slip	_____	_____
to Circulation Department		
71 File Rush (Main Catalog)	_____	_____
72 File Rush (Shelf List)	_____	_____
74 Work slip with copy?	_____	_____
with LC cards?	_____	_____
105 Was book rushed?	_____	_____
11 (Card and slips to) RUSH	_____	_____
hold file		
120 Workslip & copy to typist	_____	_____
106 Typing correct?	_____	_____
121 Correct typing	_____	_____
122 Record card statistics	_____	_____
124 Arrange and file cards)	_____	_____
125 Pull and discard slips)		
107 Guide cards needed?	_____	_____

FIGURE 10A (cont.)

IF ANSWER (ITEM 107) IS YES, HOW MANY:

126 Pull stock; type guide cards   _____ _____
106 Typing correct?   _____ _____
121 Correct typing   _____ _____
124 Arrange & file (guide cards)   _____ _____

partment), and that these sheets be numbered and placed in the book itself, so that every person performing an operation could mark the tally columns without looking for the tally sheet.

The date the book came to cataloging for processing, the date it went to circulation, and the date the cards were filed in the catalog were added to the forms and provided some interesting information on elapsed time.

The final forms, Figures 10B and 10C, were laid out using the same terminology as the original form. Lines were numbered consecutively, in addition to bearing the numbers of the flow chart boxes. The old form was kept as a summary sheet.

Unfortunately, the final sheets were still too complicated for easy use. The project staff had felt that little cataloging time would be used in making the tallies, although complaints from the catalog department staff indicated otherwise. By the time enough samples had come through to show that the catalogers were right, there was not enough time left to redesign the forms again and still have a significant sample of books and slips completing the cataloging cycle. If this study were repeated, the forms would be completely reworded, with many steps either combined or eliminated to reduce the total number of actions to be tallied, and more time would be allowed so that a greater number of items could be sent through the complete cycle. As a result of the complication of the sheets, there was some inaccuracy in the tallies.

As indicated in Chapter 2, the reference department kept records of all reference questions asked over a twelve day period. Original plans had centered around the use of a concealed microphone leading to a tape recorder, then around the use of portable tape recorders that the reference librarians could carry with them. Unfortunately, suitable machines could not be acquired on a rental basis. Therefore the reference staff volunteered to write the questions on slips of paper as the patron asked his question. This proved satisfactory, and 832 questions were recorded in a 12 day period. Several other questions were written up in such a manner as to record all conversation between the patron and the librarian as they dealt with a more complicated reference question. The first fifty-eight of the 832 questions are included in the appendix. These represent the first day's intake of questions.

No special forms had to be made or extra work done to accumulate data from the serials and acquisition department, as detailed figures were already available for this area.

It was found that existing statistical material should not be slighted when gathering information about library departments, as many departments already keep daily, weekly, monthly, or annual statistical summaries. All departments make annual reports to the librarian, and a great deal of information on policy and departmental operations can be reconstructed from a careful study of these reports. The annual report of the librarian and of the university, or taxing body, are of value, especially for the financial information they contain.

Organization charts are important to a library and to that library's personnel in several ways. They show graphically the positions within the organization, the working relationships between one position and another, staff and line relationships, and to a degree, at least, the boundries of responsibility for each position. One of the first analytical tasks the project staff undertook was drawing a complete set of organization charts for the UIC library at the time of the project, as it was expected to be at the end of phase 1 of new campus construction, and as it was expected to be at the time of the library's full administrative development.

Figure 11 shows present organization; Figure 12 is projected
to 1964; and Figure 13 assumes final building construction and
20,000 students after six years on a new campus. Both the
1964 and the 1970 charts may very well change.

The project staff members from General Electric and from
the UIC Library would never have been able to gather the information necessary for the study in the short time allotted
them without the enthusiastic support of all the staff of the
library. Starting with the initial flow charting, the amount
of overtime put in by department heads and other professional staff members, and the amount of time they took from
their regular duties to furnish those bits of information which
only they could supply, was amazing and encouraging. The
clerical staff, on whom most of the burden fell for keeping
the day to day statistics, also did yeoman service. Any
library that undertakes a major systems study and does not
get such support from all of its staff will not, in any probability, be able to either complete or implement the study
successfully. Everyone must be convinced of the value of
the study and be willing to go out of his way to see that the
understanding necessary for success is achieved.

FIGURE 10B

UNIVERSITY OF ILLINOIS   GIFT MONOGRAPH
Chicago Undergraduate Division   (WITH SLIPS)

Catalog Department 13 86 Cards with LC
Statistical   deal.   _____
Work Sheet

14 52 Search entries;
record on top
Item Number   GIFT MONO-   card.   _____
GRAPH
(WITH SLIPS) 15 53 Check hold shelf. ____

Date Started _____
16 85 Book with slips
1 76 Unit card main _____   found?   _____
entry in catalog?
2 26 Discard 1 slip _____ 17 56 Add LC deal to
to surplus.   book and slips. _____
3 25 Stamp 1 slip
"catalog"   _____ 18 75 Forward book,
slips, and LC
5 File into main   deal to cataloger.____
catalog

4 78 Order LC cards.   19 91 Rush book?   _____

45 Start LC deal. _____ 20 92 Completely new
title?   _____
5 47 Discard 1 slip
to surplus.   _____ 21 29 Pull kindred shelf
6 79 Cutter?   _____   list card, etc. _____
22 99 Unit entry
28 Cutter on 1 slip?   identical?   _____

7 80 Book here?   _____ 23 100 Added part or
volume?   _____
8 81 Remaining 3
slips in book? _____ 24 93 Exact copy with
9 84 Order LC cards?_____   book?   _____

10 45 Start LC deal. _____ 25 30 Begin copy search.____

11 54 Shelve on hold   26 94 Exact copy found.____
shelf.
_____ 27 96 LC card (copy)
12 8 LC replies to   found?   _____
order.   _____

GIFT MONOGRAPH (WITH SLIPS)

28 95 Kindred copy found? _____

29 31 Prepare copy? _____

30 97 Order LC cards? _____

31 32 Transcribe copy. _____

32 34 Pull tracing re-cord, all cards. _____

33 35 Suggest changes on work slip. _____

34 98 All entries verified? _____

35 33 Search all entries. _____

36 101 Tentative call number available? _____

37 36 Classify, using DC tables. _____

    37 Add tentative call number to slip.

38 102 Tentative call number accepted. _____

39 38 Search and refine call number.

40 39 Assign definitive call number. _____

    40 Record in book and on slips. _____

    41 Count for book statistics.

41 103 Book for reference? _____

42 42 Pull blank from stock. _____

    43 Type card and pocket. _____

    44 Paste in pocket, and date due slip.

43 69 Label spine. _____

44 104 Book preparation correct? _____

45 70 Correct errors. _____

46 73 Send book and faculty slip to circ. dept. _____

Date to Circulation _____

47 71 File rush (Main Catalog)

48 72 File rush (Shelf List). _____

49 74 Work slip with copy? _____

50 74 Work slip with LC cards? _____

51 105 Was book rushed? _____

52 11 (Card and slips to) RUSH hold file.

53 120 Workslip and copy to typist.

54 106 Typing correct? _____

55 121 Correct typing. _____

56 122 Record card statistics _____

57 124 Arrange and file cards _____

    125 Pull and discard slips

58 107 Guide cards needed? _____

GIFT MONOGRAPH
(WITH SLIPS)

If answer (Number 58, Item
107) is YES, HOW MANY:

59 126 Pull stock; type
            guide cards.   _____
60 106 Typing correct?   _____

61 121 Correct typing.   _____

62 124 Arrange and file
            guide cards.   _____

Date Finished _____

FIGURE 10C

UNIVERSITY OF ILLINOIS   PURCHASED MONOGRAPH
Chicago Undergraduate Division   (ONE SLIP)

Catalog Department 16 83 Rush books? _____
    Statistical
    Work Sheet   17 54 Shelve on hold
                  shelf. _____

Item Number   PURCHASED   18 8 LC replies to
        MONOGRAPH   order. _____
        (ONE SLIP)

Date Started _____   19 86 Cards with LC
  1   3   deal? _____

  2 80   20 52 Search entries;
                  record on top
  3 80A Count statistics _____   card. _____
      for receipt record.   21 53 Check hold shelf. _____
  4 81
                  22 85 Book with slip
  5 57 Check hold slips   found? _____
      file _____   23 56 Add LC deal to
                  book and slips.
  6 87 Remaining 3 slips   24 75 Forward book and
      found? _____   slips to cataloger. _____
  7 88 Only 1 slip found? _____
                  25 92 Completely new
  8 58 Hold books; re-   title? _____
      check daily. _____
  9 51 Add slips to book   26 29 Pull kindred shelf
      and/or LC cards. _____   list, etc. _____
10 80 Book here? _____   27 91 Rush book? _____

11 87 Remaining 3 slips   28 99 Unit entry
      found? _____   identical? _____
12 82 LC cards on
      order? _____   29 100 Added part or
                  volume? _____
13 84 Order LC cards? _____
                  30 93 Exact copy with
14 46 Pull 1 slip from   book? _____
      surplus. _____
15 45 Start LC deal. _____   31 30 Begin copy
                  search. _____

PURCHASED MONOGRAPH
(ONE SLIP)

32 94 Exact copy found?____

33 96 LC card (copy)
        found?   ____

34 95 Kindred copy
        found?   ____

35 31 Prepare copy?   ____

36 97 Order LC cards?____

37 32 Transcribe copy. ____

38 34 Pull tracing re-
        cord, all cards. ____
39 35 Suggest changes
        on work slip.   ____
40 98 All entries
        verified?   ____

41 33 Search all
        entries.   ____

42 101 Tentative call
        number available?____

43 36 Classify, using DC
        tables.   ____
44 37 Add tentative call
        number to slip. ____
45 102 Tentative call
        number accepted. ____
46 38 Search and refine
        call number.   ____
47 39 Assign definitive
        call number.   ____
48 40 Record in book
        and on slips.   ____
49 41 Count for book
        statistics   ____
50 40B Forward book
        to labelling point.____

51 103 Book for refer-
        ence?   ____

52 42 Pull blanks from
        stock.   ____
53 43 Type card and
        pocket.   ____

54 44 Paste in pocket
        and date due slip.____
55 69 Label spine.   ____

56 104 Book preparation
        correct?   ____
57 70 Correct errors.   ____

58 73 Send book and
        faculty slip to
        circ. dept.   ____

Date to Circulation_____

59 71 File rush (Main
        Catalog)   ____
60 72 File rush (shelf
        list)   ____

61 74 Work slip with
        copy?   ____

62 74 Work slip with
        LC cards?   ____
63 105 Was book rushed?____

64 11 (Card and slips to)
        RUSH hold file. ____

65 120 Work slip and copy
        to typist.   ____
66 106 Typing correct?   ____

67 121 Correct typing.   ____

68 122 Record card
        statistics   ____

PURCHASED MONOGRAPH
(ONE SLIP)

69 124 Arrange and file
             cards   _____

70 125 Pull and discard
             slips   _____
71 107 Guide cards
             needed?   _____

If answer (Number 71, Item
   107) is YES, HOW MANY:

72 126 Pull stock; type
             guide cards.   _____
73 106 Typing correct?   _____

74 121 Correct typing.   _____

75 124 Arrange and file
             guide cards.   _____

Date Finished_____

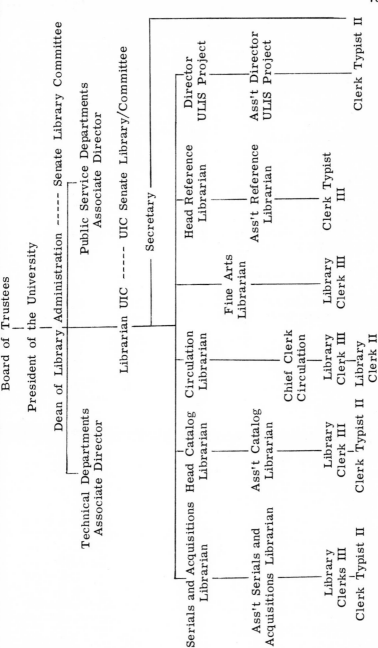

Board of Trustees

President of the University

Dean of Library Administration ----- Senate Library Committee

Librarian UIC ----- UIC Senate Library/Committee

Technical Departments
Associate Director

Public Service Departments
Associate Director

Secretary

Serials and Acquisitions
Librarian

Head Catalog
Librarian

Circulation
Librarian

Fine Arts
Librarian

Head Reference
Librarian

Director
ULIS Project

Ass't Serials and
Acquisitions Librarian

Ass't Catalog
Librarian

Chief Clerk
Circulation

Ass't Reference
Librarian

Ass't Director
ULIS Project

Library
Clerks III

Library
Clerk III

Library
Clerk III

Library
Clerk III

Clerk Typist
III

Clerk Typist II

Clerk Typist II

Library
Clerk II

Clerk Typist II

FIGURE 12

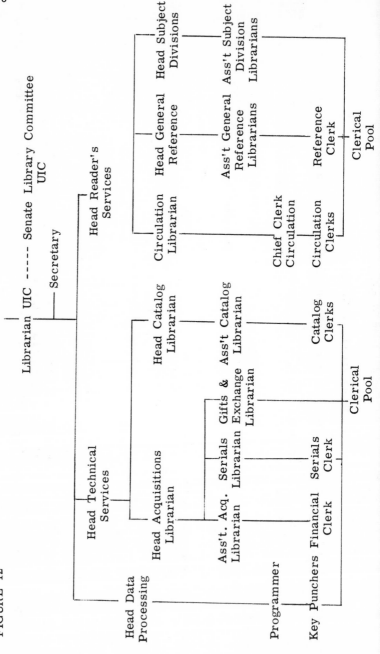

FIGURE 13

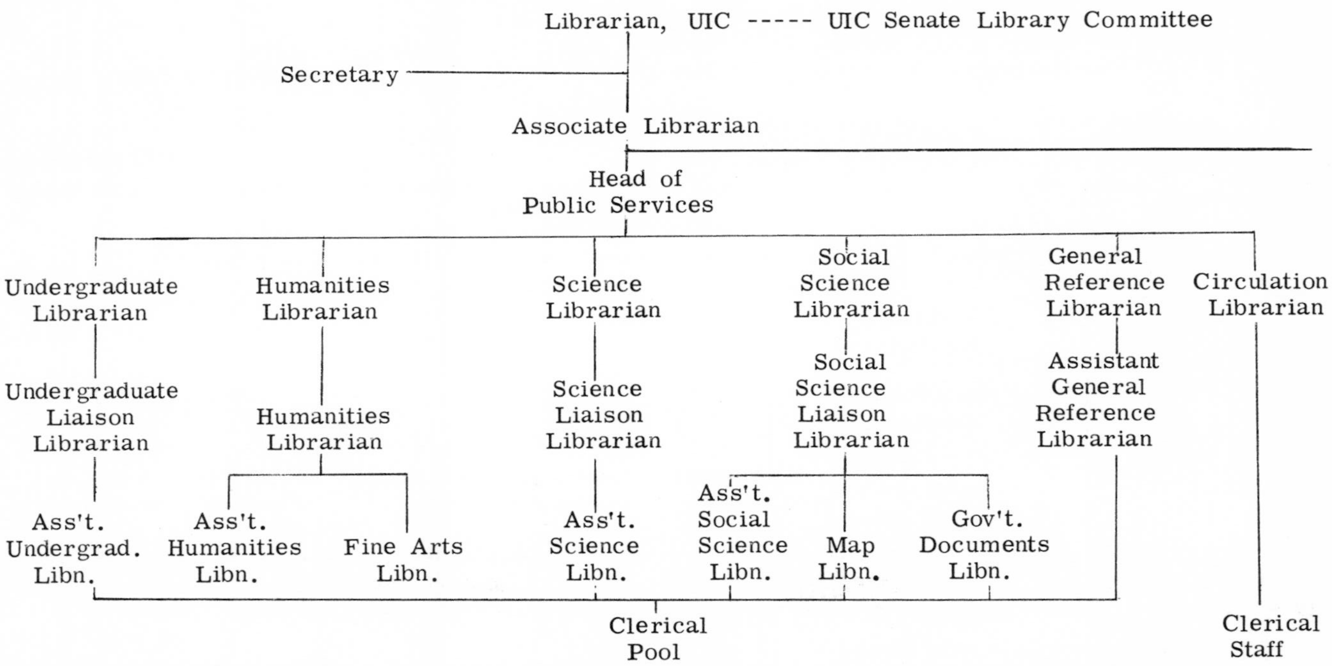

Librarian, UIC ----- UIC Senate Library Committee

Secretary

Associate Librarian

Head of Public Services

Undergraduate Librarian

Undergraduate Liaison Librarian

Ass't. Undergrad. Libn.

Humanities Librarian

Humanities Librarian

Ass't. Humanities Libn.

Fine Arts Libn.

Science Librarian

Science Liaison Librarian

Ass't. Science Libn.

Social Science Librarian

Social Science Liaison Librarian

Ass't. Social Science Libn.

Map Libn.

Gov't. Documents Libn.

General Reference Librarian

Assistant General Reference Librarian

Circulation Librarian

Clerical Staff

Clerical Pool

FIGURE 13A

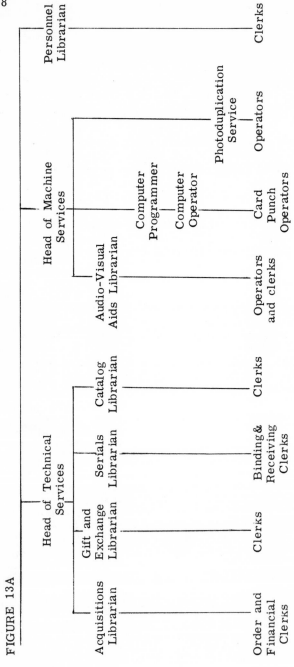

CHAPTER 5

As stated in Chapter 1, the design of advanced systems cannot begin until existing systems are set down and completely understood. This approach is the basis for successful system improvements in business, and must be the foundation of every future effort. The method of setting down systems on paper is called flow charting.

Flow charting is a graphic representation of a procedure's flow, showing the decisions that need to be made and the actions that must be taken to complete a particular task or series of tasks. Flow charts do not show who makes the individual decisions or who performs the tasks, but show the sequence in which they must be carried out.

In order to prevent confusion, four other analytical and control methods need to be defined:

1. Office Layout Charts. These are frequently called work flow diagrams, and are plans of offices or other work areas, showing the arrival and routing of materials, the movement of personnel, and layout of furniture and equipment. These charts do not show who does a job, but where it is done.

2. Job Descriptions. These show the duties of specific individuals within an organization. They are written rather than graphic, usually brief, and are normally very inclusive. They are valuable in showing the duties and decisions for which each personnel member is responsible, and are useful when hiring new personnel because they show the skills required for the position.

3. Time and Motion Study. Although time and motion studies embrace a wider field than will be used here, it is this area of management that commonly comes to mind when the term "efficiency expert" is used. For the purposes of this report, the term shall mean the scientific evaluation and establishment of standards and methods for best doing a specific task (e.g., inserting a form in a typewriter, typing, and removing it; or pasting a pocket in a book). The term also includes organization of the work area.

4. Procedure Manuals. A procedures manual (or standard instruction manual, code of procedure, systems manual, or some other standard title) follows the completion of flow charts, office layout, job descriptions, time and motion studies, etc. A procedures manual usually includes procedures, organization, and

policy. It could include some flow charts, would probably include an organization chart, and would list the procedures in detail. Such manuals are useful in training new employees, give older employees a place to check the method of performing infrequently done tasks, and are a source of company or library policy for all levels of personnel.

Once again, all studies of systems and procedures should start with flow charting. An automated or machine controlled action cannot work if there are errors in planning. Any error, no matter how small, will cause the equipment either to stop or to produce meaningless results. (In the jargon of the machine trade, this is called the "Disposal Theory" -- garbage in = garbage out).

The flow chart itself can be as elementary or as detailed as desired, as long as it is consistent in showing the whole system. Each form or shape on the chart should have a standard meaning so far as that particular set of charts is concerned, and the same parameters should apply each time a particular symbol is used. Such a situation is similar to that of standardized traffic signs, where an octagonal sign always means "stop" and a round sign always indicates a railway crossing. There is no universally standardized set of flow chart symbols, but a few conventional shapes have become established.

The General Electric Company has set standards for itself, as has IBM, the National Association of Machine Ac-
countants, and others. For library use, the IBM diagram-
ming template (X24-5884-5) seems to provide all of the shapes
required

The symbols used in the UIC flow charts are shown below, with an explanation of each one. Additional symbols
could have been used to further break down the action in the
action boxes, but the project staff felt it better to keep the
charts as simple as possible.

Question Box. The question in such a box
must always be answerable with a "yes" or a
"no." If there are three or more choices, two or more
questions must be asked.

Action Box. Any action taken is put in a rec-
tangular box. The size of a box is determined
only by the length of the note required to explain the action,
and does not indicate either type or importance of the action.

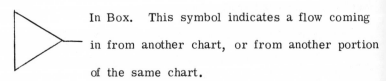

In Box. This symbol indicates a flow coming
in from another chart, or from another portion
of the same chart.

Out Box. The opposite of an in box. The point at which the flow line will be picked up again is written in the box e.g., To A-10, Blk 27 (To chart A-10, Block 27).

Hold File. Material comes in, is held for a stated period, and then goes out again. If it goes in and comes out at the same point, a double-ended arrow is used; if it goes in at one point and comes out at another, two arrows are used.

Start or Stop. The circle can have either meaning, depending on the notation written in it.

Explanation. This has a completely non-standard use as employed in these charts. It is used in this study to give explanations to the person reading the flow charts, and has no significance relating to the system itself. It is used only in the catalog department flow charts.

Y Yes Line. Leads from a question box to the box which answers "yes."

N No Line. Leads from a question box to the box which answers "no."

26 Box Number. This sample question box is marked "26." All boxes in a flow chart are

numbered after the chart is completed. Numbers are usuall[y]
assigned from left to right and from top to bottom, and are
continued from one page to the next until the set is completed.
Box function is ignored when assigning box numbers.

The project staff (and the entire library staff) found flow
charting to be an almost self-perpetuating endeavor. Once
started, system errors which had been buried in detail became glaringly obvious, were changed, and flow charts had
to be redrawn to make them a reflection of current operation. However, if errors exposed by a system study are
corrected, the savings from improved operation should pay
for the effort involved in the study.

The operations in the UIC Library at the time of initial
flow charting are not presented as a model of library efficiency, but as a fairly typical example. Many of the routines have been changed since the initial flow charting was
completed, some of them radically, and the flow charts are
continually in process of revision. A portion of the acquisitions routine is shown in both old and new form. Explanations of the flow charts, which appear in the appendix, are
given below. Departments are listed in alphabetical order.

Acquisitions Department. The UIC Library allocates approximately one third of its book budget to the academic

departments for the purchase of monographs. Records are
kept for individual fund allocations, and periodic meetings
are held with departmental representatives to discuss their
purchases.

Order requests are ordinarily submitted on Royal-McBee
Keysort cards designed for the University of Illinois Library.
Orders submitted on other forms are retyped in the acquisitions department. The order cards are coded across the top
and down the right side by notching in fixed fields to indicate
the following information: if recommended by a library staff
member; if out-of-print; if microprint; if approved for purchase; if a partial or a complete order; first two letters of
author's name; if verified; if searched; and fund allocation.

All searching and verification is done by the catalog department, and the cards are returned to acquisitions when
searching has been completed. An eight-part manifold form
is typed for each title approved for purchase. These forms
are not pre-printed, and are furnished in strips of ten sets
with one-use carbons. The colors and uses of each copy
from the set is as follows:

1. Light Yellow. "On order" slip; filed in the public
    catalog.

2. White. Stapled to original copy of purchase order
    sheet; individual items are not typed on purchase order.

3. Goldenrod. Acquisitions department fund slip; sent
    to catalog department with book, used as temporary
    shelflist; eventually sent to book fund representative.

4. Pink. Library of Congress card order slip; may be
    used as a temporary catalog slip if the LC entry is
    radically different from entry under which the item
    was ordered.

5. Green. Catalog department workslip.

6. Dark Yellow. Cataloging department slip placed in
    the card catalog to replace the "on order" slip. It
    bears the call number, and is destroyed when the
    permanent cards are filed.

7. Blue. Duplicate purchase order; stapled to the dup-
    licate purchase order sheet and filed in the acquisi-
    tions department.

8. Salmon. Faculty notification slip; left in the book
    when it leaves cataloging, and used by the circulation
    department to notify the requesting faculty member
    that material is ready for use.

Purchase orders are accompanied by blank invoice-vou-
chers to be filled out by the vendor. In those cases where
the vendor refuses to use the university form or charges
extra for doing so (an ever-increasing number), vouchers
are prepared by the library on the basis of dealer's invoices

Each voucher is signed by the acquisitions librarian and sent to the Librarian's office, where it is dated, the file copy is detached, and the remaining three copies are transmitted to the business office. Monthly financial reports are prepared in the acquisitions department, and copies are distributed to the UIC Librarian, the Director of Libraries and Head of Acquisitions at the main campus (Urbana), and the UIC business office.

Flow charts for the acquisitions department and other library departments are included in the appendix. For the benefit of those who do not wish to examine the entire set, Figures 14 and 14A show the creation of the financial records. Figures 15, 15A, 15B, 15C, and 15D show the same procedures after expansion and modification.

Cataloging Department. Cataloging flow charts are complicated by the need to delineate three separate flows on one set of charts. Most departmental operations can be shown on this one set, with separate charts for analytic and series entries, and for the treatment of cataloged serials.

The catalog department receives five basic types of materials: (1) manifold sets of five slips for materials on order; (2) gift or block purchase materials, which arrive in the department with the manifold set in the book; (3) purchased

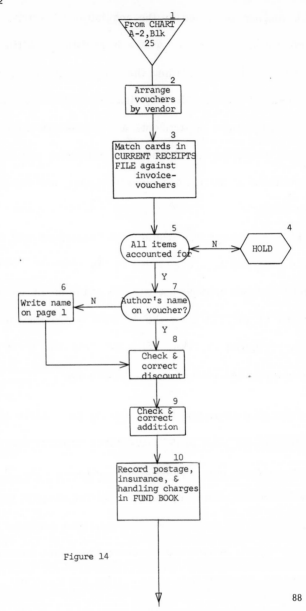

Figure 14

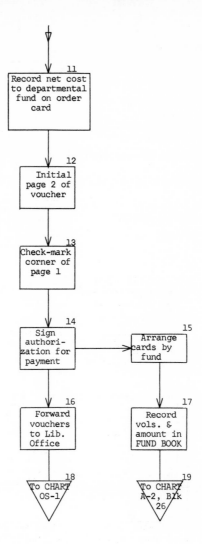

Figure 14A

89

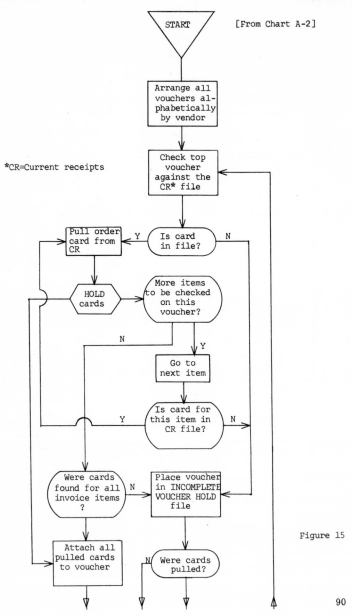

[From Chart A-2]

*CR=Current receipts

Figure 15

90

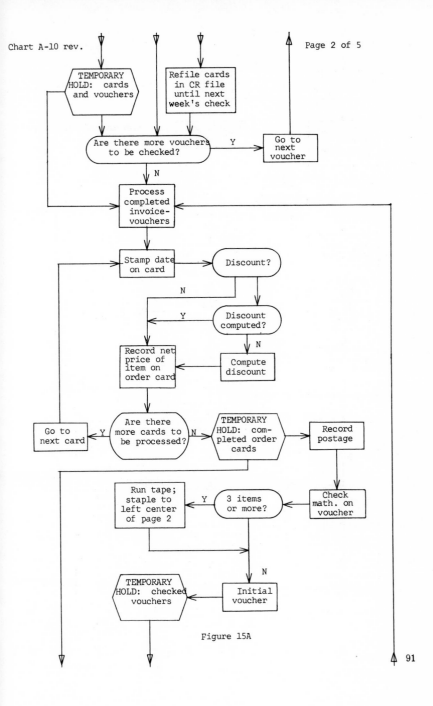

Figure 15A

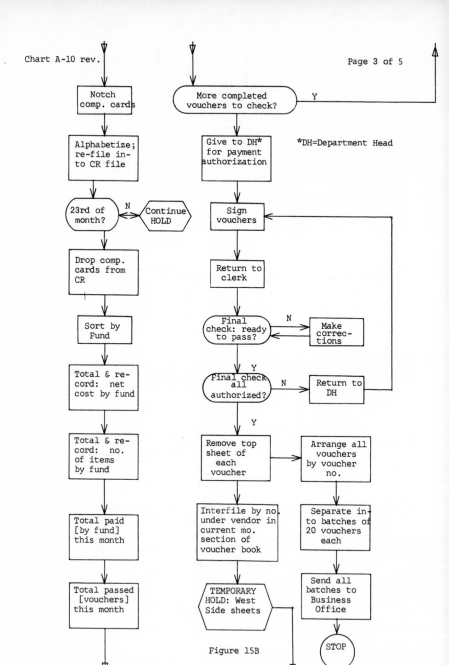

Figure 15B

*DH=Department Head

92

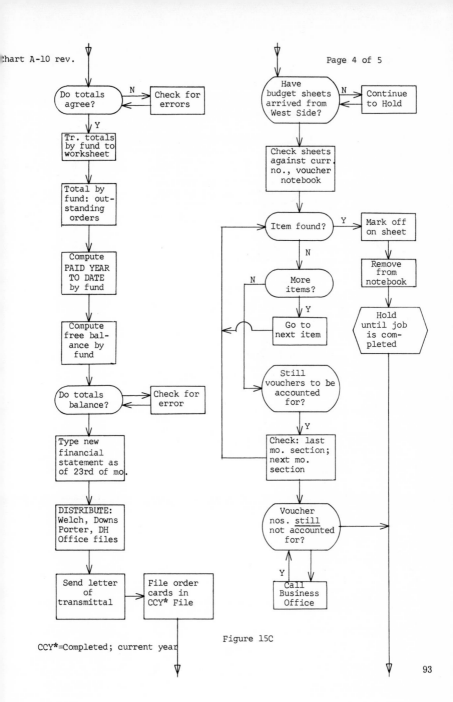

Figure 15C

CCY*=Completed; current year

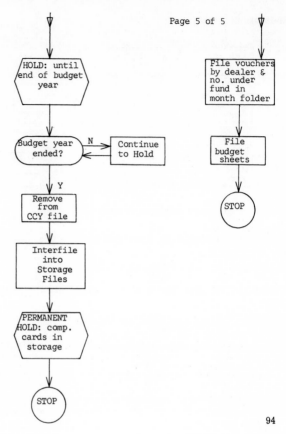

94

Figure 15D

monographs with one slip in the book; (4) serial pieces already posted on the serials records, and accompanied by a
set of serials manifold slips; and (5) shipments of Library
of Congress cards

Because the UIC library staff feels that the patron is best
served by limiting the number of files he must use, a number of temporary records are filed to make "in process" information available to both the public and the service staff.
In addition to the temporary catalog slips already discussed
in connection with the acquisition department manifold sets,
temporary slips are filed in the shelf list, and dummy
slips are filed every time a shelf list card is removed.

Library of Congress cards may be ordered at any of
three points in the cataloging operation. Most of them are
ordered as soon as manifold sets arrive from the acquisitions department. Other orders, especially for out-of-print
items and materials hard to obtain, may be held until the
material actually arrives in the catalog department. All gift
and block purchase materials fall into this category. If not
ordered at either of these points, the cards may be ordered
after the material goes to the cataloger. Analytic cards are
ordered at one point only in the analytic procedure.

When catalog cards are not available from the Library of

Congress the UIC produces its own on a Cardmaster mimeo-graph.

Circulation Department. When working with the proce-dures concerned with inanimate objects such as books, it is reasonably simple to create a linear flow chart of the opera-tion, even though human decisions are involved at many points. But whenever the interaction of one human being with another is charted, the result is artificial because the chart must make a linear flow of mental processes that are largely matrix in approach. As a result, the mental pro-cesses delineated in both the circulation department and ref-erence department systems do not actually follow the pro-cesses of the human mind. The mind grasps meaning from the memory of past experiences, from vocal inflections, facial expressions, and other non-chartable actions of too subtle a nature to be captured on flow charts.

The UIC circulation system is a manual operation using Royal-McBee Keysort cards printed especially for the pur-pose. Each card has punch fields along all four edges. The top may be notched to indicate a reserve book, a faculty charge, or that the book is in processing, missing, at the bindery, lost and paid, or overdue. It may also be punched to indicate that the book is part of the uncataloged paperback collection. One side of the card contains fixed fields that allow notching for the first and second digits of the call number. The rest of the holes on the card are used to indicate date due; there are thirty-six of these, with a code allowing each hole to indicate one week. These cards are kept in a pocket in the back of the book. Both card and pocket bear the call number, author, and title. Cards are filled out by the patron, giving his name, address, and student identification number; a clerk at the circulation desk stamps both card and due slip with a hand stamp. When the book is returned to the library, the date on the due slip is cancelled by stamping it out with a pattern stamp. Each card may be used for fourteen circulations before being replaced.

In addition to the regular collection, the UIC circulation desk controls a large collection of paperback books[1-2], a small collection of disk recordings, a growing number of foreign language tapes which must be placed on tape playback equipment so that students can listen to them on earphones checked out from the circulation desk, chess sets that are checked out to members of the chess club, and all interlibrary loans. The circulation department also administers final examinations to students in the Chicago area who have completed extension courses.

Because the library for the UIC "campus" is located 2,200 feet from the shore on a pier extending 3,000 feet into

Lake Michigan, a partially duplicated collection of reserve
materials has been established at the shore end of the pier
in the Reserve Book Station.

Library Office. As pointed out under the discussion of
acquisitions department flow charts, the invoice-voucher procedures are carried out in this office. The Librarian's secretary is also charged with keeping library accounts balanced
with the summary sheets issued by the business office of the
University of Illinois at the Medical Center.

In addition to routine administrative tasks and correspon-
dence, the staff in the Librarian's office handles the clerical
routines for supplies, furniture and equipment inventories,
student payroll records, and for hiring new employees.

Reference Department. The UIC reference staff is made
up of the department head and three assistant reference librarians. All four of these people spend a major portion of
their time at the public reference desk. Each of the assistants is in charge of a specialized part of the reference collection in addition to his general work: one is in charge
of government documents, one supervises the map collection,
and one maintains the pamphlet collections. Special bibliographic assignments, e.g., debate topic bibliographies, National Discussion Question bibliographies, and lists for sem-

inars and other special groups, are prepared on assignment from the head of the reference department.

The "print out" facility of the reference department, which appears several times in the flow charts, is a clerk with her electric typewriter.

Serials Department. The main function of the serials group, which is administratively part of the acquisitions department, is maintenance of the Central Serials Record (CSR). This records all active continuations, giving information as to issues held and date of receipt, binding and financial information, information as to missing issues and incomplete volumes, etc. The CSR also includes holdings information for "dead" periodical runs. The file is made up of four Acme file units of 13 drawers each; entries are on 5 x 8 inch cards, filed alphabetically by title or catalog entry. All questions pertaining to serials are answered at this point; in some cases, the service departments send patrons directly to the serials department for help. No problems of staffing or of service have arisen because both public service and technical service divisions are open the same hours (8 a.m.- 4:30 p.m., Monday - Friday).

All serials cataloging is carried out in the cataloging department. Serials department procedures are limited to order and financial routines, and to the operations of checking in, claiming, binding, etc.

One area of library administration that has received far too little attention is that of cost analysis. Librarians often add new services or modify old ones with little idea of the exact cost of the operation. Many of them do not know how much present operations cost the library, and have only an inkling of the load new ones will put on their budgets.

In order to have some figures with which to make future comparisons, the project staff computed the cost, on a per piece basis, of three of the UIC Library departments: serials-acquisitions, cataloging, and circulation. Every item of expense charged against these three departments was totaled, the number of operations for each department was added together, and divided into the total cost of operating the department. Rental of space, heat, light, and janitorial service were not included because these are figured as university overhead and are not broken down on a departmental basis. The cost of departmental telephone service was included. Figures are for the year 1959-60.

Serials and Acquisition Department

Academic salaries.	$10,108.57
Clerical salaries.	14,640.00
Student wages.	687.70
	$25,436.27

Postage.	85.00
Supplies.	250.00
	$25,771.27

Serials items.

Checked in	14,930
Cataloged Serials	798
Binding	962
Withdrawals	71
Orders placed	150
	16,911

Acquisitions items.

Added	3,341
Withdrawn	29
Orders placed	936
	4,306

Total added.	4,139
Total withdrawn	100
Total orders placed	1,086
	5,325

COST $4.84 each

Repairs.

Plating	4,300
Re-Label	152
Repair	207
Reinforce	486
Inserts	47
Drymount	62
	5,254

Total Serials items	16,911
Total Acquisitions items	4,927
Total repairs (less plating)	954
	22,171

COST $1.16 each

Catalog Department

Academic salaries.	$13,139.94
Clerical salaries.	10,444.00
Student wages.	882.05
	$24,465.99

Postage.	5.00
Supplies.	225.00
	$24,965.99

Cataloged items.

Titles cataloged	2,549
Analytics	84
Items recataloged	248
	2,881

COST (On a title basis) $8.67 each

Items handled.

Books	4,314
Pamphlets	755
Films	55
Microcards	408
Maps	2
Phonodiscs	120
Items withdrawn	99
	5,780

COST (On a per item basis) $4.32 each

Circulation Department

Academic salaries.	$ 7,262.43
Clerical salaries.	17,905.00
Student wages.	2,135.37
	$27,302.80

Postage.	300.00
Supplies.	500.00
	$28,102.80

Total transaction of the department.
59,045

COST (On a total cost of the department
        basis) $ .4760 each.

Non-circulation items in the budget

Book selection	$1,157.64
Display	683.00
Mail delivery	472.50
Guard relief	236.25
Messenger service	225.00
Housekeeping	1,075.00
	$3,849.39

COST (On a circulation only basis) $ .4108 each.

This is a very brief look at library cost analysis, and it
undoubtedly leaves much to be desired in method. The reaction of most librarians to cost figures in these ranges
borders on the incredulous. However, these figures, at
least those for the circulation department, compare favorably
with those calculated at the Brooklyn Public Library in 1951-
52, where the factors omitted from the UIC analysis were
probably included.[3] Difficult as it is to believe, a new title
costing $5.00 costs $18.51 at UIC by the time it gets to the
shelf, and a gift book costs the UIC library over $13. to
accept, check, and catalog.

The UIC staff feels that with proper reorganization the
work load of these three departments could be increased
somewhat without increasing the size of the staff. This
would lower the unit costs, although the inclusion of fixed
overhead, which should be added to show overall cost to the
university, would probably bring it right back up again.

Additional investigation should be made of cost factors
for several different kinds and sizes of libraries. Studies of
this type would give librarians figures against which they
could compare their own unit costs.

REFERENCES

1. De Young, Charles D. Operation paperback. in
    Library Journal, 84:1185-8, April 15, 1959.

2. De Young, Charles D. Operation paperback: a second
    look. in Library Journal, 85:3023-26, September 15,
    1960.

3. St. John, Francis R. Management improvements in
    libraries. in College and Research Libraries, 14:174-7,
    April, 1953.

CHAPTER 6

Three basic assumptions need to be restated at this point. The first is that the function of a book as a container of information is separate and distinct from the function of a book as an artifact of civilization. This is not to say that a book cannot fulfill both functions at the same time. Materials, as discussed in this report, are not considered from the point of view of the rare book librarian or from that of a lover of books as books. Books are considered, instead, from the viewpoint of those who are primarily interested in their contents and whose purpose is to make this knowledge more widely available and easier to use.

The second assumption is that a librarian can love books as books and at the same time operate a library on an efficient and businesslike basis. If the use of machines or the scientific analysis of systems is necessary to being an efficient or businesslike librarian, this seems a logical direction to take. Both efficiency and a knowledge of books are necessary.

One of the major findings of the project was that any service-oriented philosophy of librarianship for the machine age will require more efficient methods.

If maximum service to users is to be realized, the flow
of both subject and control information must be improved.
The first reason for improving the flow is that present costs
are much too high. Even if these UIC costs are not unreasonable when compared to other libraries of similar size and
kind, it seems ridiculous to pay $8.67 to catalog one title.
These cataloging costs, plus the $4.84 cost of selecting and
acquiring the material in the first place, make a book almost
too valuable to circulate. Also, a circulation cost of 41 cents
per transaction seems to call for careful investigation of ways
to cut costs.

Every year the percentage of the library budget spent on
generating control information has increased over the percentage spent for the subject information itself. Librarians
have done practically nothing to reverse this trend. The application of data processing techniques plus adaptation of the
best of traditional library methods may help to solve this
problem.

Second, some types of control information, necessary to
serve both the user and the library staff, are not now available at a price libraries can afford to pay. The need for
highly specialized subject bibliographies and lists arranged
by multiple descriptive factors should be examined. Potential

use and cost are among the obvious factors to be studied in determining the variety and number of such lists, and information of dubious value should not be furnished simply because it is possible.

Third, some kinds of control information are not available during evening and week-end hours. A user should not be considered a second-class patron because he is unable to use the library's facilities during normal "office hours." The non-availability of control records such as serials files, official catalogs, shelflists, and on-order records causes waste of time and effort and creates ill will for the library.

The fourth reason for wanting to improve information flow is that some documents should be redirected and more widely disseminated if maximum use is to be made of them. Catalogs that may be used only in the library have a limited usefulness and may generate desires on the part of faculty members to have collections in their own locations. The investigations carried out during the course of the systems project indicate that new systems making use of machines can make control documents available to all who need them.

If full advantage is to be taken of opportunities for improved information flow in the library, there must be a corresponding improvement in the methods of handling routine technical operations. These operations include the selection, acquisitions and financial processes, and circulation and overdue routines. This requires standardization of cataloging, and much of the present, traditional library methodology will have to be eliminated or adapted and brought up to date.

Several things need to be done if improved methods are to be worked out and put into use.

First, there must be a careful analysis of the library, its service goals, and its methods, including those aspects of the present system which must be retained for geographic, legal, or sentimental reasons. This self-examination gives staff members time to face the idea of changing present procedures, forces them to realize that present methods may not be the most desirable in their particular situation, and gives them practice in flow charting, systems analysis, and other techniques necessary in planning new systems.

Second, there must be careful examination of available machines, methods, systems, forms, etc., that are useful in a library environment or can be modified to make them useful. The librarians in charge of data processing and systems development must have access to journals, books, and other sources of information on developments in the fields under study.

Third, a more progressive attitude must be fostered in

the thinking of librarians at all staff levels. It is recognized
that library administrators will be the ones who untimately
decide whether or not changes will be made in the existing
system, but it should not be forgotten that it is the line staff
who will either make or break the new system through their
attitude toward it and their ability to work with it. A program of education of the staff members of any library making
major system changes is a prime requirement.

Fourth, decisions must be made as to the proper utilization of equipment suitable for new systems. Machines currently on the market can be either rented or purchased.
Most corporations of moderate size or complexity have electronic computers and installations of tabulating equipment.
Most university campuses also have similar installations in
the business office, the statistical office, or in the engineering department. Libraries without suitable equipment within
their own organization can rent time on computers, and can
rent the use of tabulating equipment and operators on an
hourly basis from service bureaus, or other agencies.

Another major finding of the project staff was that electronic computers are capable of manipulating bibliographic
data and generating the documents and control records necessary to smooth operation of a library. The use of such
capability seems desirable. However, systems using elec-

tronic computers have different requirements than systems
that are manual or that evolved from manual systems.   A
chart (Figure 16) compares present manual library systems,
semi-automatic systems, and a fully automated system.   The
first two are "conventional," and the third is an "unconven-
tional" system.

Most libraries use conventional manual systems, and a
few use semi-automatic ones; but none uses a fully automated system, or even a small segment of one.   As can be
seen from the chart, manual systems are people-operated.
All routines are carried out by hand.   Semi-automatic systems are based on exactly the same procedures, but some
operations are done mechanically.   The fully automated system is based on completely different principles than the other
two, in that there is only one input, partially automatic, per
entry and a multitude of ways that the data can be retrieved,
printed out, or changed without requiring human action other
than a decision as to the form of output required.

For libraries unable to purchase computers, the leasing
of equipment may be a solution.   To illustrate the purchase
and rental costs of three computers suitable for library work,
a table is included to show comparative costs.   It should be
kept in mind that the cost of maintenance plus the salaries

FIGURE 16

COMPARISON OF TWO CONVENTIONAL SYSTEMS WITH A NON-CONVENTIONAL SYSTEM

| Operations | Conventional Systems | | Non-Conventional Systems |
	Current Practice	Semi-Automatic	Automatic
Putting information into a system			
Acquisitions	People	Punched cards	Tape or cards plus retrieval function
Identification	Typewriter, pen and ink, pencil	Updated punched cards	Telegraphic abstract & auto-indexing
Subject Analysis			
Input	Paper	Cards punched	Punched cards and punched tape to computer
Arranging	Hand filing	Sorter and collator	
Storage	Catalog cards & books	Catalog cards, books, and punched cards	Magnetic tape, thermoplastic film, and random access memories
Taking information out of a system			
Request formulation	Patron	Patron to librarian to punched cards	Programmed
Retrieval	Patron	Collation	Internal matching
Output	Written	Print out by tabulator	Print out by computer
Circulation	Manual	Tab card control	Automatic patron operated

of programmers and operators is about equal to the average
monthly rental.

Rental and Purchase Cost
of Medium Sized Computers

Manufacturer	Model	Purchase	Monthly Rental
International Business Machines Corporation	IBM 1401	$280,000.00	$5500.00
Minneapolis-Honeywell Regulator Company	Honeywell 400	$390,000.00	$8000.00
National Cash Register Company	NCR 315	$225,000.00+	$4400.00+

If a library operation is not large enough to justify having
a computer immediately at hand (and few of them are, especially if information retrieval is not involved), the use of
a service bureau is a logical choice. Rental of an IBM 1401
computer with a magnetic tape input and output costs $105.00
per hour. The cost of forms and programming are extra.

It is important that the librarian be the one to translate
these new techniques into the language of the library and that
this job not be left in the hands of computer personnel. It
is easier to train a librarian in the techniques of programming than it is to make a librarian out of a physicist or
mathematician trained in computer and machine technology.
Being a librarian implies a state of mind as well as special
training. It is only by being in charge that the librarian will

be able to insist on arranging and handling bibliographic information in a manner convenient and easy for the patron to use, and meeting the basic objectives of the library and the predominence of a service-centered philosophy.

Unfortunately, professional librarians trained in machine techniques are virtually non-existent. A few librarians, usually connected with university libraries, are taking computer courses. It is unfortunate that training of this nature is usually in mathematical analysis which is not cognate to the business operations that will remain the frontier of library mechanization for years to come.

CHAPTER 7

Any organization's work is made up of dozens of sub-systems. Most of these have been developed as the need arose and have little relationship to each other. These fragmented routines are also complete entities and do not support and are not supported by the other routines of the organization. Usually, documents created for one system are not used in any other system partly because the documents are not compatable and partly because the systems are not internally related.

The proposed system developed by General Electric during the ULIS Project has two important aspects which have appeared in the better business systems for some time.

First, the proposed systems applications are based on the total system approach. Each department of the library has been taken into consideration as the parts of the proposed system were designed and the effects of each part on each other part were carefully thought out before final approval to the proposal. Thought was also given to the relationships of the library system to the systems of other departments in the University and their requirements and needs.

Second, each part of the system has been made both in-
dependent and interdependent. If one record could be devised
which would do for several parts of the system this was done.
A certain amount of independence of the parts from the whole
was necessary, however; for, if one part failed to perform
as expected, the staff did not want the whole system to col-
lapse. Eventual improvements in certain parts of the system are expected as soon as equipment, now in the development stage, is perfected. The system should be flexible
enough to take advantage of any other new machines or methods.

Flexibility is also given these sub-systems by the choice
of a computer over a punched card installation. In a tabula-
tor installation all catalogs must be arranged in some permanent order if the total length of the entry exceeds eighty
spaces, as sorters and collators cannot sort entries when
more than one punched card per entry is used. A complete
punched card operation is not a good intermediary step between manual and automated systems, as decisions not compatible with computer-based systems frequently must be made
in order to make a punched card system work.

Chapter VI stated as a major finding of the ULIS Project
that an electronic computer was necessary if a fully automated library system was to be adopted. Electronic computers

come in many sizes and are built for many different functions, not all of which are compatible. It is therefore important that criteria be established for selection of the proper
electronic computer, whether for purchase, rental, or use at
a service bureau.

In general the environmental requirements for today's
computers are much less critical than were those of four or
five years ago. While even the smallest computer requires
an air conditioned room and its own electrical circuits (i.e.
transformer fed directly from the sub-station) practically no
other special installation problems exist unless extremes of
temperature or humidity are present in the area in which it
is to be installed. Modular library buildings have floors
strong enough to support the weight of a computer of almost
any size. Some older structures would not support the required 150 pounds per square foot maximum weight in all
areas. A discussion of computer environment in libraries
is really more or less academic, as only the largest library
systems will be able to afford their own machines at this
time. However, the future may bring an especially designed
library computer at a much lower price which would put
automated systems within the range of many libraries.

Computer based systems start with data which are punched into cards or punched into paper tape (sometimes as a

by-product of typing the original record) and these are fed
into the computer. All electronic computer actions are unde
the control of the program, which in most cases is stored
in a deck of punched cards or tapes and is fed into the computer just ahead of the data. During computation the data
stored on magnetic tape are transferred from the tape to the
computer and stored temporarily in a magnetic memory. The
data in the computer are then manipulated according to the
instructions in the program. The results of the computation
are printed out, if so ordered, and/or put on magnetic tape.
Direct print out from computer memory is called "on line
printing." Data are frequently stored on magnetic tape and
printed out at the convenience of the operator. This is re-
ferred to as "off line printing."

A computer should be capable of accepting input from
punched cards, punched paper tape, or magnetic tape; transferring the data from the input device to the memory; making
the computation or manipulation; printing out or putting the
results on tape or both simultaneously.

Other criteria for a computer, and the basis from which
all cost computations were made, are a transfer rate from
tape to memory of at least 15,000 alpha-numeric characters
per second, end of record gap of .75", character density of

200 to the inch, and a forward speed for the tape drive of 75 inches per second.

The printing unit should be able to handle a 120 character line at the rate of 600 lines per minute. It is important, moreover, that the paper speed should be raised when passing portions which are not to be printed.

The card reader, which accepts the data and the program input, must read the cards at 400 per minute. Some readers operate in the 2000 cpm range but this speed is not necessary because even 400 cpm is nearly twice the available transfer rate criteria set above.

The more the magnetic core storage holds, the better for library applications, and the memory should hold at least 4000 characters.

The final criteria for a library computer is that it handle variable field alpha-numeric information. It is important that the word and record length be variable as bibliographic entries vary in length.

An electronic computer which meets the above specifications, and can be expanded to exceed them, is the IBM 1401 Data Processing System. The 1401 System is made up of the 1401 processing unit, a 1402 card read-punch, a 1403 printer, and up to six 729 tape units. This is not to say that this is the only electronic computer which will do the job.

In fact, at least two other machines in roughly the same price class are now on the market and could be used. These are the Honeywell 400 and the NCR 315. There are also several large scale computers that would handle library work but rental of these costs $300 per hour or more.

The important factors in selection of a computer suitable for library automation are magnetic tape facility, speed of transfer from tape to memory, and speed of print out. These factors are nearly the antithesis of criteria for the selection of a computer for scientific use, i.e., mathematical computation.

A difficult first step in implementing any library automation project will be the identification of the parts of a potential bibliographic citation. Many persons, when first considering automated libraries, state that all books (or all indexes or the LC Catalogs or etc.) should be put on magnetic tape so information could be printed out in any order or selectively printed. This is not a practical use for electronic computers. For example, the Reader's Guide to Periodical Literature from 1890 to February 1961 contains 53,581 pages. A random sampling of the page count shows an average of 5,250 characters per page. 5,250 characters x 53,581 pages = 281,300,250 characters in the Reader's Guide. Magnetic tape usually comes on 10-1/2" reels containing 2,400' of 1/2" wide tape. Using a density of 200 characters per inch plus an end of record gap of .75", a reel of magnetic tape will hold 5,484,000 characters. $281,300,250 \div 5,484,000 = 52$ reels of tape. Assuming that the tape drive could make a search at 75" per second it would take 6.4 minutes to search one reel and 332.8 minutes to search the whole file. At \$105.00 per hour computer rental cost, the cost of one linear search would come to \$582.75. Obviously putting the tools of the library on tape would make them economically impossible to use.

Some machine adherents state that large scale random access machines are the answer as linear searches would not have to be made. The major fault with random access memories available today is their small size. The CRAM units with the NCR 315 will hold 5,555,200 characters per cartridge. These cartridges can be removed from the file and stored like a tape reel. Magnetic discs, (up to five) for use with the IBM 1410 will hold up to 100,000,000 characters. Reports of RAMAC units with capacities up to 1,000,000,000 characters have been made but for storage of library books or tools even these are too small.

Storing the shelf list is a different story, however. 100,000 titles will have about 30,000,000 characters and this is within the capacity of many present machines. Note that

it is not necessary to put the whole card catalog into the
computer as each title needs to be represented only once and
can be ordered out in any arrangement, i.e. author first,
title first, etc.

But before the library shelf list can be put into any kind
of machine readable form the parts of the bibliographic citation for each entry must be identified. In its simplest form
identification of the parts of the "bibliographic string," as it
can be called, would have to be done only upon those parts
which would usually be used as headings. In a small university library with a general collection these would be relatively few, but specialized libraries and special collections would
make the potential number swell. It would seem best to provide for all eventualities in the first place so the work would
not have to be done over again if a bibliography were needed
on an unlisted heading. A typical "bibliographic string"
would be as follows:

(A) MACKENZIE, SIR COMPTON (AD) 1833- (T) MY
RECORD OF MUSIC (PL) NEW YORK (PU) G. P.
PUTNAM AND SONS (D) 1955 (PA) 280 (IL) YES
(S) 24CM(CN) 780.92/M156M.

Sample Bibliographic String

On an LC entry this "bibliographic string" would look

like this:

780.92   MacKenzie, Sir Compton, 1833-
M156M
            My record of music. New York,
    G. P. Putnam and Sons, 1955.
 	
        280p.   illus.   24cm.
 	
                    ◯

Sample Catalog Card

It is anticipated that about 1,000 possible parts exist in

the bibliographical string.

Assumptions:

1. 1,000 definitions will eventually be required.

2. 900 definitions can be accounted for on the initial

    survey.

3. Let t be measured in weeks.

4. Assume a rate, K, of less than or equal to 10%,

    where K is the percentage of remaining definitions

    to be found in a given week.

5. A differential equation of the form

$$y' = -Ky$$

    was assumed where y is the number of changes to

be made in week t. One would reasonably expect

an exponential decay process.

1) Solving 5. we have

$$y = ce^{-Kt}$$

2) Let c = 1,000 - 900 = 100; K = .10; t = 50 weeks.

$$y = 100e^{-(.10)(50)}$$

$$y \cong 1 \text{ change.}$$

If a preliminary list of definitions in which 90% of the
total list of definitions is accounted for, ten new additions
will be added every week once the program is started. By
the end of one year the rate of adding new definitions will
have dropped off to one per week. That is to say, at the
beginning, one book out of 200 will introduce four to five
new definitions. At the end of the year, only one book out
of 400-500 would introduce one change.

In addition to the identification of parts of the bibliographic string a sequence number of some kind has to be formu-
lated to identify each item in the shelf list. This number
should be written by either unskilled clerks or by the computer. Use of the call number first was brought out but it
is necessary to have the number assigned at the time the
item is ordered and the call number is, of course, not ready
this early in the procedures. The LC card order number

was also considered but this would mean a computer with a large enough internal memory to take the whole shelf list at one time as the LC card order number would be essentially in random order. The IBM 1401 in its largest form would handle only 16,000 characters so that unordered material would have to go through a lengthy sorting process before it could be used for anything at all.

On September 14, 1959, H. P. Luhn of IBM addressed the American Chemical Society and in describing his KWIC Index also described "a derived code for the identification of bibliographic items." This code was mechanically generated from the name of the author, the year of publication, and the title of the document. For example, the code for Mr. Luhn's talk would be LUHNHP59KCI. This represents the first four letters of the author's last name (LUHN), the initials of his given name (HP), the last two digits of the date of publication (59), and the first letters of the first three significant words in the title (KCI).

A similar code has been proposed for use with library bibliographical entries. As it is generated as part of the order cycle, two of its features are of particular interest to acquisitions departments. It is calculated that duplicates of Mr. Luhn's code will occur once every 17,000 times. This should be improved for general library use. Although dup-

licates could occur once every 18,545 times in the project
derived sequence number, the practical limit is really much
higher than this.   For example: David Judson Haykin's book
Subject headings - a practical guide, which was ordered
April 20, 1961, would have the sequence number HAYKDJSH
1201, where the code equals the first four letters of the
author's last name (HAYK), the initials of his first two
names (DJ), the first letters of the first two significant words
of the title (SH), the day of the year of the order (120), and
the last digit of the current year (1).   This would keep entries in a rough alphabetical order by author and author
ordered print outs could be assembled with only one pass
through the computer.

One group of problems, which will have to be faced eventually by machine-minded librarians, is the most important
one of filing rules.   It is easy enough to say that a computer
will put an unordered list in order by author or by title.
However, the computer program for doing this does not exist.
Should the programmer start on new filing rules based upon
nothing but machine requirements and ignore the complexities
of both the ALA and LC filing rules or should he try and
program the standard (?) filing rules presently used in most
libraries?   Other questions in the same vein are: What is to
be done with Arabic numerals versus those written out?

How about non-English languages? and Where do non-Roman
alphabets get filed? These questions will have to remain
unanswered for the present.

Acquisitions Department. The proposed system for the
acquisitions department is based on one prime requirement,
viz. any new system must be equal to or better than the
present one in simplicity, accuracy, and the cost of operation. And the key to all of these is, as Thoreau says in
Walden, "Simplify, simplify."

General flow charts of General Electric's proposed acquisitions routines are shown in Figures 17 and 17A. The
routine for ordering an item starts the same way as present
routines; the request is sent to the department on an edge
notched card. Once the items have been approved for purchase and verified, the information is keypunched into IBM
cards. These cards contain all the information known about
the orders; author, title, date, publisher, vendor, fund,
and anything else that can be discovered in routine verification. The notched cards are saved until the end of the budget year, microfilmed for a permanent record of approval
signatures, and destroyed. The IBM cards are fed weekly
into the computer, which in turn prints the purchase order,
the LC card order form, punches the check-in card, and

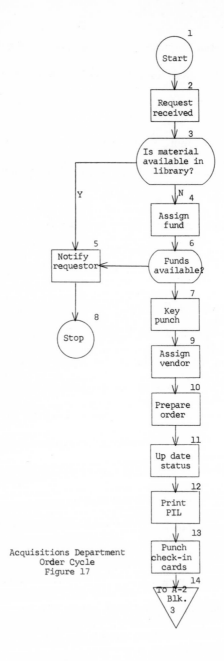

Acquisitions Department
Order Cycle
Figure 17

128

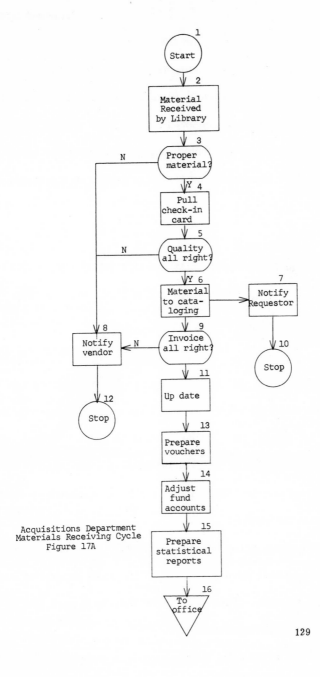

Acquisitions Department
Materials Receiving Cycle
Figure 17A

129

puts all the information on the Processing Information List
tape. The Processing Information List (PIL) is then printed,
probably off line. Figure 18 is a sample page from a typical PIL. The first line of the entry (see sample entry) contains the machine generated sequence number (by which the
entries are arranged) and the information on the status

MACKSCMR1921   (M) ON ORDER (F)RNYP (B)00.

MACKENZIE, SIR COMPTON. MY RECORD
OF MUSIC. NEW YORK, G. P. PUTNAM AND
SONS, 1955.

Processing Information List Sample Entry

of the material (M) which is written out so patrons can use
it, the financial record (F), and the bibliographic information,
i.e. LC cards. (B). Codes should be set up so that information for the staff only would take up less space. This
would, of course, leave more room for explanatory information for the patron.

As orders would be sent out weekly, a separate routine
would probably have to be set up for rush items that could
not be delayed. This might even lead to a once per week
one-sheet PIL supplement.

As the Processing Information List would carry all entries

from the time the order was placed until it was added to the
catalog, as well as all items removed from circulation, several classes of material would have to be enumerated for
the patron's use. The report from the General Electric
Company included the following possibilities: wrong material
sent, cataloging, searching, cancelled, on order, checked in,
bindery, new book shelf, out of stock, incomplete information,
damaged material, and reorder on (date). The financial
information which, as stated, would be coded for use of the
staff only, would include: received, not yet paid (RNYP) and
received and passed for payment (RAPFP). Bibliographic
information, which would also be coded for staff use, would
have: on order (OO), card order received and checked in
(RI), and reorder (RO) as its states of being.

It would also be possible to encumber funds automatically
as both the price (list) of the item and the fund number
would be initially punched. An alternative is the possibility
of encumbering funds with an average price for books in that
subject field. Fund representatives would have their previous
balance, tentative encumbrance, tentative balance, and actual
balance. This would prevent overspending of library funds
allocated to departments and would help them spread their
spending more evenly over the entire year.

FIGURE 18

4.5 PROCESSING INFORMATION LIST   31 JULY 1961

ALEXC LE2121   (M) ON ORDER   (F)   (B) 00
ALEXANDER, CARTER, HOW TO LOCATE EDUCATIONAL
INFORMATION AND DATA; AN AID TO QUICK UTILIZATION
OF THE LITERATURE OF EDUCATION. 3RD ED., REV.
AND ENL. NEW YORK, BUREAU OF PUBLICATIONS,
TEACHERS COLLEGE, COLUMBIA UNIVERSITY, 1950.

BARBTHWW1941   (M) DAMAGED   (F)   (B)00
                      MATERIAL   RNYP
BARBER, THOMAS H., WHERE WE ARE AT. NEW YORK,
SCRIBNER, 1950.

BUCHRMBE2021   (M) BINDERY   (F)   (B)
BUCHSBAUM, RALPH MORRIS, BASIC ECOLOGY PITTS-
BURGH, BOXWOOD PRESS, 1951

CHICU IG2011   (M) OUT OF STOCK   (F)   (B)
CHICAGO UNIVERSITY, INTRODUCTORY GENERAL COURSE
IN THE PHYSICAL SCIENCES. CHICAGO, UNIVERSITY OF
CHICAGO PRESS, 1949-50.

COOKMTVV2101   (M) ON ORDER   (F)   (B)
COOK, MELVILLE THURSTON, VIRUSES AND VIRUS DI-
SEASES OF PLANTS. MINNEAPOLIS, MINNESOTA, BUR-
GESS PUBLISHING CO., 1947.

FAEGMEYC1991   (M) CANCELLED   (F)   (B)
FAEGE, MARION ELLISON (LYON), YOUR CHILD FROM
6 to 12. WASHINGTON, U.S.GOVERNMENT PRINTING
OFFICE 1949.

FENTN PF2051   (M) CHECKED IN   (F)   (B) 00
                                        RNYP
FENTON, NORMAN, THE PRISONERS FAMILY/A STUDY OF
FAMILY COUNSELING IN AN ADULT CORRECTION SYSTEM.
PALO ALTO, CALIF.   PUBLISHED FOR THE AMERICAN
CORRECTIONAL ASSOCIATION BY PACIFIC BOOKS, 1959.

FICHJHSR2041   (M) ON ORDER   (F)   (B)
FICHTER, JOSEPH HENRY, SOCIAL RELATIONS IN THE
URBAN PARISH, CHICAGO, UNIVERSITY OF CHICAGO
PRESS, 1954.

FITEEDS11971   (M) SEARCHING   (F)   (B)
FITE, EMERSON DAVID, SOCIAL AND INDUSTRIAL CONDI-
TIONS IN THE NORTH DURING THE CIVIL WAR.   NEW
YORK, THE MACMILLAN CO., 1910.

GIBSRESA2021   (M) CHECKED IN   (F)   (B) RO
                                        RAPFP
GIBSON, RALPH EDWARD, SCIENCE ART AND EDUCATION.
IN SMITHSONIAN INSTITUTION ANNUAL REPORT, WASH-
INGTON, 1954.

GLASDVSM1981   (M) ON ORDER   (F)   (B) 00
GLASS, DAVID VICTOR, SOCIAL MOBILITY IN BRITAIN.
GLENCOE ILLINOIS, FREE PRESS, 1954.

JORDE GL2071   (M) REORDER ON   (F)   (B)
                       3 SEPT
JORDAN, ELIFAH, THE GOOD LIFE.   CHICAGO, CHICAGO
UNIVERSITY PRESS, 1949.

KAESH BB2051   (M) CATALOGING   (F)   (B)RI
                                        RAPFP
KAESE, HAROLD, THE BOSTON BRAVES.   NEW YORK,
G.P. PUTNAM'S SONS, 1948.

Also, to keep the work load of the acquisitions staff more even and prevent the rush of orders which frequently comes at the end of the budget year, quarterly allocation of funds might be required. A computer could easily handle the bookkeeping involved in the fund allocation routine.

Gift and exchange material would be added to the PIL as soon as it arrived and slack time was available at the key-punch machine. The entries would be taken from the title page by the keypunch operator and no effort would be made to sort out duplicates or verify entries beyond one initial sorting by the acquisitions librarian. Doubtful pieces would probably be checked against the catalog during the preliminary sort. Verification and cataloging of these materials would take place only in slack periods (as they are now handled) in the cataloging department, but they would be available for "use" by being listed, albeit imperfectly, in the PIL until they had been completely cataloged.

The check-in cards, punched as part of the original order cycle, would be gang punched with the date. These dates would be used to construct statistical reports on work loads and process rates so a more efficient job of administering could be done because of the better information available.

When material arrives it would be checked against the Processing Information List, one of the two check-in cards pulled and used to up date the PIL. The other check-in card would be pulled when the invoice arrives and also be used for up dating purposes. After checking for damage (in which case a notice would be sent and the material and the invoice held) the book would be sent to cataloging. The invoice check-in card would have the actual price of the item punched into it and be used to up date the financial records and the fund reports. All reports, forms, etc. would be produced by the computer.

The most expensive part of this proposed acquisitions system is, of course, the Processing Information List. The potential cost for this item can be figured in the following way:

Assume:

1. Page size: 11" x 14".

2. Page layout: 2 columns.

3. Lines per page: 54.

4. Characters per title: 300.

5. Number of titles per tape record: 10.

6. Number of titles per UNIT: 1000.

7. Average processing time for a piece of material, ten weeks.

8. The design load of 24,000 titles per year will be assumed as equivalent to 500 per week.

Calculations:

1. Number of pages required to print 1000 titles: 56.

2. Number of lines to be printed per 1000 titles:

    = (Number of pages per 1000 titles) x (Number of

    lines per page)

    = 56 pages x 54 lines.

    = 3,024 lines per 1000 titles.

3. Time required to print 1000 titles:

    = (Number of lines per 1000 titles)
      _____
      (Number of lines per minute printer speed)

    = 3,024 lines per 1000 titles
      _____
      600 lines per minute

    = 5.04 minutes.

4. Estimated cost to print 1000 titles per issue

    = (Machine rental per hour) x

    (Number of minutes per 1000 titles)
    _____
    (Number of minutes per hour)

    = ($100 per hour) x (5.04 minutes per 1000 titles)
                        _____
                        (60 minutes per hour)

    = $8.00-$9.00 per 1000 titles per issue.

5. Numbers of items to be printed per issue of the Processing Information List.

$$\begin{cases} = \text{Lower bound:} \left(\dfrac{\text{Number of items}}{\text{Week}}\right)\left(\begin{array}{l}\text{Number of weeks}\\ \quad \text{to process} \quad -1\end{array}\right)\\[3ex] = \text{Upper bound:} \left(\dfrac{\text{Number of items}}{\text{Week}}\right)\left(\begin{array}{l}\text{Number of weeks}\\ \quad \text{to process} \quad +4\end{array}\right) \end{cases}$$

$$\begin{cases} = \text{Lower bound:} \left(\dfrac{500 \text{ items}}{\text{Week}}\right) \ (10 \text{ weeks} - 1 \text{ week})\\[3ex] = \text{Upper bound:} \left(\dfrac{500 \text{ items}}{\text{Week}}\right) \ \ 10 \text{ weeks} + 4 \text{ weeks}) \end{cases}$$

$$\begin{cases} = \text{Lower bound:} \quad 4500 \text{ items.}\\[2ex] = \text{Upper bound:} \quad 7000 \text{ items.} \end{cases}$$

6. Estimated cost to print one issue of the Processing Information List.

   = (Number of 1000 titles per issue) x
   (Cost to print 1000 titles)

   $=$ Lower bound: (4.5) x ($9.00)

   Upper bound: (7.0) x ($9.00)

   $=$ Lower bound: $40.50 per issue

   Upper bound: $63.00 per issue

7. Estimated cost per year to print one issue per week of the Processing Information List.

   = (Number of weeks per year) x (cost per issue)

   $=$ Lower bound: (52) x ($40.50)

   Upper bound: (52) x ($63.00)

Lower bound: $2,106 per year
=
Upper bound: $3,276 per year

Note that the range of the price from the upper bound to the lower bound is entirely dependent upon the amount of time an item is in process from ordering to the shelves, i.e. is listed in the PIL.   This directly affects the size and therefore the cost of the list.   Anything done to reduce the time taken for the acquisitions - cataloging cycle will immediately and directly reflect in a cost reduction.

Cataloging Department.   The primary function of the cataloging department, i.e. the intellectual effort in assigning subject headings and subject classifications and in describing the book, for those items which have not been so assigned previously, will not be changed.   Automation will affect cataloging in eliminating the clerical burden of maintaining the catalogs and shelf lists and in preparing book cards, pockets, and labels.   The preparation of book cards and pockets can probably be eliminated once new circulation and cataloging systems are operational.

A general flow chart showing the proposed cataloging department operation is given in Figure 19.

The areas in the catalog department which should gain most from the project are: maintenance of the card catalog,

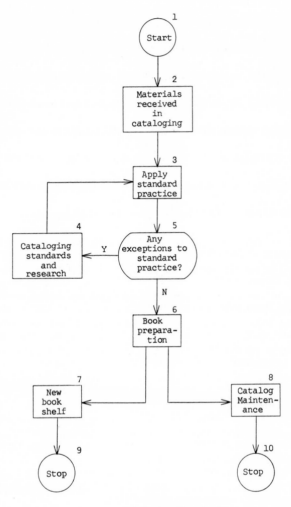

Cataloging Department
Figure 19

139

which is very expensive and should be replaced with two
levels of book catalogs, the Total Holdings Edition (THE)
and the Monthly Edition (ME); notification of interested faculty members and selected students of new acquisitions through
the Current Dissemination of Information List; and the better
use of subject headings with the Permutation of Subject Headings Index (POSH).

As proposed, the cataloging information starts with the
Processing Information List. All items are up-dated with
corrected or new information as this information is generated
or found. In cataloging, this process is continued, and by
the time the book is completely cataloged the entry in the
Processing Information List is complete. The completed
entry is held in the PIL until the next Monthly Edition of the
book catalog is to be printed. Essentially, the book catalog
lists the same information as a typical catalog card. There
is more information available about the item on the tape but
it is suppressed during printing.

At the beginning of each month all completed entries in
the PIL are added to the Monthly Edition. The ME is cumulative and contains all items cataloged since the last edition
of the Total Holdings (the main book catalog). Once the new
ME is issued the previous edition can be destroyed. Eventually it becomes cheaper to print a new edition of the THE.

The Total Holdings Edition contains full bibliographical entries under author, title, and all subject headings. It would be possible and cheaper to produce only the full author entry and skeleton entries under title and subject after the manner of the Cumulative Book Index. All cost figures, however, are calculated on a full entry basis.

The costs for both the Monthly Edition and the Total Holdings Edition are estimated at about $33,000.00 per year. Present catalog maintenance costs do not include the cost of LC cards or the cost of typing and revising cards when LC cards are not available. The costs of ME and THE do not include keypunching the information into the IBM cards or the cost of the LC copy.

It is assumed by General Electric that the UIC Library technical services will be able to handle 24,000 pieces per year or about 2000 per month. Each title will be listed under up to five entries, an average of 2.4 for author - title and 2.6 per subject. Each entry will contain an average of 300 characters. See the appendix for cost calculations on offset printing. It totals $57.16 per 1000 entries.

Calculations:

1. Cost of preparing Total Holdings Edition is given by the
    following:

    $$\$THE = (\text{Number of 1000 titles in the edition}) \times (\text{Cost of entering one unit})$$

    $$\$THE = (A + BM)C_1$$

    where A = the number of 1000 entries appearing in
    the last edition of the THE, B = the number of 1000
    entries being added to the Monthly Edition each month,
    M = the number of months since the last THE, and C_1 =
    the cost to enter 1000 entries in the THE.

2. Cost of preparing the Monthly Edition over a period of
    M months as given by:

    $$\$ME = (\text{Number of 1000 entries in month 1}) \times (\text{Cost per 1000 entries})$$

    $$+ (\text{Number of 1000 entries in month 1} + \text{month 2}) \times (\text{Cost per 1000 entries})$$

    $$+ (\text{Number of 1000 entries in month 1} + \text{month 2} \ldots + \text{Month } (M-1)) \times (\text{Cost per 1000 entries})$$

    $$= \left\{ \frac{B}{2} \ M \ (M-1) \right\} C_2$$

    where M is the number of months since the last THE.
    Note that $(M-1)$ is used instead of $(M+1)$ since the last
    ME is not printed; all new entries plus all of the $(M-1)$
    ME data goes into the next edition of the THE.

B is the number of 1000 entries being added to the
Monthly Edition each month.

C_2 is the cost to enter 1000 entries in the ME.

3. The equations appearing in 1. and 2. can be solved
    simultaneously to give the optimum interval of months
    (m) between successive publications of the THE

$$\$THE = (AC_1) + (BC_1) \ M$$

$$\$ME = + \left(\frac{BC_2}{2}\right) \ M + \left(\frac{BC_2}{2}\right) \ M^2$$

Solving for M gives

$$M^2 - \left(\frac{2C_1}{C_2} + 1\right) M - \frac{2AC_1}{BC_2} = 0$$

Based on the assumptions in terms of 1000 titles

C_1 = \$57.16

C_2 = \$9.00

A = 60

B = 2

Substituting

$$M^2 - 14M - 381 = 0$$

Solving

$$M = \frac{14 + \sqrt{196 + 1524}}{2}$$

$$\simeq 28 \text{ Months}$$

It must be kept in mind that M is the optimum interval (in the sense of least cost) expressed in terms of months that gives the lowest combination of production costs for the THE and the ME.

The values for M, multiplied by the number of titles processed per month, are now added to the former value of A to give a new value of A. The formula is solved again to obtain the next interval which will be optimal for the production of the next Total Holdings Edition. This calculation has been carried out so:

$$M_1 = 28 \text{ months}$$

$$M_2 = 36 \text{ months}$$

$$M_3 = 42 \text{ months}$$

4. Estimated costs of producing book catalogs for a five year span.

The sum of M_1 and M_2 is a span of 64 months, and the following calculation will be carried out on this 64 month base and later annualized.

The cost of producing the monthly edition is given by

$$\$ME = \left\{ \frac{B}{2} \ M \ (M-1) \right\} C_2$$

$$= \left\{ \frac{2}{2} \ M \ (M-1) \right\} \$9$$

$$= \$9 \ M \ (M-1)$$

Letting $M = M_1 = 28$

$$\$THE = (60 + 2.28) \ \$57.16 = \$6631.$$

Letting $M = M_2 = 36$

$$\$THE = (116 + 2.36) \ \$57.16 = \$10,746.$$

Adding the costs for the Monthly Edition and the Total Holdings Edition for a year the estimated costs for one year is $6660.00. This cost represents the cost of one card being filed in the catalog (or one entry per title). Since there is an average of five entries per title the total cost would be about $33,300.00 per year.

It might be noted here that although the optimum span for production of the Total Holdings Edition is more than one year it might be well to schedule a new edition of it once each year even if it is more expensive, as budget items which cannot be scheduled into each annual budget have a tendency to get postponed. It would be false economy to let the Total Holdings Edition get one day beyond its planned age.

It would be better instead to produce it a little more frequently than necessary.

The library will be in a good position to notify faculty members and selected students of new material arriving in the library.   The items can be ordered out by author, subject heading, or classification number.   Patrons wishing to participate in the dissemination program will have the terms in which they are interested punched into cards and put on tape.   A match will be made against the new entries for the Monthly Edition and a notice of each item of interest will automatically be sent.   A pre-punched response card could be included each time or at intervals.   Such a card would have to be returned to insure that a patron's name remain on the list.   For instance: three consecutive no response mailings would drop the patron from the dissemination system.

No cost figures have been developed for this dissemination system.   A chart was made by the contractor showing the dissemination possibilities in the present system, in a proposed system using a computer, and in two microfilm catalog systems, one using reels of film and manually operated readers and one using DACOM, which is a computer controlled searching system which has 16mm microfilm as output (See Figure 20).

The chart is largely self-explanatory except for lines as noted. Many of the variations on the chart are up to the installing library and its budget. By and large, these variables do not affect the basic system. Frequency is a good example. It is envisioned that the UIC proposed dissemination system would cycle once per month. The basic system would not be affected if the cycle time were one day or twice each year. The dissemination system would be primarily for faculty members who would sign up for the service. A few selected students might also be put on the list for the term of a specific project. This individual service would have to be gauged against the cost of providing this service through a departmental library.

In Chapter 3, the permutation on subject headings or POSH Index was discussed at some length. Suffice it to say here that specialized bibliographies are possible using the 120 space line and minimum of bibliographic information by permuting on the significant words in the LC subject headings.

The costs for a POSH Index are figured on the basis of using it for the subject listing for the book catalog; both Monthly Edition and the Total Holdings Edition. The cost amounts for this are the same as for the actual projected use of the index for specialized bibliographies. The cost of

FIGURE 20

Retrospective Search Monographic Entries	UIC 1962	UIC 1964 Duplicated	UIC 1964 Photo-Offset	UIC 1964 With Computer	Microfilm Manual	Microfilm DACOM
A Divided Catalog	No	Cards	Book	Cards or Book	Reel	Reel
B Dictionary Catalog-Public	Card	Cards	Book	Cards or Book	Reel	Reel
C Shelf List - Staff use	Card	Cards	Book	Cards or Book	Reel	Reel
Current Accessions						
Author	No	Yes	Yes	Yes	Yes	Yes
Subject – Alphabetical	No	Yes	Subject Headings	Yes	Subject Headings	Yes
Subject – Classified	No	Yes	Decimal Class.	Permuted	Decimal Class.	Permuted
Published	No	Expensive	Yes	Yes	Yes	Yes
Frequency (week-month)			See Text	See Text		
Subscription			See Text	See Text		
Cumulative	No	No	Yes	Book Yes	Yes	Yes
Individual service of current accessions			See Text	See Text		
Fullness of citation			See Text	See Text		
Order of Entries			See Text	See Text		
Frequency of service (daily, weekly, monthly, etc.)			See Text	See Text		
Distribution	No	Yes	Photo-copy	Yes	No	
Dewey Numbers - 16th Ed.			See Text	Yes		Yes
Index Terms						

offset printing is $18.48 per 1000 entries.   Development of
this cost is shown in the appendix.

Estimated cost of production of the Permutation on Subject Headings Catalog.   The formula expressing the intervals
for the POSH index is the same as the one for ME and THE.

$$M^2 - \left(\frac{2C_1 + 1}{C_2}\right) \quad M \quad - \quad \frac{2AC_1}{BC_2} \quad = \quad 0$$

Where the constants now have the values:

C_1 = $18.50

C_2 =   3.00

B   =   2

A   =   60

Solving for M

M_1 =   26

M_2 =   33

Substituting these values in the formula for the Monthly
Edition

$POSH: M_1 = $3   (26) (25)   = $1950.

$POSH: M_2 = $3   (33) (32)   = $3168.

Solving for the Total Holdings Edition

$POSH: TH   = $18.50 $\left[60 + (2 \times 26)\right]$ = $2072.

$POSH: TH   = $18.50 $\left[112 + (2 \times 33)\right]$ = $3293.

Summing the values for the monthly and the total holdings editions for a POSH Index and annualizing: $2148. Estimating costs using a combination of the full entry book catalog for authors-titles and the POSH Index for subject headings.

Assuming 2.4 author entries per title

Annual rate for authors: $6660 x 2.4 = $15,984.

Assuming 2.6 subject heading entries per title

Annual rate for subject headings:

$2148 x 2.6 = $5585.

This yields a book catalog production cost of $21,569.

Circulation Department.   The development of the proposed sub-system for the circulation department is somewhat more nebulous than those of the other departments as no machine exists which will do all of the things the project staff feels is necessary.   Therefore a start will probably be made with a semi-hand system using the punched card of the final system without the fully automatic handling.

The flow chart (Figure 21, and 21A) shows a two phase system.   The first phase checks the book out and cancels the check-out records on the return.   The second phase shows the Daily Circulation List, overdue notices, and faculty holdings lists in preparation.

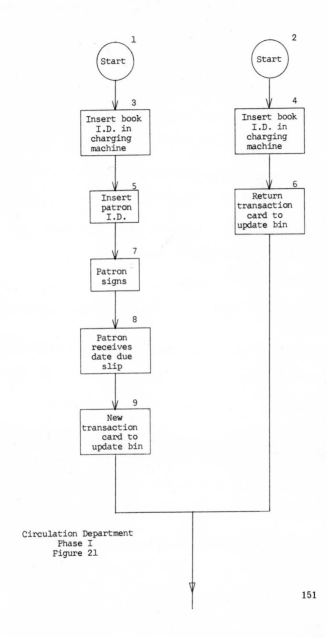

Circulation Department
    Phase I
    Figure 21

151

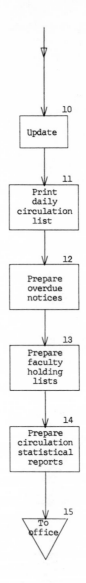

10 Update

11 Print daily circulation list

12 Prepare overdue notices

13 Prepare faculty holding lists

14 Prepare circulation statistical reports

15 To office

152

Circulation Department
Phase II
Figure 21A

The charging machine, from phase one, must:

1. Be simple enough to be operated by college freshmen.

2. Be economical enough so that several can be used,
   i.e. $200 - $300 each.

3. Have a reliability factor of not more than one
   failure in 250,000.

4. Accept 2 input documents: the patron's plastic ID
   card and the IBM book card, and also punch fixed
   data in the source document such as station number and date due.

The circulation staff feels that each station should generate its own documents and not transmit the data to a central
office in the manner of the Datex Corporation's DL - 210
System. A machine which would do both would be ideal.
Until the ideal machine is built, especially adapted hand or
electrically driven source data recorders will probably be
used. Machines of this type are manufactured by Datanamics,
Inc. and Dashew Business Machines, Inc. It is also considered important that two or three completely manual machines
be kept in reserve if the recording of circulation data uses
electric or electronic equipment.

To use these machines the patron would insert his plastic

ID card and the plastic coated IBM book card. If they are
inserted correctly the cards would be returned after a source
document had been punched which would contain the patron's
ID number, the call number of the book, the date due, and
the station number. In addition to this punched information,
the patron's name, address, and ID number could be im-
printed on the face of the card. The source document would
be made in duplicate so that one copy could remain with the
book and act as the return card. This second source document would also be the date due card and would have the
date due both pre-printed and pre-punched on it. If necessary, it would also be possible to have the student sign the
original source document before the charging process
begins.

The punched book card is generated by the computer from
the tape originally made as part of the acquisitions process
and up dated during the cataloging routines. This card is
kept in the book at all times and a fee would be charged for
any books returned without it. The possibility of having the
call number on the book in machine readable form is being
investigated. If this effort is successful the book card in
any form could be done away with.

The source record card would be used to print a list of
all material checked out of the library. This list, called

the Daily Circulation List, would be produced by the computer each evening after the library closed and would be ready before opening time the next morning. It would only be produced five days per week even if the library were open longer hours than this. General Electric's proposed form, (Figure 22), allows 14 positions for the call number and three for the date due. Because it will be necessary to add the patron's ID number, the size and cost of the list will be increased about 50% because only four rows instead of six can be accommodated. As this will use only 114 of the 120 available spaces, the call number of each item could be expanded to 15 spaces at no additional cost. An analysis of the call numbers at the UIC Library was made and it was found that 98% of the call numbers took 14 spaces or less. If this system were adopted, it would probably be well to put a limit of 15 spaces on call numbers and not allow the cataloging department to assign any over that length. There are also other advantages in having fixed length numbers when machine uses are contemplated. Note that the date due is given as a three digit number. This is the number of the day of the year. For example, January 1 is 001, May 24 is 144, and December 6 is 340.

Every book not on the shelf would be listed in the Daily Circulation List. Locations, such as repair, display, or

FIGURE 22

DAILY CIRCULATION LIST   31 JULY 1961

Call No.		Call No.		Call No.		Call No.	
016.371A375H3	220	330.942H669C	213	506S664A	223	616.01B619M2	213
016.5515T519B	223	330.973F546S	215	509.2E14YM	221	616.8H323A	221
016.62S741B	208	331.88S824S	219	510J27T	214	618.92M681P	213
016.813H859G	221	332.6D546S	212	510P868M	216	620.11F514C	223
919I29D	207	335G583F	220	510.78M151M	208	620.78N736P	222
025.129S535U	219	336.73W739F	219	517G716C	215	620.9C951E	209
125.2D796B	222	337E56I	209	517M648A	223	621.04B326E	220
031T289	212	338.7D734M	212	519W628C	213	621.381B418M	215
131.32D486S	216	339.973B234W	215	526.98T671M	206	621.384M322E	215
136.7U58CX	223	341.1G654U	207	530C532I	214	623.8L429D	221
136.7W493A	213	343.73F334D	221	532B358I	213	624.154C516F	205
136.73U58CA	220	347.7B583C	223	535H893N	215	631.3W663S	209
136.7352G389I	216	352.8P269U	222	537.1J15I	213	632.3C771V	221
151.2Y46P	222	355.48B963S	220	539.1F359E	209	636.7K55H	216
160B974R	215	364.36B393F	214	539.2K62I	212	641.5L524C	216
170J82G	220	365F342P	221	541.3W517P	219	658.1P145S	214
195B898YS	216	368.03C443D	214	554.8B859I	219	668.4R658M	220
220.88W875B	213	371B296T	216	549K91G	208	671L7430	222
270.6L973YLI	223	371.1B355T	222	551.31E19G	216	701B422W	223
277.3B598P	209	371.335D328M	215	553.8H148D	213	709R283AR	220
282.73F445R	220	371.425M823B	221	572G618E	215	709.6G846F	223
301.15B862S2	219	378.12C397T	216	572H572E	222	720C874A	222
301.158C233I	222	388N277B	220	574.9B921B	209	720.9K49H	221
301.3C592I	216	396G592R	212	575F699M	215	722.5B985A	212
323.1091N	223	412L759S	221	580.92B946H	206	728S632H	219
323.3G549S	213	420K35C	223	591.5B835A	216	741.91K63	223

cataloging, could be listed in place of the patron's ID number and the date due, or these could be carried in the Monthly Edition. It would be much cheaper to put them in the Daily Circulation List. It would be assumed that the DCL would read "down the columns." However, if the internal core memory of the computer is too small, and for forty 120 space lines it would have to be 4800 characters plus space for the programs, the entries would have to be printed across the page from left to right. This is because the computer prints out the whole 120 space line in one pass. If "down the column" reading is needed, the memory must hold the whole page so that items No. 1, No. 41, No. 81, and No. 121 can be printed at the same time.

When a book is returned, the date due card is removed and the book is sent to the shelf. The card is gang punched or pre-punched for return and is used to delete the entry from the circulation tape. If librarians fear that the wrong card will get into the wrong book, then the card could be verified by several different methods before being sent to update the tape. If verification were made, the cost of circulation would be doubled.

The cost of the DCL, including complete maintainance of the circulation files but not sending of overdue notices or faculty lists, is figured in the following way.

Assumptions:

1. Page size: 11" x 14"

2. Page layout: 6 columns

3. Lines per page: 57

4. Print positions per entry:

> 14 + blank for call number and
>
> 3 + 2 blanks for date due,
>
> = 20 print positions per entry.

5. Call number of greater length than 14 will occupy two lines of printing.

6. One unit: 100,000 entries.

7. Number of early returns equals the number of over-dues.

8. 100,000 circulation transactions per year is equivalent to 400 per day.

9. Number of days in the circulation cycle: 14.

10. Printed five times per week.

11. Patron ID number will not be printed.

Calculations:

1. Number of entries per page:

> = (Number of columns per page) x (Number of lines per page)
>
> = 6 x 57
>
> = 342 entries per page.

2. Number of transactions per cycle:

    = (Number of transactions per day) x
         (Number of days in cycle)

    = (400) x (14)

    = 5600 transactions.

3. Number of pages in the DCL per day (5600 entries):

    = $\dfrac{\text{(Number of transactions per cycle)}}{\text{(Number of entries per page)}}$

    = $\dfrac{5600}{342}$

    = 17 pages.

4. Number of lines per printing per transactions per

    cycle:

    = (Number of lines per page) x (Number of pages)

    = 57 x 17

    = 969 lines.

5. Time to print one transaction cycle:

    = $\dfrac{\text{(Number of lines of printing}}{\text{(Number of lines per minute printing speed)}}$

    = $\dfrac{969}{600}$

    = 1.615 minutes.

6. Time to print DCL per year per unit:

    = (Number of days per week) x (Number of weeks
         per year) x (Number of minutes to print one unit)

    = 5   x   52   x   1.615

= 420 minutes per year.

7. Cost to print the DCL per year per unit;

= (Machine rental per hour) x
$$\frac{(\text{Number of printing minutes per year})}{(\text{Number of minutes per hour})}$$

= \$100 x $\frac{420}{60}$

= \$700 per year per unit.

8. Cost to handle CUD estimated load on DCL per year:

= (Number of units per year) x (Cost per unit)

= 4 x \$700

= \$2800 per year.

Serials Department.   The serials department revolves around the Central Serials Record, which, as was explained in Chapter 5, is on 5" x 8" Acme cards.   These cards are arranged by title of the periodical and are not available as an ordered list of all kinds of serials information.   Five other files have been set up to supplement the central check-in file.   They are: financial records, bindery file of duplicate bindery slips, dead titles file, purchase order file, and index file.

The proposed serials system is based on a book form of the Central Serials Record (CSR) and its supplementary files. The broad flow charts for the proposed serials operation show (Figures 23, 23A, and 23B) both the materials check-in procedure and the order cycle procedure.

Serials material which arrives in the mail is sorted and put into alphabetical order. A punched card is then pulled from a tub file to match each item received and the card is put into a received bin. The card is later gang punched for date received and used to update the tape from which the Weekly Periodical List and, eventually the Annual Periodical Holdings List are made.   Material received from the bindery and indexes received from the vendor are checked in the same way, except the cards are in separate trays in the tub file.

The Weekly Periodical List is arranged alphabetically by title and the entries contain, in addition to the title, the date the last issue was received, the expected date of arrival of the next issue, issues being claimed, issues that are missing and have been reordered, volumes or part volumes at the bindery, and indexes on order. A preliminary sample page was made using the specifications set down by the contractor (Figure 24). The project staff felt that the information contained in this list was inadequate but as the necessary information is to be on the master tape, it would only be a matter of programming to get the proper data.

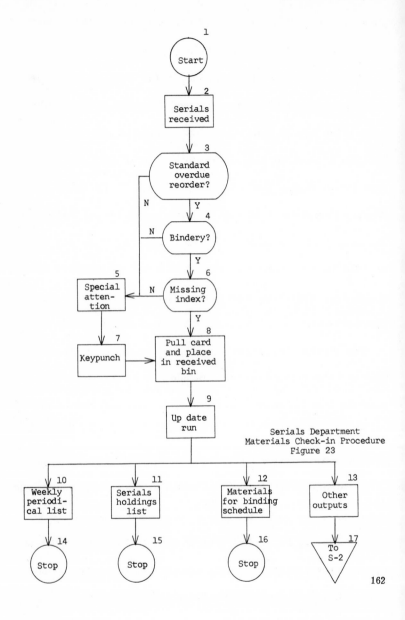

Serials Department
Materials Check-in Procedure
Figure 23

162

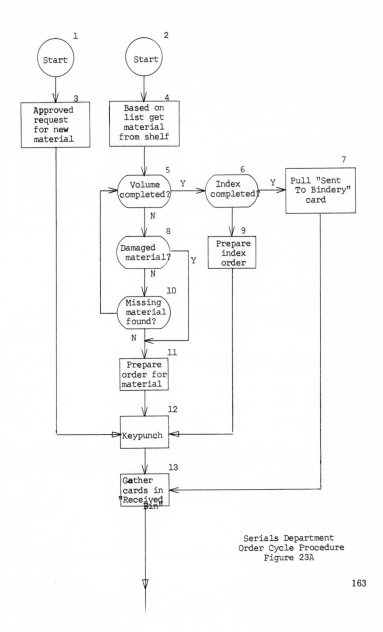

Serials Department
Order Cycle Procedure
Figure 23A

163

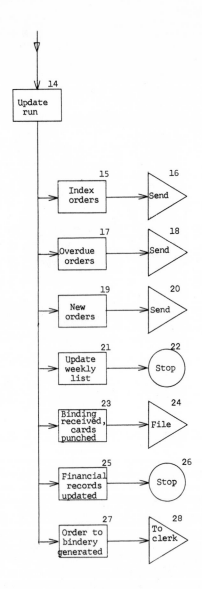

Serials Department
Order Cycle Procedure
Figure 23B

164

FIGURE 24   WEEKLY LIST OF CURRENT PERIODICALS   24-28 JULY

TITLE	CV#	I/Y	ADA	TITLE	CV#	I/Y	ADA
ACOUSTICAL SOC OF AM BU	16	4	15	FAMILY HANDYMAN	27	6	12
ACTA CYTOLOGICA	27	3	5	FLUGWELT	51	12	10
AGRICULTURAL RESEARCH	37	12	7	FUSION	18	4	5
AM CATHOLIC SOC REVIEW	75	4	5	FUEL OIL NEWS	121	12	20
AMERICAN RECORD GUIDE	10	12	5	GIFTED CHILD	10	4	7
ANLS OF HUMAN GENETICS	87	4	4	HARVARD BUSINESS REVIEW	39	6	10
AR FUR OHREN NASEN UND	221	2	8	HOTEL WORLD RV & HT MG	62	48	WED
ARTS MAGAZINE	73	10	7	INDUSTRIAL ARTS TEACHE	17	5	6
AUSTRALIAN METEORL MAG	42	4	5	INST RAD ENG PROC	51	12	7
BELL SYSTEM TECHNICA J	62	6	7	INTER-AMER ELON AFFAIR	27	4	4
BOOKS AND BOOKMEN	51	12	16	INT REV OF MISSIONS	118	4	8
BR NUCLEAR ENG CONF JL	17	4	24	JOBS AND FUTURES	20	10	16
BUSINESS EDUCATION WOR	22	10	5	JOURNAL OF COMMER ART	55	12	16
CANADIAN BEE JOURNAL	50	12	17	JL OF MACHINE ACCOUNTG	17	11	19
CANNING TRADE	72	52	TUE	JL OF REHABILITATION	62	6	5
CHEMISCH WEEKBLAD	16	52	FRI	LIBRARY JOURNAL	122	22	FRI
CHRISTIAN SCIENC MONIT	182	312	12	LIFE AND HEALTH	31	12	10
COMMERCE	50	12	5	LIFE MAGAZINE	24	52	MON
CONTROL ENGINEERING	21	12	10	LISTENER	8	52	MON
CURRENT SOCIOLOGY	17	3	11	MANCHESTER GUARDIAN	156	252	MON

(CV#)   Current Vol. Number
(I/Y)   Issues Per Year
(ADA)   Average Day of Arrival

The expected date of arrival of the next issue is the triggering date for the claim slip, which is automatically sent to the vendor if the issue is more than a set number of days late. When an issue is claimed, a missing issue is reordered or an item is sent to the bindery, a card is punched for filing in the tub file as a future check-in card.

Each title has all of its bibliographic and financial information on the master periodicals tape. This tape is used to generate a set of punched cards, one for each issue, one for each index, and one for each bound volume, which are filed in the tub file as received cards. It should not take any longer to pull the correct card from the tub file when an issue arrives and put the card in the received bin for tape updating than it does to check in the periodical by present methods.

There are two ways to have the computer punch out the check-in cards. First, they can be punched out once per month and the monthly batch filed as one unit. If there are any cards left over at the end of the month, they would be potential claim cards and could be either kept separate (making another place to look if an issue is late) or inter-filed in the tub with the new month's cards. Second, the cards could be punched out only once per year. This would make only one filing and refiling per year instead of twelve but would increase the initial size of the file from 5500 cards to 65,000. It would take three 68" tub files to hold 65,000 cards.

The proposal is to start with the current materials only. The data for the balance of the CSR would be punched during slack periods. This would be completed in about two years.

Usually, binding schedules call for large numbers of periodicals to be bound in January and July of each year. An effort to even out the binding load for both the serials staff and the bindery personnel has resulted in a plan to schedule some binding each month depending on end-of-volume date, frequency of binding, promptness of index arrival ,etc. This plan would be affected by missing issues, which would call for rescheduling if the volume were not ready to send when scheduled.

Financial records and orders for new subscriptions would be printed once per year from the master serials tape. Any notices of changes of title, periodical price, frequency, or any other thing affecting the master tape would have to be punched and then used to update the tape record.

The cost of the Weekly Serials List would be less than $50.00 per month. It has been estimated that savings in the reference department would be $700.00 per year if this list were available.

Assumptions:

1. Page size: 11" x 14"

2. Page layout: 2 columns per page.

3. Lines per page: 57

4. One unit: 1000 titles

5. Number of characters per title: 58

6. Number of titles per tape record: 20

7. Number of titles received per year: 6500

8. Number of serial pieces received per title per
    year: 10

Calculations:

1. Number of items per page.

    = (Number of lines per page) x
        (Number of columns per page)

    = 57   x   2

    = 114 items per page.

2. Number of pages required to print 1000 titles.

    = $\dfrac{\text{(Number of items per 1000 titles)}}{\text{(Number of items per page)}}$

    = $\dfrac{1000}{114}$

    = 9 pages.

3. Number of lines to be printed per 1000 titles.

   = (Number of pages) x (Number of lines per page)

   = 9   x   57

   = 513 lines.

4. Number of cards received per week per 1000 titles.

   $$= \frac{\text{(Number of titles) x (Number of pieces per title)}}{\text{(Number of weeks per year)}}$$

   $$= \frac{1000 \times 10}{52} \quad = \quad \frac{10000}{52}$$

   = 193 cards per week.

5. Number of cards punched per month for check-in
   cards per 1000 titles.

   $$= \frac{\text{(Number of titles) x (Number of pieces per title)}}{\text{(Number of months per year)}}$$

   $$= \frac{1000 \times 10}{12} \quad = \quad \frac{10000}{12}$$

   = 833 cards.

6. Number of seconds to transfer 1000 titles from tape
   to memory.

   $$= \frac{\left(\dfrac{\text{Number of titles}}{\substack{\text{Number of titles} \\ \text{per record}}} \right)}{\text{(Number of inches per second tape speed)}} \quad \text{x}$$

   $$\frac{\left\{ \left(\substack{\text{Number of titles} \\ \text{per record}} \right) \text{x} \dfrac{\left(\substack{\text{Number of} \\ \text{characters} \\ \text{per title}} \right) \text{x} \left(\substack{\text{EOR} \\ \text{Gap}} \right)}{\text{Number of characters per inch}} \right\}}{\text{(Number of inches per second tape speed)}}$$

$$= \left(\frac{1000}{20}\right) \quad x \quad \left\{\frac{(20 \quad x \quad 58) \; + \; .75"}{200}\right\}$$

$$\overline{\hspace{4cm} 75" \text{ per second}}$$

$$= \frac{50 \quad x \quad 6.55}{75"}$$

$$= \quad 4.37 \text{ seconds.}$$

7. Time to print 1000 titles.

$$= \frac{\text{(Number of lines to print 1000 titles)}}{\text{(Number of lines per minute printer speed)}}$$

$$= \frac{500}{600}$$

$$\simeq \quad 1 \text{ minute per 1000 titles.}$$

8. Time to print CUD estimated load.

    = (Number of units of 1000 titles) x
    (Time to print one unit)

    = 6.5 x 1

    = 6.5 minutes

9. Estimated cost to print CUD estimated load per week.

    = (Machine rental per hour) x
      $$\frac{\text{(Time to print CUD load in minutes)}}{\text{(Number of minutes per hour)}}$$

    = \$100 per hour x $\dfrac{6.5 \text{ minutes}}{60}$

    $\simeq$ \$11 per week.

10. Estimated cost to produce weekly periodical list
    per year.

    = (Number of weeks per year) x (Weekly cost)

    = 52 x 11

    = $572.

The Serials Holdings List would be produced on an annual basis and would, like all other serials records, be produced from the master serials tape. For a sample page of this list see Figure 25. If this were a little less cryptic it would probably be easier to use. The cost, of course, would double if the size of the entry were doubled.

The cost of the Serials Holdings List is calculated as follows:

Assumptions:

1. Paper size: 11" x 14"

2. Page layout: 1 column per page

3. Number of lines per title: 1

4. Number of titles per page: 80

5. Page costs for offset printing (1000 copies):
   $10 per page.

6. 1 unit = 1000 titles.

7. Number of titles received per year: 6500

FIGURE 25

SERIALS HOLDINGS LIST

AMERICAN HORTICULTURE MAGAZINE (4) VB (15-39) V40 ADA (J.A.J.O. 12)

ATLANTIC MONTHLY (12) VB (1-104) M (105-105   VB (107-206) V207 ADA-3

AVIATION WEEK (52) VB (67-72) V (73-74) ADA-FRI

CHRISTIAN CENTURY (52) VB (1-77) ADA-TUES

FOREIGN AFFAIRS (4) VB (20-38) ADA (J.A.J.O. 17)

FORTUNE (12) VB (1-63) ADA-5

HARVARD BUSINESS REVIEW (6) VB (1-16) M (17) V (18-38) ADA-10

EXAMPLE

IS READ

ATLANTIC MONTHLY (12) VB (1-104) M (105-106) VB (107-206) V 207 ADA-3

ATLANTIC MONTHLY - 12 ISSUES/YEAR. THE LIBRARY HOLDS BOUND VOLUMES 1-206;
VOLUMES 105-106 ARE MISSING; AND VOLUME 207 IS NOT BOUND.   THE AVERAGE DATE
OF ARRIVAL (ADA) IS THE THIRD OF EACH MONTH.

Calculations:

1. Number of lines of printing per 1000 titles.

    = (Number of titles) x (Number of lines per title)

    = 1000 x 1

    = 1000 lines per 1000 titles.

2. Time required to print 1000 titles.

    = (Number of lines per unit)
      ─────────────────────────────────
      (Lines per minute of printing speed)

    = 1000
      ─────
      600

    = 2 minutes per 1000 titles.

3. Time to print CUD Serials Holdings List.

    = (Number of estimated units) x
          (Time to print one unit)

    = 6.5 x 2

    = 13 minutes.

4. Cost to print Serials Holdings List.

    = (Machine rental per hour) x
          (Time to print one unit)
          ─────────────────────────
                  60

    = $100 x   13
             ─────
               60

    ≅ $22 per year per unit.

5. Number of pages to be offset printed per 1000 titles.

    = $\dfrac{\text{(Number of lines per 1000 titles)}}{\text{(Number of lines per page}}$

    = $\dfrac{1000}{80}$

    = 13 pages per 1000 titles.

6. Estimated cost to offset print 1000 copies per

    1000 titles.

    = (Number of pages per 1000 titles) x (Cost per page)

    = 13 x $10

    = $130 per 1000 copies per 1000 titles.

7. Estimated cost to offset print 1000 copies of the

    Serials Holding List.

    = (Number of units of 1000 titles) x (Cost per unit)

    = 6.5 x $130

    = $845   per year.

For discussion of the recommendations in this chapter,
please see Chapter 9.

CHAPTER 8

In the July 1945, issue of the Atlantic Monthly, Dr. Vannevar Bush, then Director of the Office of Scientific Research and Development, proposed that everyone having to deal with published materials have a desk-sized machine which would store, on microfilm, all material in which he was interested. The "Memex," as Dr. Bush called it, would be able to retrieve any of the documents stored in it and produce hard copy if needed. The key to the whole affair was the index, which was not provided. Several concrete attempts to produce machines which do what Dr. Bush envisioned have been made in recent years. These efforts have enjoyed varying degrees of success and all have stumbled over the problem of indexing.

A distinction should be made between document retrieval and information retrieval. Documents are normally retrieved by author, title, or discrete identification number. The use of any periodical index or the card catalog by author and/or title entry gives the data necessary to retrieve a document from the shelves. If an approach to these tools is through subjects, then the resultant retrieval is informational, i.e. by subject. Most documentalists do not consider the unsophisticated results of card catalog searching as true retrieval but the principle is exactly the same.

In order to search on specific subjects, in greater detail, or on two or more subjects as they are related, indexing in greater depth is necessary. The UIC Project staff felt that university libraries would not be willing or financially able to index in more depth than they are presently doing.

By and large, machines for retrieval are both document and information retrievers. The operational aspects of six of these systems are listed below.

The Rapid Selector. Dr. Vannevar Bush set the stage in several articles written just after WW II for this first retrieval machine effort. The United States Department of Agriculture, under the leadership of its librarian, Dr. Ralph R. Shaw, took Dr. Bush's idea and built a prototype retrieval machine. It was called the Rapid Selector. The storage medium, like most of the subsequent devices, was on microfilm (35mm.) and coding was by a series of binary dots on the film preceding each document image. The index code was punched into cards for the retrieval and placed in the "comparator," which reads the pattern and compares it to the dots on the film. A 2:1 microfilm copy of the correct

image is made when a match is recognized. A later version
was taken over by the Bureau of Standards and then by the
Navy Department's Bureau of Ships. BUSHIPS has worked
with it and, using the same principles, has built an improved model of the Rapid Selector and it is part of their Publications and Information Retrieval Branch work. Recent information on the Rapid Selector is available in a brochure:
The Bureau of Ships Rapid Selector (Navy Department, Bureau of Ships, Code 240, December 23, 1959, 10p.) and in
a magazine article by Howard R. Ball, Head, Publications
and Information Retrieval Branch, titled Bureau of Ships
Rapid Selector (Bureau of Ships Journal 10:6-7, November
1961). A still later version, noted below, was built by
F.M.A., Inc. and installed in the Navy Department Bureau
of Ships in 1962.

Media. Media (Magnavox Electronic Data Image Appara-
tus) is strictly a document retrieval machine. Each document is assigned a number, filmed, and the film clip is
filed in a metal, open topped capsule. The capsule is placed in a special filing cabinet and the location of the capsule
by cabinet, drawer, and location within the drawer are noted.
When the document image is needed again, the number must
be looked up in an index. The first part of the number is

the cabinet, the next part the drawer, the next part the location in the drawer.   The capsule is placed in the selector-
reproducer and the last part of the 17 digit number is keyed
into the machine.   The selector checks the numbers on each
of the 200 media cards in the capsule, makes a photocopy of
the correct one, and returns the stack of film clips to the
capsule.   Additions to the capsules are filed by hand.

Along with the 17 digit location number on the media
card, there is room for a 17 digit code for subject, author,
or other information.   However, no system seems to have
been developed for using this extra code.   Media cards are
16mm   film pieces which can contain two 11" x 14" documents.   Photo reduction is 30x.

FileSearch.   FMA, Incorporated, has developed a microfilm storage and retrieval machine called FileSearch.   The
storage medium is either 35mm or 70mm microfilm with a
photo reduction of 25:1.   Retrieved documents can be viewed
on a projection screen, printed out as hard copy, or printed
out as a 1:1 film copy.   Each document is analyzed and indexed "according to the user's desires."   The index number,
title subjects, or whatever system is used, is typed on a
Flexowriter which produces a punched card containing up to
56 characters of coded information.   This card and the doc-

ument are put into the recording unit which photographs the document and the binary coded information. Up to 1000 feet of film can be spliced together.

A retrieval request is typed on the Flexowriter and the punched card is inserted in the retrieval unit along with the "appropriate" reel of film. Each time a match occurs the film is stopped and projected onto the screen. If a copy, either hard or on film, is desired the correct button is pushed and the copy is made. The search continues after the whole article is copied or read. One thousand feet of film can be searched in five minutes.

Minicard. Minicard is the name selected by Eastman Kodak Company for their microfilm storage and retrieval machine. 16mm microfilm, cut into 32mm lengths and put on storage sticks in lots of 2000 cards, is the storage medium. Each minicard can hold up to 12 legal sized documents or up to 455 characters of binary coded information or any combination of code and document images. The reduction ratio is 60:1.

The code is input on paper tape produced by a tape typewriter. The document and the tape are combined in the Minicard Camera to produce the minicards. After processing, the film pieces are stored on metal rods. The original

film is filed permanently and a duplicate is made for the
working file.

Retrieval is made by punching a paper tape with the correct code words and feeding the tape and the right film magazine into the Minicard Selector. The selected films are
deposited on a storage stick, duplicated, and returned to the
file. The patron checks the selections on the Minicard View-
er and has full-size copies made on the Enlarger-Processor
of the ones he needs. Minicard was built on contract for
the Rome Air Development Center, U. S. Air Force.

Walnut. The latest effort in government sponsored large
capacity document storage and retrieval systems is Walnut,
built by International Business Machines Corporation for the
Central Intelligence Agency.

Basically this retrieval system is in two parts: an adaptation of a RAMAC computer to retrieve document addresses
when queried with either individual or coordinate terms
which match the index terms inserted at the time the document was microfilmed and filed in the retrieval device.

All documents are indexed and microfilmed upon receipt.
Standard 35mm film is used. The index terms and a unique
document number are assigned, punched into paper tape, and
put into the RAMAC index. An input control card with the

document number and page count is loaded into the image
converter where the document image is further reduced and
transferred to the image strip. The file location of the document image is punched into the input control card which, in
turn, is fed into the address section of the index.

The image converter puts the image on a strip of film
which holds 99 page images in three rows of 33 images each.
These strips are filed in image cells containing 50 strips.
The image cells are stored in a bin containing 40 cells in
each of five concentric circular rows. This gives a capacity
of 990,000 images per image storage bin. As many bins as
necessary can be used.

When information is needed, the requestor states his
needs in terms of the index entries. These terms are
punched into paper tape and matching entries are printed out
and address cards are punched. The user selects the entries
he wishes to have reproduced and these address cards are
fed into the retrieval mechanism of the storage bin. The
address card has an aperture containing a piece of undevel-
oped film large enough to receive four document images. As
the address card is read, the bin is rotated to the correct
cell row and shifted to the right circle. The film is removed by a pincer like device which has selected the correct
strip of the 50 in the cell and raised it to the correct image

height.   The optical system is indexed to the right image
row on the strip and an exposure is made. As soon as the
address card is read it is moved into position to receive the
image from the strip in the cell. A mercury vapor lamp
makes the exposure and the film in the aperture card is
fixed by heat. It is then stacked for the user who can read
it on an optical reader or put it in a printer for hard copy.

Verac.   The AVCO Corporation is working on a document
storage and retrieval device called Verac. This machine
differs from the others outlined above in that the photo reduction is as high as 240:1.

Again, no system has been advocated for information retrieval. The user will have to have his own system.

The Verac machine records a page of text on a sheet of
film which would have the images placed serially in discrete
locations. Several film sheets would be stacked together in
the retrieval device. The capacity of each "block" of film
would be 1,000,000 images. This would mean 100 rows of
100 images per sheet of film and 100 sheets to the "block."

Output would be printed onto microfilm and hard copy obtained through a Xerox Copyflo.

The precision involved in the AVCO machine is much
greater than that of the other retrieval devices. Misregister

would give the wrong image rather than a truncated one. It
was hoped that there would be a readout screen, similar to
the one on FileSearch, but optical problems dealing with such
great reductions made the use of a two stage all photographic
printout mandatory.

Each of these information retrieval systems is an ingeni-
ous solution to difficult problems in mechanics, optics, and
chemistry. Unfortunately, all of them rely upon user developed indexing systems which are only as good as the index-
ers and the depth to which they are permitted to go.

The ULIS Project staff does not believe that most university and public libraries will be able to afford indexing or
cataloging in greater depth than that which they now do. They
cannot afford it for two reasons: the financial cost is too
great and the teaching functions of the university library level
demand that the user learn research techniques while using
the library. It is recommended that further consideration
of information retrieval systems be dropped as long as these
systems are in their present state of development.

There is, however, one area of mechanization which has
great possibilities in university libraries and has not at this
point been exploited. This is facsimile transmission. The
expensive part of facsimile transmitters is not the machines
themselves but the electronic connections between the ma-

chines. The best reception is made over either coaxial cable or microwave towers. It is possible to use leased telephone lines, but greatly increased transmission times are encountered in this application.

Tentative plans at UIC call for a microwave hookup between the main University of Illinois campus at Champaign-Urbana and the two Chicago campuses in order to carry television instructional programs. If this network is built, the expense to the UIC Library should not exceed $6,000.00 to install one receiver and transmitter. This would place the three and one half million volume library resources of the main campus at the disposal of the faculty and students of the UIC. All this is possible, but careful analysis of the load potential must be made to see if it is of real value.

Transmission of pages of books, periodicals, maps, pamphlets, memos, letters, drawings, pictures, or anything written or drawn could be done during non-television hours. Requests could be sent to Urbana by telephone or Telautograph. The replies would be batched and transmitted that night so less than 24 hour service could be given. The copies received at UIC would be given to the user who could destroy them when they had served their purpose. Whether or not this would be more economical than special delivery mail service remains to be determined.

Facsimile equipment is in two parts: the receiver and the transmitter (or scanner). They cost about $2,500.00 each or rent for about $200.00 per month per pair. Requirements for library centered facsimile machines include provision for sending copies of pages of bound books or parts of very large maps and other odd-sized materials. Receivers should be automatic so they would not have to be manned when in operation. Copy does not have to be archival quality but the resolution should be fairly fine if small book type or map entries are to be usable. Unfortunately, type sizes smaller than 10 point do not transmit well on these machines because present equipment is limited to a definition of 100 lines per inch or less.

Three companies make equipment in this field. They are Fairchild Camera and Instrument Corporation, Alden Electronic and Impulse Recording Equipment Company, and the Hogan Facsimile Corporation. The Hogan Corporation built a special high speed facsimile printout device for the Navy Department, Bureau of Ships, to transmit engineering drawings from one shipyard to another. This multiplex recorder operates at the rate of 4320 square inches per minute. Most others receive at the rate of about 30 square inches per minute.   This is equivalent to about three minutes per 8-1/2

x 11" page over microwave or six minutes over leased

telephone lines.

REFERENCES

1.   Bush, Vannevar.   "As we may think."   in Atlantic

       Monthly, 176:101-8, July 1945.

CHAPTER 9

Chapter 6 listed the findings of the project up to the receipt of the report of the General Electric Company, the systems contractor. Nearly all of Chapter 7 was taken from their report, Improving information flow in a university library. This final chapter will evaluate certain portions of the General Electric report and state the recommendations of the UIC project staff members, based on the overall study. Most UIC comments on the GE report were stated in Chapter 7, Proposed Systems.

The sample page of the Processing Information List contains no reference to the dealer information which must be included if this list is to be of great value to the library. Fund information will also have to be included, although this can be a three digit code. All this information will be on the magnetic tape, so the entries on the PIL will be a matter of programming. However, the cost as given in Chapter 7 will be less than the actual cost. More work is required to determine what pieces of information are needed in the entry.

The gift and exchange book procedure as outlined in the General Electric report is a completely separate system set up to handle these items. According to the proposed system the acquisitions librarian makes a preliminary sort and the balance of the books are sent to the keypunch operator, who enters the information from the title page into cards. These cards are then used to add these gift and exchange items to the Processing Information List. The books, which are very low priority items, are then sent to storage and are cataloged during slack periods. The entry on the PIL keeps the book's existence in the library before the public service staff.

The acquisitions staff felt that there is no need to set up a separate procedure just for gift and exchange material and the keypunch operator should not be placed in a decision-making situation. It would probably be better to start gift and exchange books in the regular book cycle, i.e. have the order clerk enter known information on the process slip, have the title and author verified, and search the catalog. At this point the process slip would be sent to the keypunch operator. The information on the slip would be punched and added to the PIL.

The entries in the Monthly Edition and the Total Holdings Edition will be as complete as the LC entries. It is not felt that additional cataloging can be afforded, although special files, which are now made by subject librarians and are considered vital in the operation of the public service area, should be done by the cataloging department. Once this additional information is in machine readable form, printing special lists or adding items to the regular entry will be relatively simple.

The cost figures for the additions to the book catalog are not as complete as desired. The costs of reproducing 25 copies of the Monthly Edition seem to need particular attention.

The cost calculations for the cataloging department are based upon a full entry under author, title, and all subject headings. Additional calculations cover the cost of using the POSH Index as the subject part of the main catalog. The intention of the UIC Project staff was, however, to use the POSH Index only for specialized bibliographies printed for the subject divisions. As suggested before, significant savings could be effected if full bibliographic information were given only under the main entry and skeleton information under the added entries. Anything which will cut the length of the entry will save money, but deletions which made the entry less valuable would be foolish.

The circulation department's Daily Circulation List will have to have the ID number of the patron added to each entry. This will raise the cost of this document by 50% per year, as the number of the columns of entries per page will de-

crease from six to four. The GE report stated, as one of
the parameters of this list, that anonymity of the patron was
essential. With this in mind they eliminated reference to
the patron but the circulation staff must be able to identify
the patron in order that books may be recalled for other use
as necessary.

The two serials department lists also needed some attention. The sample page of the Weekly Periodical List was
so lacking in relevancy that it was removed from the report
as circulated. It is, however, included in this final report
as comment can accompany it. The Weekly Periodical List
(Weekly List of Current Periodicals) contained a 22 space
title, the current volume number, the number of issues per
year, and the average date of arrival of each issue. The
entry should include all of the information in the Serials
Holdings List plus total information for any new titles added
since the last issue of the list. The full entry should include holdings, volume numbers and dates, date of last issue
received, arrival date of last issue received, any issues
missing, reordered, or claimed, any volumes at the bindery,
and a code for handling the index (arrives as part of the
last issue in the volume, sent to all subscribers, must be
sent for each time, no index available, etc.)

The weekly list entries, at least the title and holdings, will probably be abbreviated rather than stated in full and the title cross references used in the Serials Holdings List will be eliminated in order to conserve space. Also, serials arriving less frequently than once per year will be omitted from the weekly list.

These proposed changes in the two serials lists will require substantial upward adjustment in the costs given in Chapter 7 for the serials documents.

It is obvious from the above discussion of details concerning the documents proposed by the General Electric Company's Information Systems Section, that the major conclusion of the ULIS Project staff is that a university library can benefit from the application of data processing and systems analysis techniques.

It is further concluded that librarians actually have little choice in applying new techniques, in that something must be done to cut costs, improve efficiency, place the professional librarian in a professional position, and improve service to library users. As time is running out, this action must be taken at once if the library is to remain a dynamic force.

It is therefore recommended that implementation of the University Library Information Systems Project be started without delay. Before an actually operating library can be put on a fully automated basis the following tasks must be accomplished:

1. The basic form of the bibliographic entry must be established and a code devised so that bibliographic lists can be ordered out on any and all pertinent parts of the entry. This list should include codes for all classes of material handled in libraries.

2. A code should be established which will enable periodical titles to be arranged alphabetically. The code should be generated mechanically if possible.

3. A code should be established which would enable entries of books to be arranged alphabetically. This code should also be generated mechanically.

4. A decision must be made to either adapt present filing rules to machine use or to write a completely new set of machine-oriented library filing rules.

5. The adapting of present filing rules or the writing of new ones must be done.

6. A central clearing house for gathering library automation information and coordinating the efforts of those libraries adopting new techniques should be established. This could be a part of the Library of Congress, the American Library Association, or a

library interested in working with the problem. The University of Illinois at Congress Circle might be the most logical location. It is near ALA, near the site of the Midwinter Conference, near the geographic center of transportation, and has done basic investigation in this area.

7. The mathematical models listed in Chapter 7 of this report must be tested for validity in an actual library situation and changes and additions made as necessary.

8. The library of the University of Illinois at Congress Circle should be made the library in which these experiments and studies be carried out because of its unique position in past experience, present size, and proposed future development.

PART TWO

APPENDICES

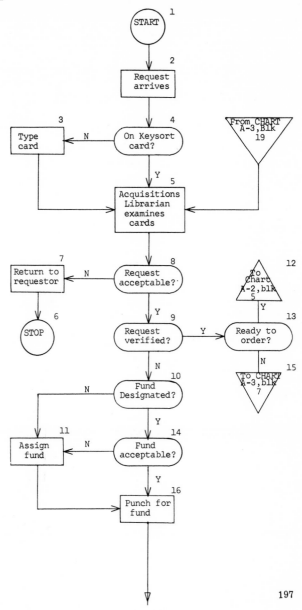

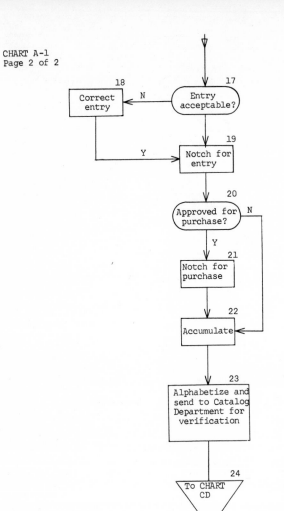

198

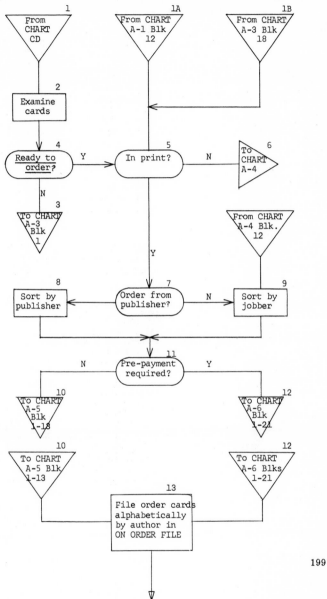

199

200

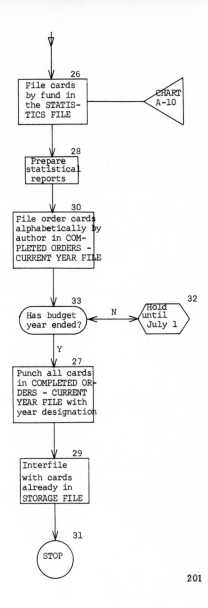

26
File cards
by fund in
the STATIS-
TICS FILE

CHART
A-10

28
Prepare
statistical
reports

30
File order cards
alphabetically by
author in COM-
PLETED ORDERS -
CURRENT YEAR FILE

33
Has budget
year ended?

N

32
Hold
until
July 1

Y

27
Punch all cards
in COMPLETED OR-
DERS - CURRENT
YEAR FILE with
year designation

29
Interfile
with cards
already in
STORAGE FILE

31
STOP

201

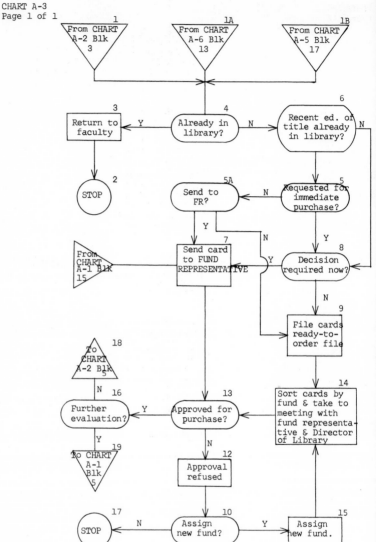

202

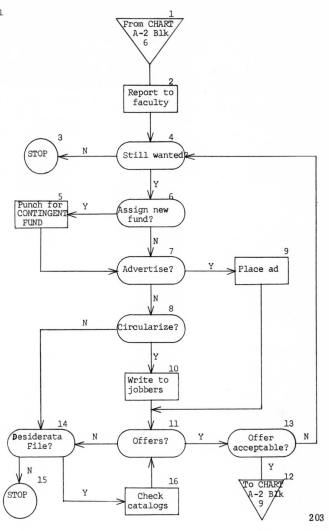

203

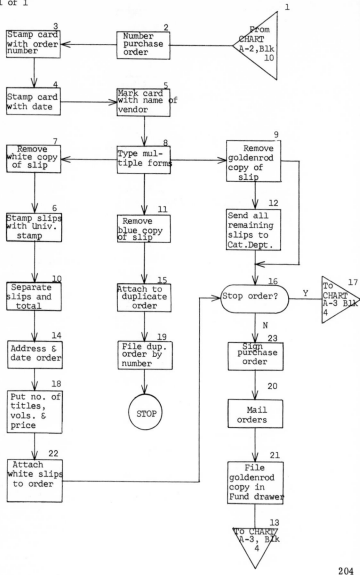

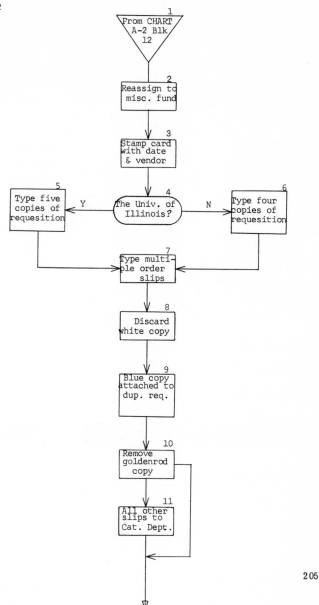

12 Stop order?

Y

13 To CHART A-3 Blk 4

N

14 Send all but dept. copy of requisition to Library Office

15 Hold goldenrod slip, order card & dept. copy of requisition for requisition no.

16 Get number

N

17 Does office send number?

Y

18 Put requisition number on order card, goldenrod slip, & dept. copy of requisition

19 File goldenrod slip in FUND DRAWER

20 File dup. requisition

21 To CHART A-2 Blk 13

206

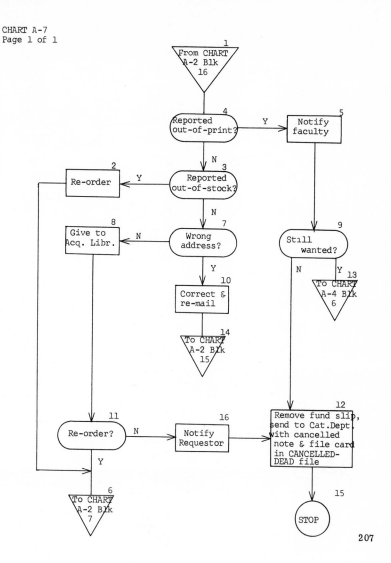

207

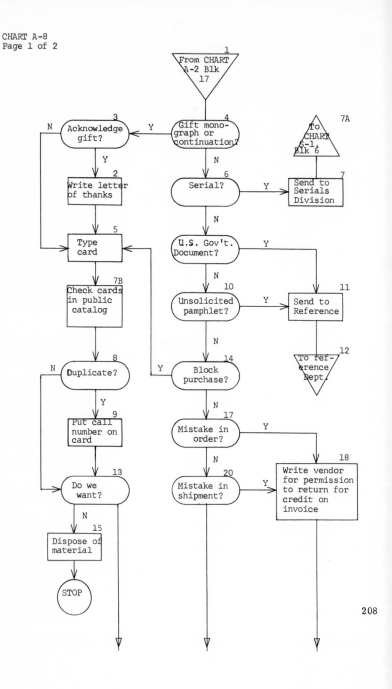

208

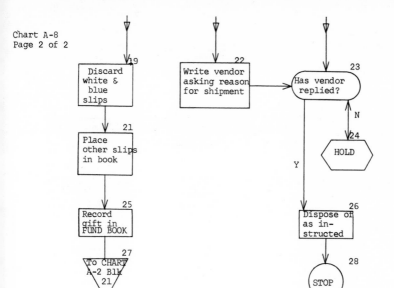

19
Discard
white &
blue
slips

22
Write vendor
asking reason
for shipment

23
Has vendor
replied?

N

24
HOLD

21
Place
other slips
in book

25
Record
gift in
FUND BOOK

Y

27
To CHART
A-2 Blk
21

26
Dispose of
as in-
structed

28
STOP

209

1 From CHART A-2, Blk 20

4 Compare order card & fund slip with title page

2 Book or pamphlet?

3 Phonodisk or painting?

8 Agree?

7 To CHART A-8, Blk 17

5&6 Material to Map Librarian

11 Acceptable condition?

10 To CHART A-8, Blk 18

9 Material to Fine Arts Librarian

15 To be cataloged

14 Reference pamphlet?

16 Stamp covers

13 Underline first letter of author entry on title page

12 Distribute as per instructions on card-- including Serials

20 Material to Reference

17 Mark processing date in gutter of page following title page

18 STOP

19 Stamp edges

210

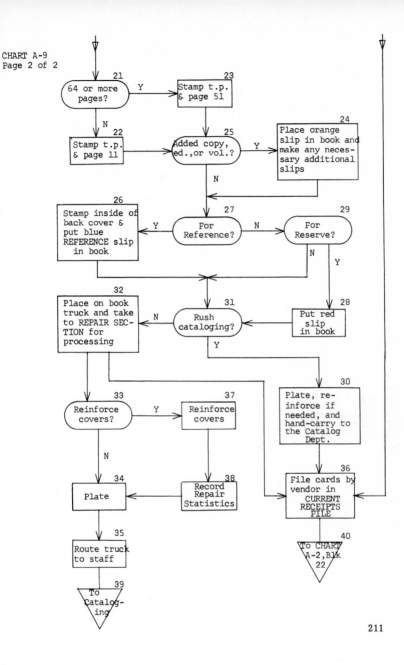

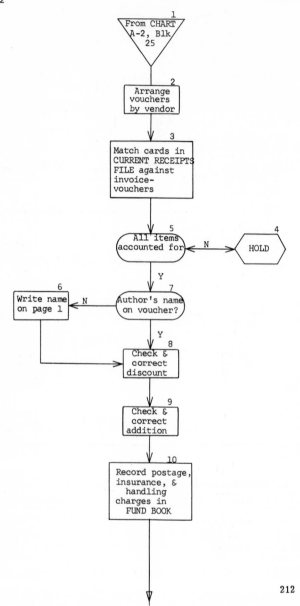

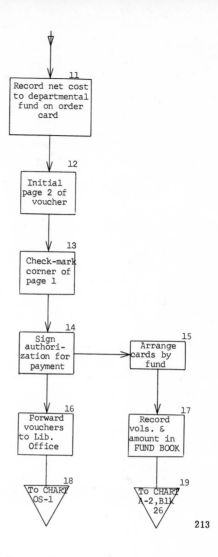

213

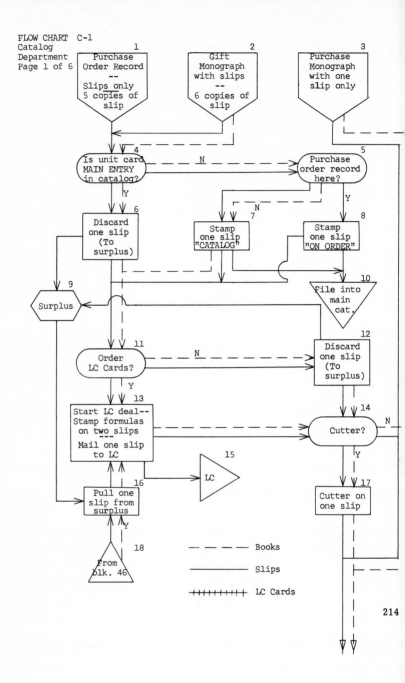

FLOW CHART C-1
Catalog
Department
Page 1 of 6

1 Purchase Order Record -- Slips only 5 copies of slip

2 Gift Monograph with slips -- 6 copies of slip

3 Purchase Monograph with one slip only

4 Is unit card MAIN ENTRY in catalog?

5 Purchase order record here?

6 Discard one slip (To surplus)

7 Stamp one slip "CATALOG"

8 Stamp one slip "ON ORDER"

9 Surplus

10 File into main cat.

11 Order LC Cards?

12 Discard one slip (To surplus)

13 Start LC deal-- Stamp formulas on two slips Mail one slip to LC

14 Cutter?

15 LC

16 Pull one slip from surplus

17 Cutter on one slip

18 From blk. 46

- - - - - Books

——— Slips

++++++++++ LC Cards

214

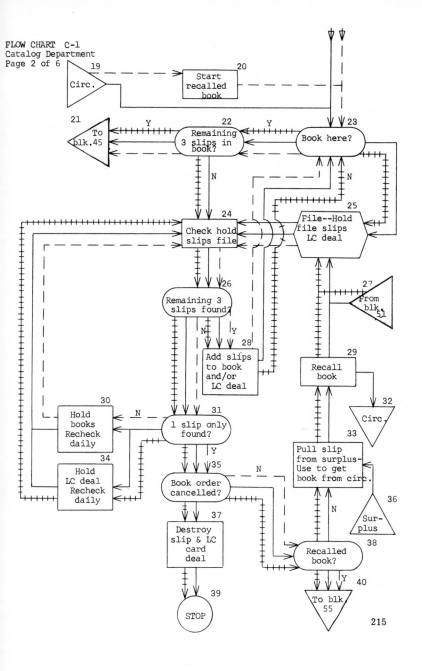

215

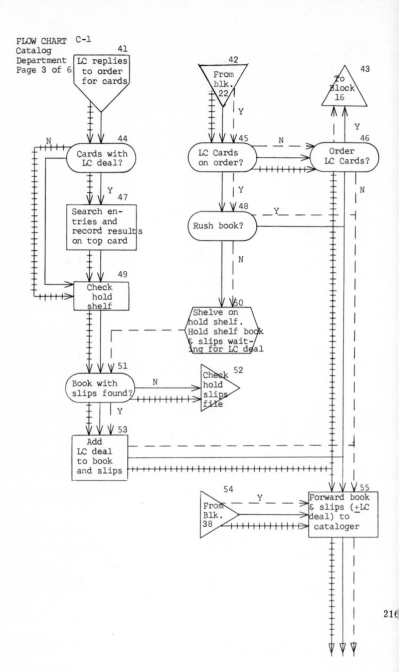

FLOW CHART C-1
Catalog
Department
Page 3 of 6

41 LC replies to order for cards

42 From blk. 22

43 To Block 16

44 Cards with LC deal?

45 LC Cards on order?

46 Order LC Cards?

47 Search entries and record results on top card

48 Rush book?

49 Check hold shelf

50 Shelve on hold shelf. Hold shelf book & slips waiting for LC deal

51 Book with slips found?

52 Check hold slips file

53 Add LC deal to book and slips

54 From Blk. 38

55 Forward book & slips (+LC deal) to cataloger

216

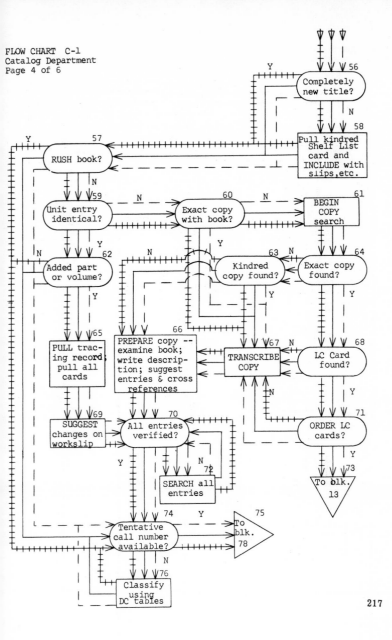

217

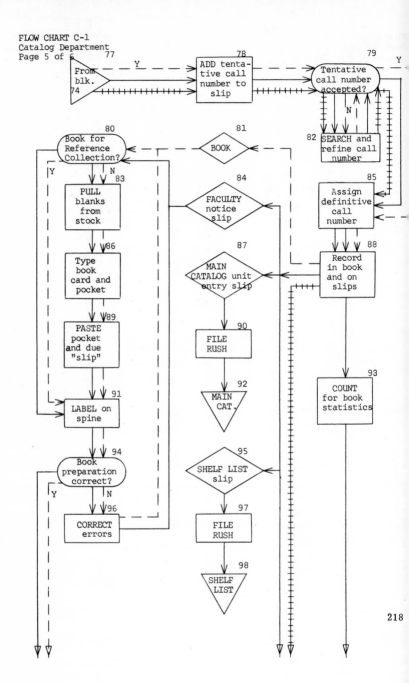

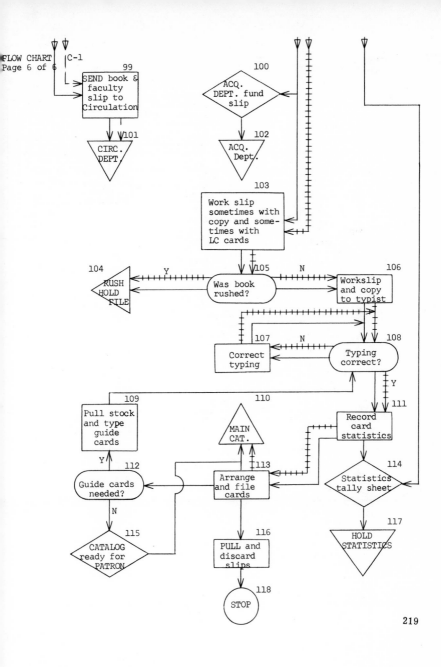

99 SEND book & faculty slip to Circulation

101 CIRC. DEPT.

100 ACQ. DEPT. fund slip

102 ACQ. Dept.

103 Work slip sometimes with copy and sometimes with LC cards

104 RUSH HOLD FILE

105 Was book rushed?

106 Workslip and copy to typist

107 Correct typing

108 Typing correct?

109 Pull stock and type guide cards

110 MAIN CAT.

111 Record card statistics

112 Guide cards needed?

113 Arrange and file cards

114 Statistics tally sheet

115 CATALOG ready for PATRON

116 PULL and discard slips

117 HOLD STATISTICS

118 STOP

219

CHART C-2
Page 1 of 1

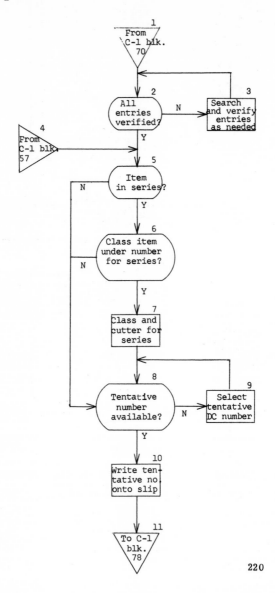

1 From C-1 blk. 70

2 All entries verified?

N → 3 Search and verify entries as needed

Y

4 From C-1 blk. 57

5 Item in series?

N

Y

6 Class item under number for series?

N

Y

7 Class and cutter for series

8 Tentative number available?

N → 9 Select tentative DC number

Y

10 Write tentative no. onto slip

11 To C-1 blk. 78

220

CHART C-3
Page 1 of 3

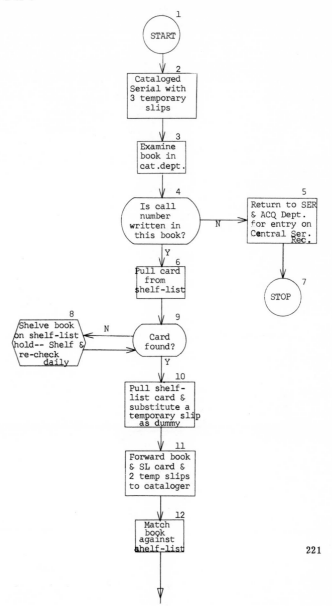

1 START

2 Cataloged Serial with 3 temporary slips

3 Examine book in cat.dept.

4 Is call number written in this book?

5 Return to SER & ACQ Dept. for entry on Central Ser. Rec.

N

Y

6 Pull card from shelf-list

7 STOP

8 Shelve book on shelf-list hold-- Shelf & re-check daily

N

9 Card found?

Y

10 Pull shelf-list card & substitute a temporary slip as dummy

11 Forward book & SL card & 2 temp slips to cataloger

12 Match book against shelf-list

221

CHART C-3
Page 2 of 3

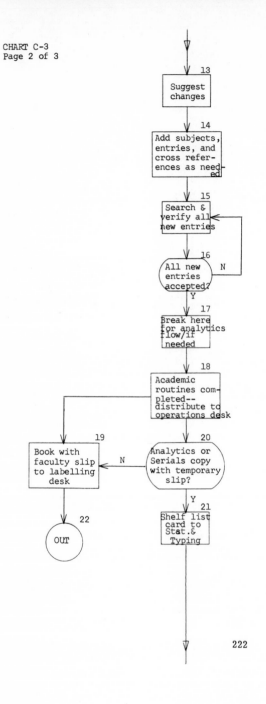

13 Suggest changes

14 Add subjects, entries, and cross references as needed

15 Search & verify all new entries

16 All new entries accepted?   N

Y

17 Break here for analytics flow/if needed

18 Academic routines completed-- distribute to operations desk

19 Book with faculty slip to labelling desk

N

20 Analytics or Serials copy with temporary slip?

Y

21 Shelf list card to Stat.& Typing

22 OUT

222

CHART C-3
Page 3 of 3

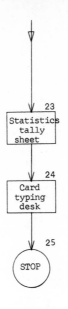

23
Statistics
tally
sheet

24
Card
typing
desk

25
STOP

223

CHART C-4
Page 1 of 2

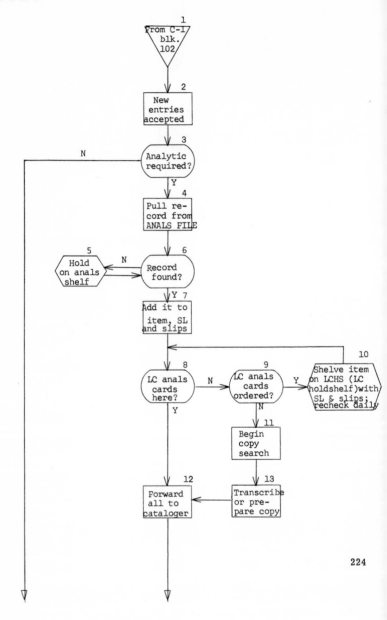

1
From C-1
blk.
102

2
New
entries
accepted

3
Analytic
required?

N

Y

4
Pull re-
cord from
ANALS FILE

5
Hold
on anals
shelf

N

6
Record
found?

Y 7
Add it to
item, SL
and slips

8
LC anals
cards
here?

N

9
LC anals
cards
ordered?

Y

10
Shelve item
on LCHS (LC
holdshelf)with
SL & slips;
recheck daily

Y

N

11
Begin
copy
search

12
Forward
all to
cataloger

13
Transcribe
or pre-
pare copy

224

CHART C-4
Page 2 of 2

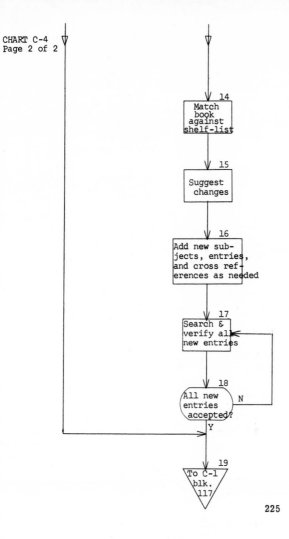

225

CHART D-1, Sheet 1
Charge Out Procedures

226

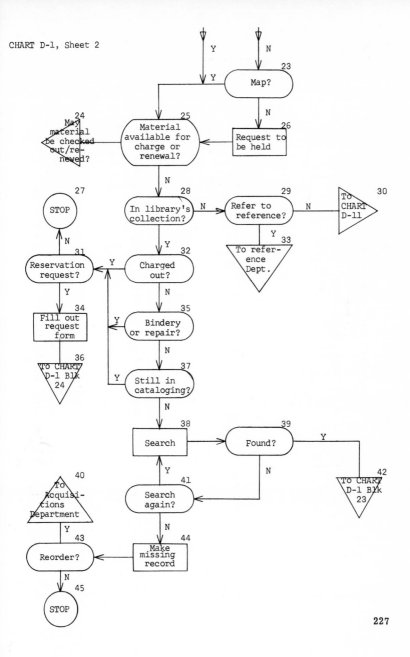

CHART D-2
Return Procedures

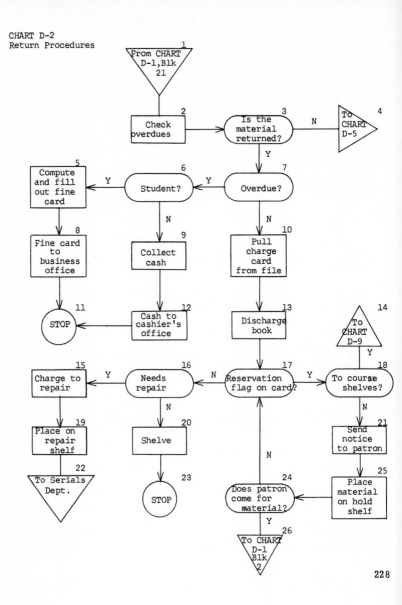

228

CHART D-3
Information and
Reference Request
Procedures

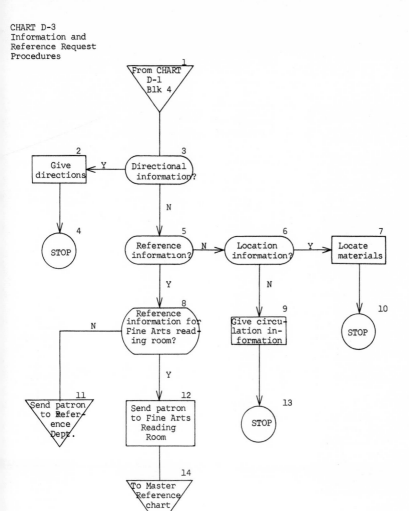

1
From CHART
D-1
Blk 4

2
Give
directions

3
Directional
information?

Y

N

4
STOP

5
Reference
information?

N

6
Location
information?

Y

7
Locate
materials

Y

N

8
Reference
information for
Fine Arts read-
ing room?

9
Give circu-
lation in-
formation

10
STOP

N

Y

11
Send patron
to Refer-
ence
Dept.

12
Send patron
to Fine Arts
Reading
Room

13
STOP

14
To Master
Reference
chart

229

CHART D-4
Circulation Processing
Procedures

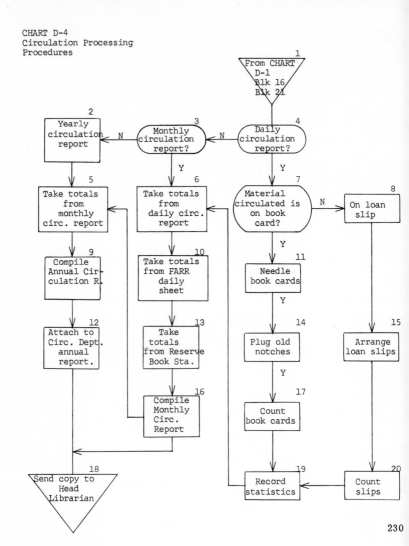

CHART D-5
Overdue Notice
Procedures

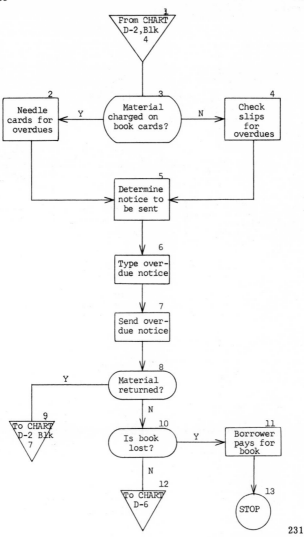

From CHART D-2, Blk 4 → Material charged on book cards? → (Y) Needle cards for overdues / (N) Check slips for overdues → Determine notice to be sent → Type overdue notice → Send overdue notice → Material returned? → (Y) To CHART D-2 Blk 7 / (N) Is book lost? → (Y) Borrower pays for book → STOP / (N) To CHART D-6

231

CHART D-6
Delinquent Student
Procedures

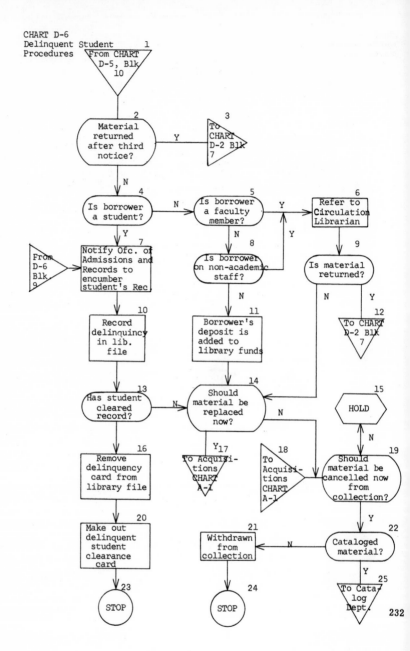

1 From CHART D-5, Blk 10

2 Material returned after third notice?
3 To CHART D-2 Blk 7

4 Is borrower a student?
5 Is borrower a faculty member?
6 Refer to Circulation Librarian

7 Notify Ofc. of Admissions and Records to encumber student's Rec.
From D-6 Blk 9

8 Is borrower on non-academic staff?
9 Is material returned?

10 Record delinquincy in lib. file
11 Borrower's deposit is added to library funds
12 To CHART D-2 Blk 7

13 Has student cleared record?
14 Should material be replaced now?
15 HOLD

16 Remove delinquency card from library file
17 To Acquisitions CHART A-1
18 To Acquisitions CHART A-1
19 Should material be cancelled now from collection?

20 Make out delinquent student clearance card
21 Withdrawn from collection
22 Cataloged material?

23 STOP
24 STOP
25 To Catalog Dept.

232

CHART D-7
End of Semester
Procedures

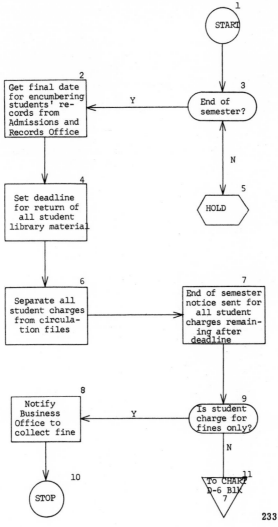

1 START

2 Get final date for encumbering students' re-cords from Admissions and Records Office

3 End of semester?

Y

N

5 HOLD

4 Set deadline for return of all student library material

6 Separate all student charges from circula-tion files

7 End of semester notice sent for all student charges remain-ing after deadline

8 Notify Business Office to collect fine

9 Is student charge for fines only?

Y

N

10 STOP

11 To CHART D-6 BLK 7

CHART D-8
Student Withdrawal
Procedures

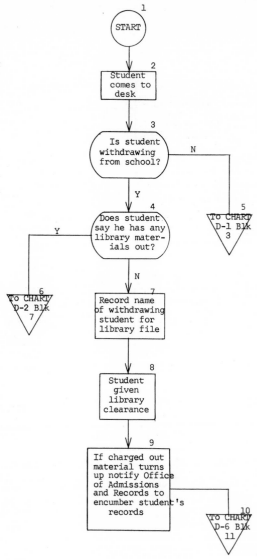

1
START

2
Student
comes to
desk

3
Is student
withdrawing
from school?

N

5
To CHART
D-1 Blk
3

Y

4
Does student
say he has any
library mater-
ials out?

Y

6
To CHART
D-2 Blk
7

N

7
Record name
of withdrawing
student for
library file

8
Student
given
library
clearance

9
If charged out
material turns
up notify Office
of Admissions
and Records to
encumber student's
records

10
To CHART
D-6 Blk
11

234

CHART D-9
Reserve Materials
Processing
Procedures

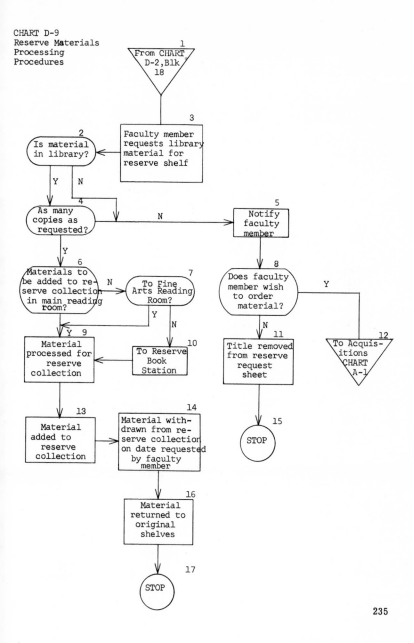

1
From CHART
D-2, Blk
18

3
Faculty member
requests library
material for
reserve shelf

2
Is material
in library?

Y   N

4
As many
copies as
requested?

N

5
Notify
faculty
member

Y

6
Materials to
be added to re-
serve collection
in main reading
room?

N

7
To Fine
Arts Reading
Room?

Y

N

8
Does faculty
member wish
to order
material?

Y

N

9
Material
processed for
reserve
collection

10
To Reserve
Book
Station

11
Title removed
from reserve
request
sheet

12
To Acquis-
itions
CHART
A-1

13
Material
added to
reserve
collection

14
Material with-
drawn from re-
serve collection
on date requested
by faculty
member

15
STOP

16
Material
returned to
original
shelves

17
STOP

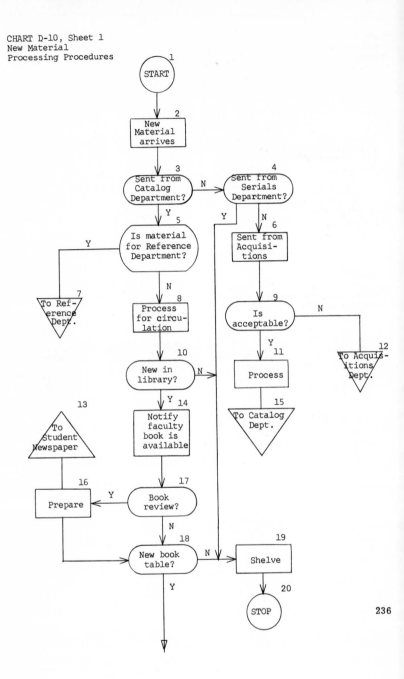

236

CHART D-10, Sheet 2
New Material
Processing Procedures

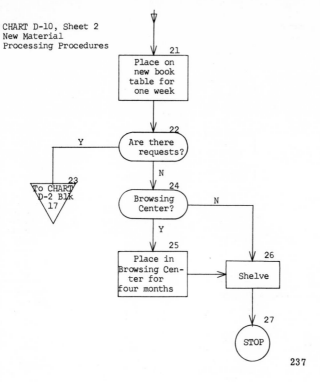

21 Place on new book table for one week

22 Are there requests?

Y → **23** To CHART D-2 Blk 17

N

24 Browsing Center?

N →

Y

25 Place in Browsing Center for four months →

26 Shelve

27 STOP

237

CHART D-11, Sheet 1
Inter-Library Loans
Borrowed

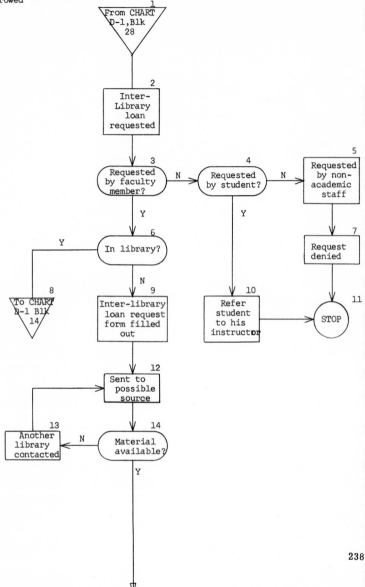

CHART D-11, Sheet 2
Inter-Library Loans,
Borrowed

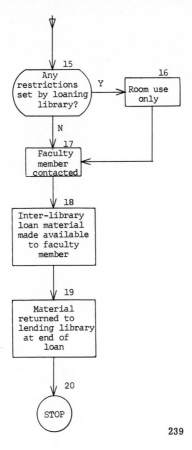

CHART D-12
Inter-Library Loans,
Lent

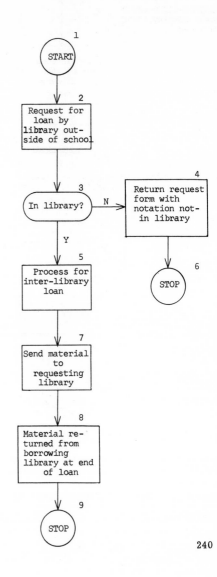

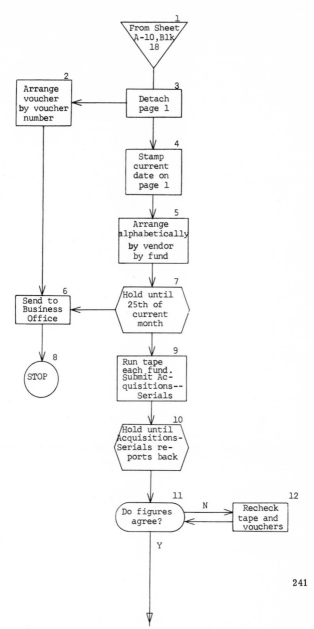

1
From Sheet
A-10,Blk
18

2
Arrange
voucher
by voucher
number

3
Detach
page 1

4
Stamp
current
date on
page 1

5
Arrange
alphabetically
by vendor
by fund

7
Hold until
25th of
current
month

6
Send to
Business
Office

8
STOP

9
Run tape
each fund.
Submit Ac-
quisitions--
Serials

10
Hold until
Acquisitions-
Serials re-
ports back

11
Do figures
agree?

12
Recheck
tape and
vouchers

N

Y

241

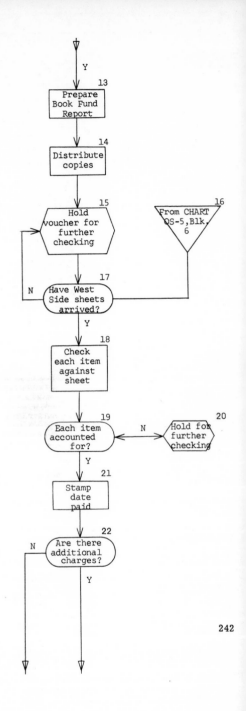

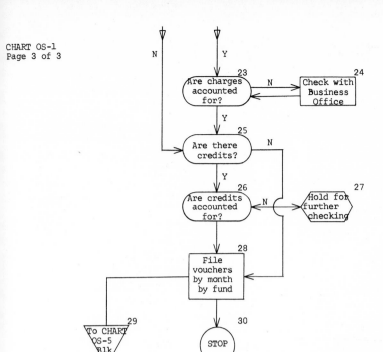

243

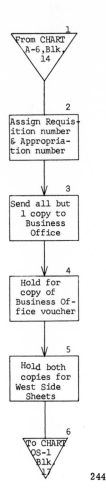

244

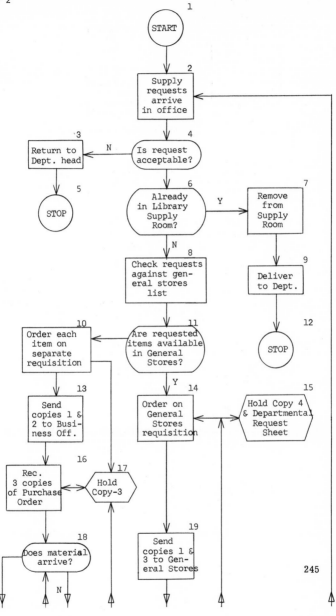

245

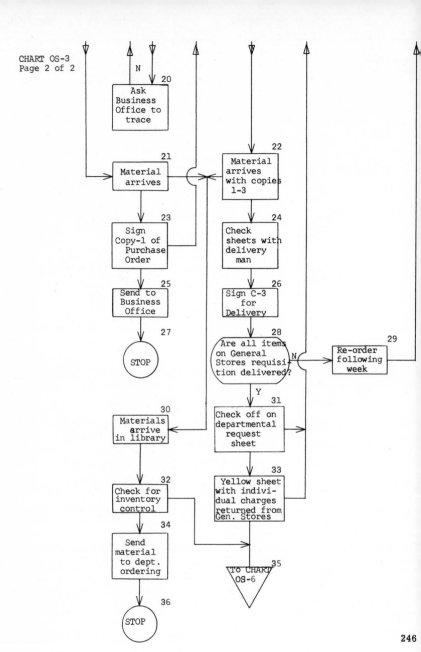

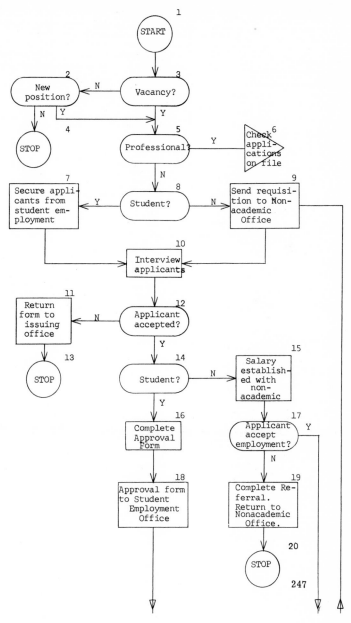

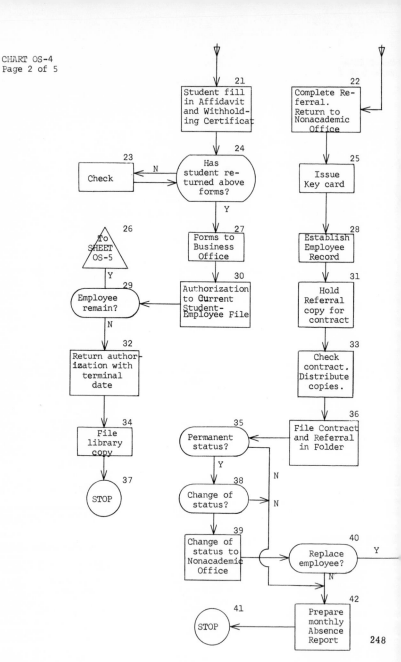

248

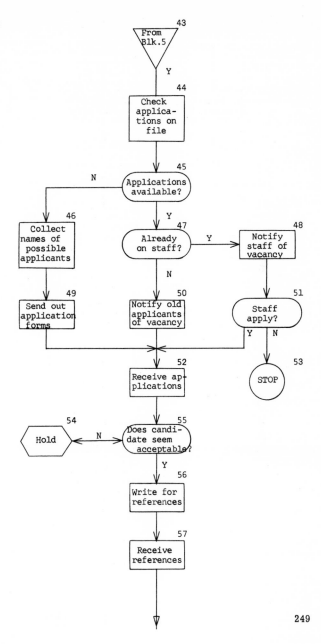

249

58 Is position offered?

N → 59 File papers → 61 STOP

Y

60 Is position accepted?

N → File papers

Y

62 Prepare, distribute recommendations for Appointment papers

63 First employment by University of Illinois?

N →

Y

64 Secure Loyalty Oath and W-2 forms from Candidate

65 Arrange for physical examination

66 Issue key cards

67 Arrange for Building Pass Permit

68 Notify other candidates

250

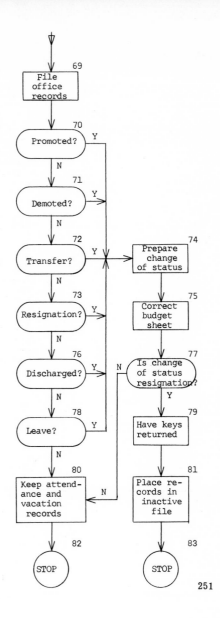

251

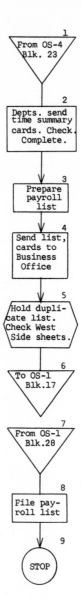

1
From OS-4
Blk. 23

2
Depts. send
time summary
cards. Check.
Complete.

3
Prepare
payroll
list

4
Send list,
cards to
Business
Office

5
Hold dupli-
cate list.
Check West
Side sheets.

6
To OS-1
Blk.17

7
From OS-1
Blk.28

8
File pay-
roll list

9
STOP

252

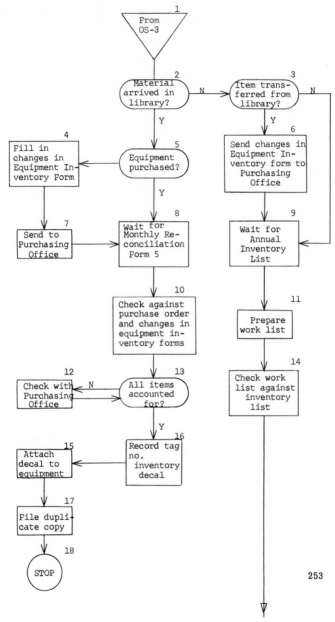

253

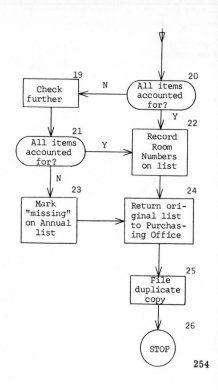

254

MASTER SHEET
Reference Department

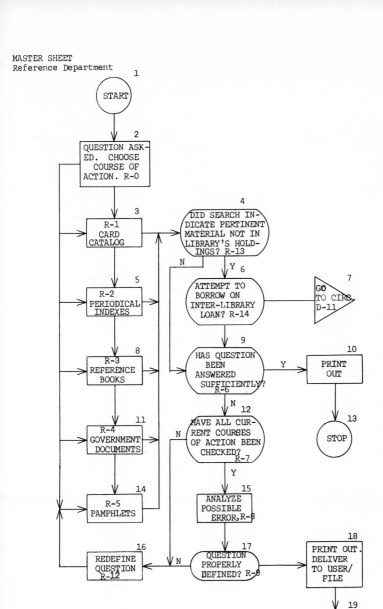

255

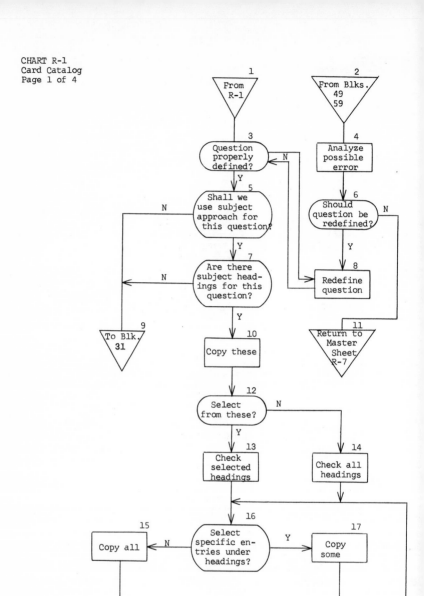

256

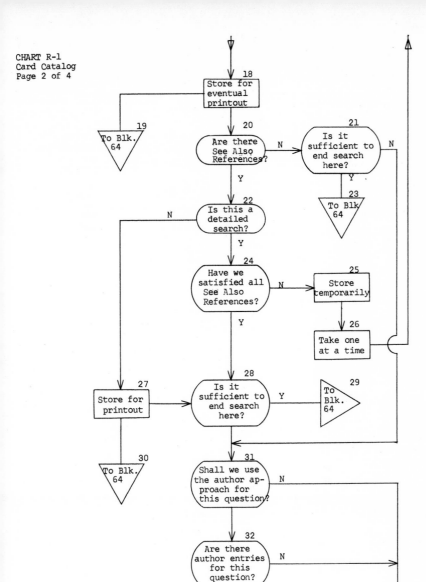

257

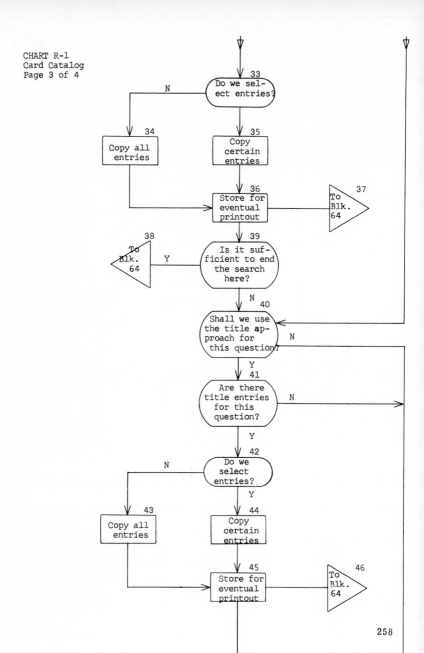

258

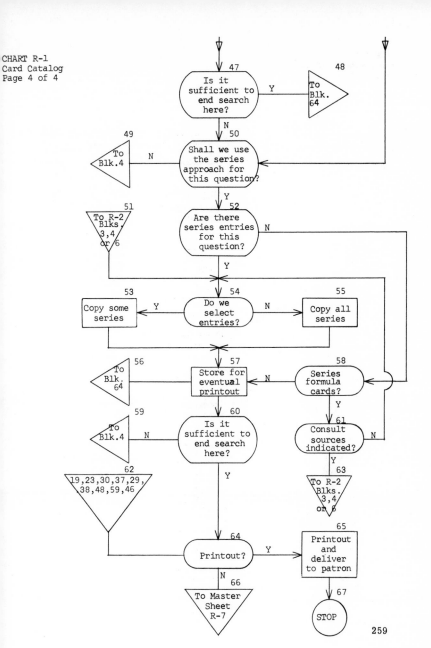

259

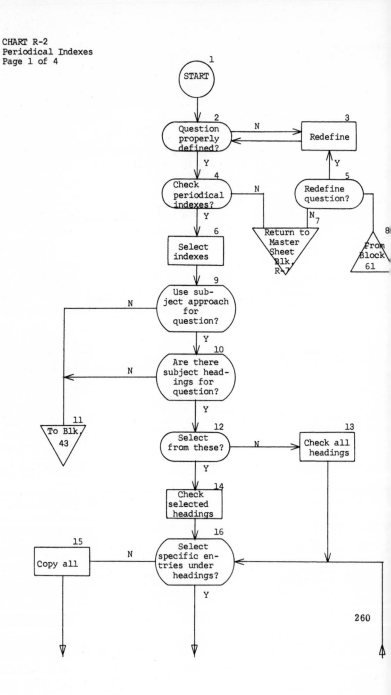

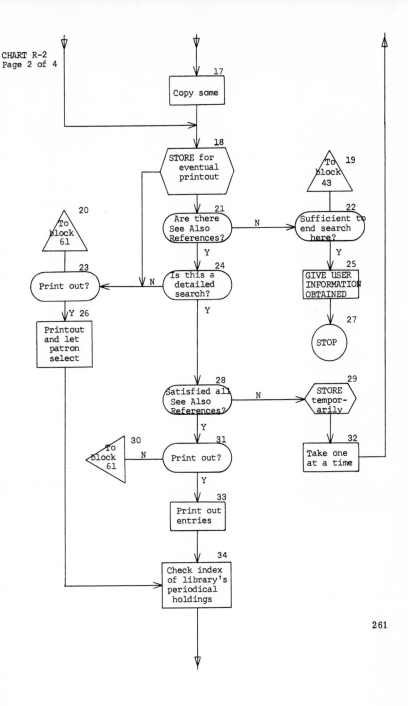

261

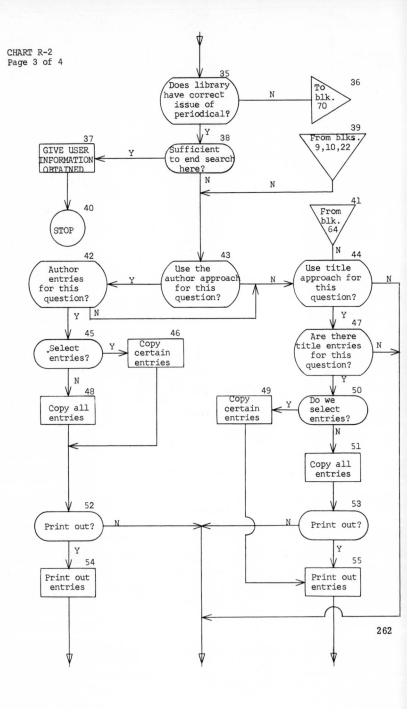

262

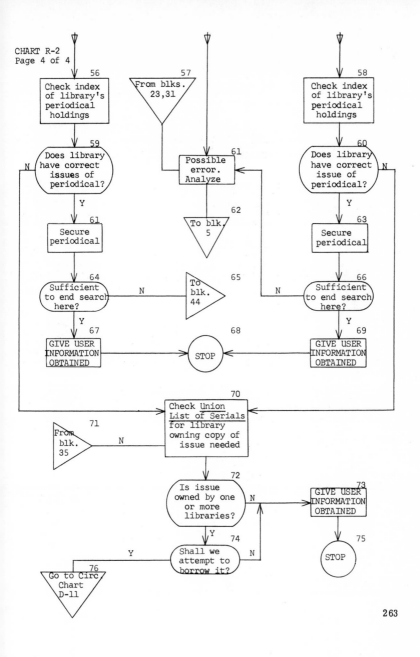

263

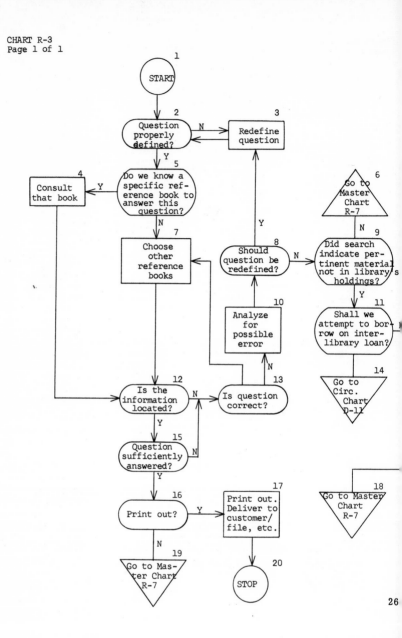

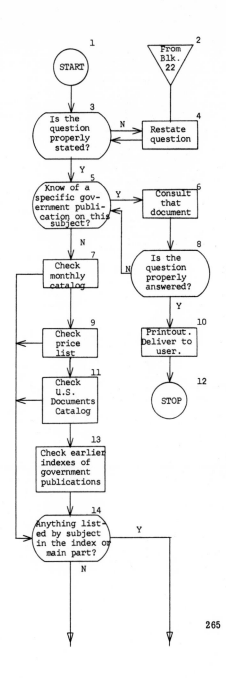

265

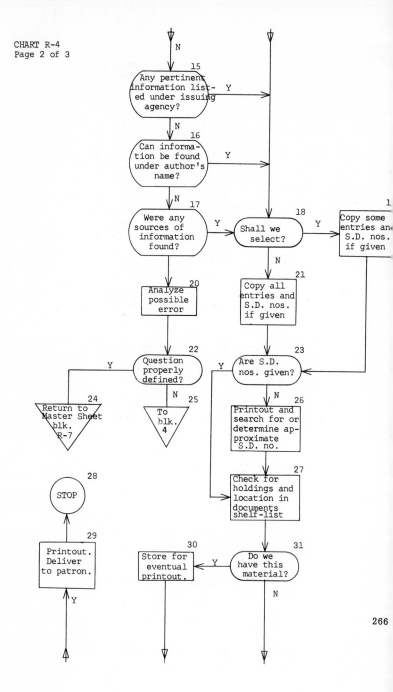

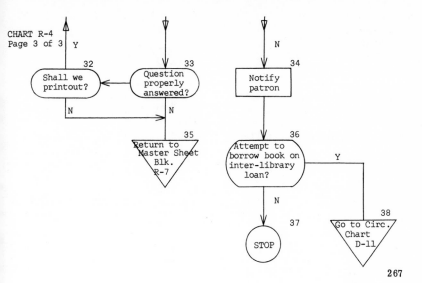

267

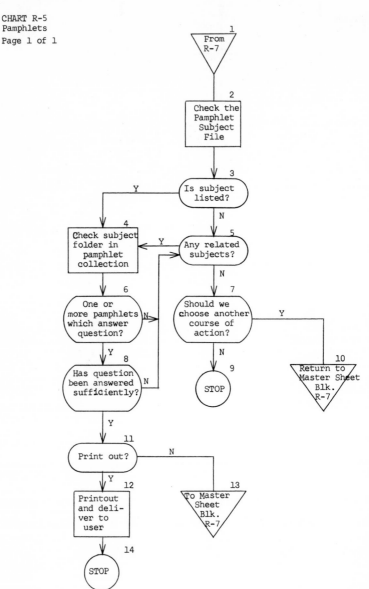

268

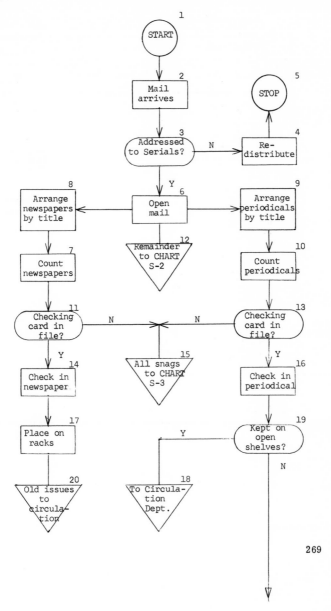

269

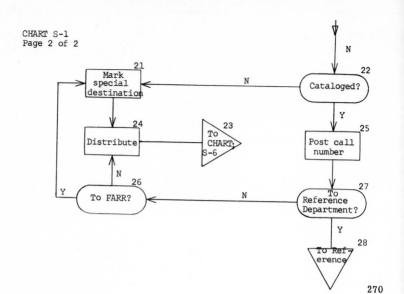

270

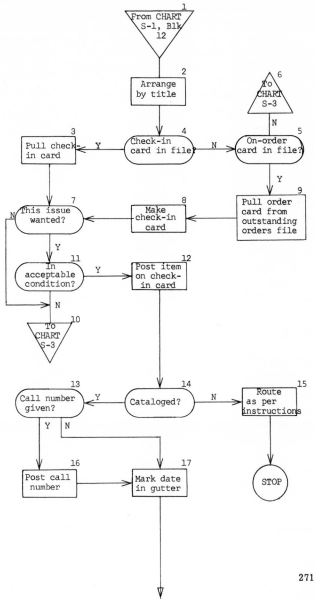

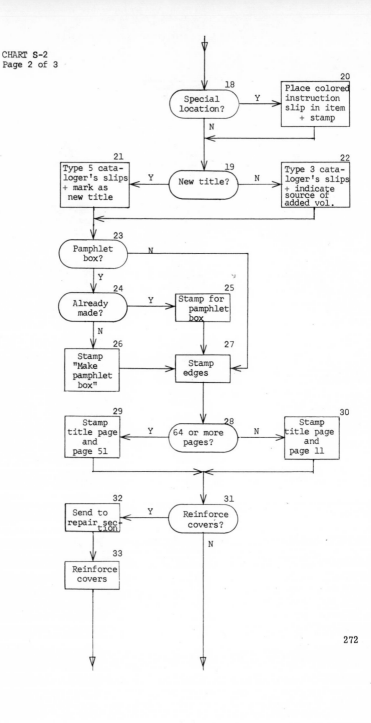

272

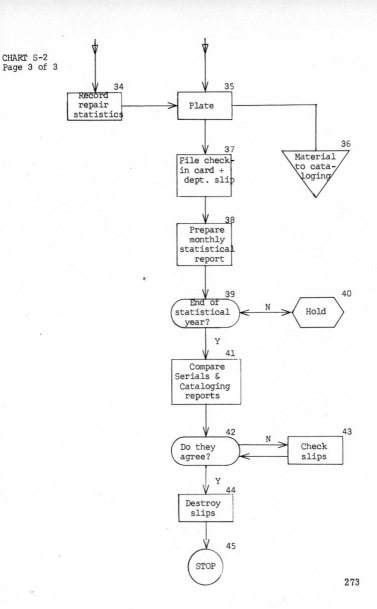

273

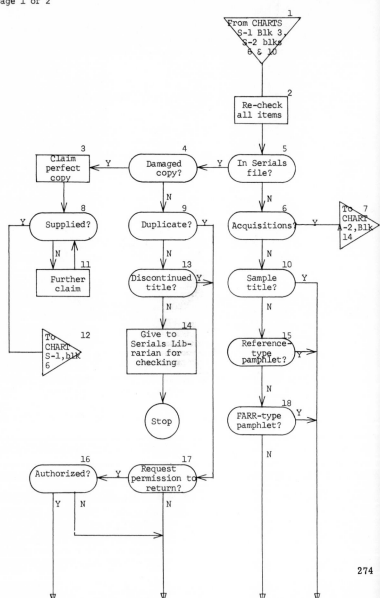

1. From CHARTS S-1 Blk 3, S-2 blks 8 & 10

2. Re-check all items

3. Claim perfect copy

4. Damaged copy?

5. In Serials file?

6. Acquisitions?

7. To CHART A-2, Blk 14

8. Supplied?

9. Duplicate?

10. Sample title?

11. Further claim

12. To CHART S-1, blk 6

13. Discontinued title?

14. Give to Serials Librarian for checking

15. Reference-type pamphlet?

16. Authorized?

17. Request permission to return?

18. FARR-type pamphlet?

Stop

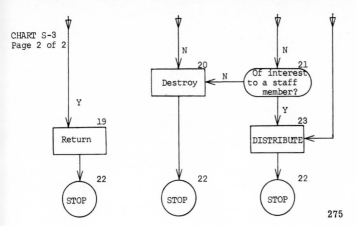

275

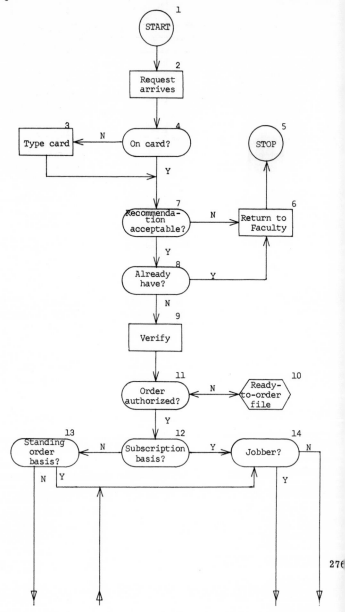

276

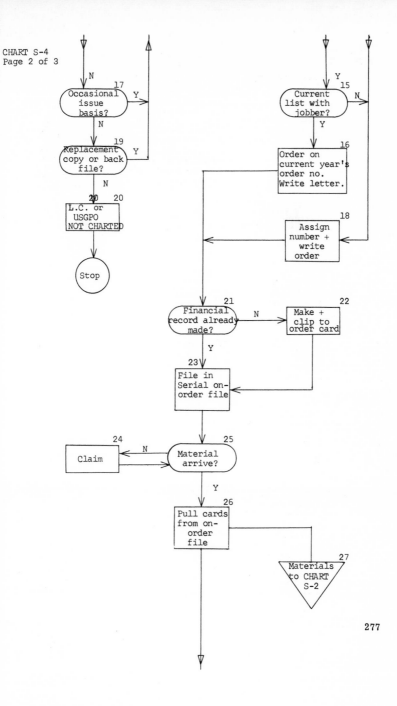

277

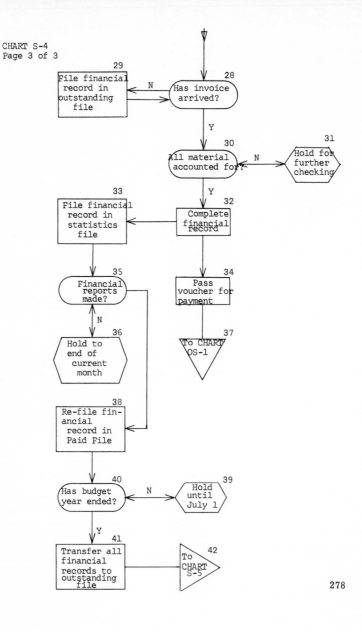

278

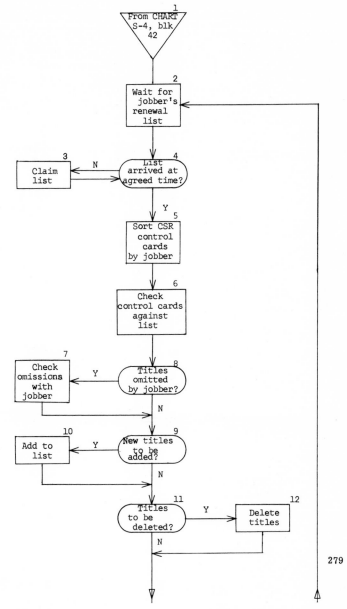

279

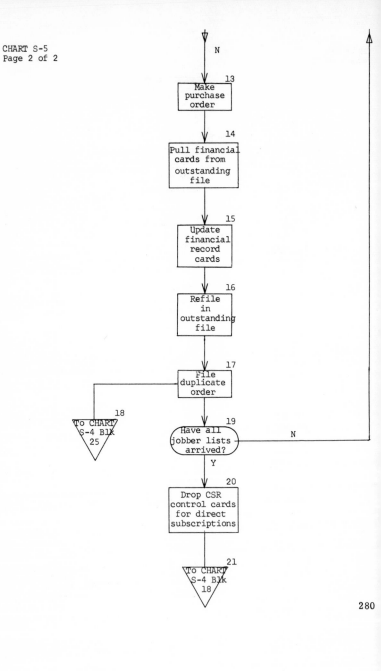

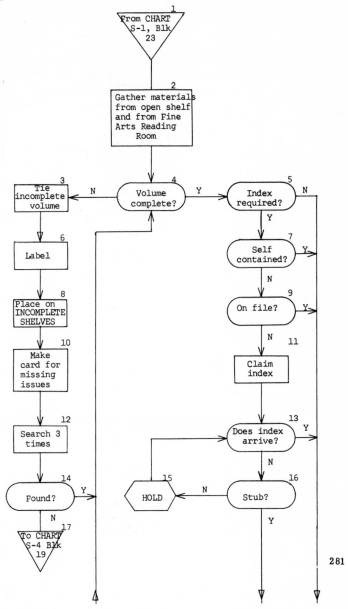

281

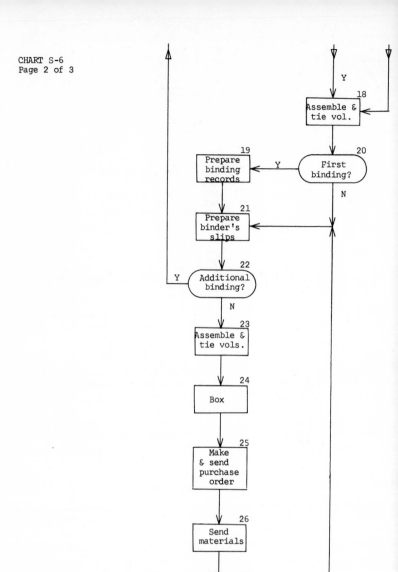

282

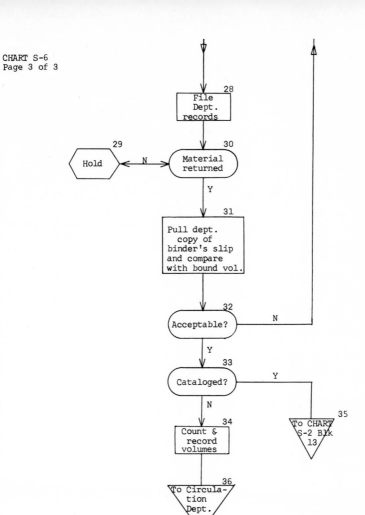

283

ESSAYS

WHAT I EXPECT THE ULIS PROJECT TO ACCOMPLISH

The project will have to reflect in some degree the divergent viewpoints of those who are concerned with it. Each of these viewpoints is valid in its own right and the expectations are, therefore, justified. To sacrifice one to any other would not be playing fair with those who have a right to expect some return from the project. The delicate part seems to be in achieving a balance between the elements. Each deserves some satisfactory recognition of its interests and desires.

Although there may be more than one group favoring either side, the main division seems to be between a practical and a theoretical solution. This is not to say that any one group favors one side and only one side, but that they are predominantly interested in either a practical or a theoretical approach. Without attempting to make the study all things to all men, the project should be capable of satisfying both elements.

Obviously, the UIC Library is interested in some concrete proposals in relation to its own needs. I believe they have a right to expect them, but I do not think this means a full-blown machine operation now. Rather, I would hope that it means a clarification of staff thinking and a development of an over-all philosophy of service which will allow a consideration of the mechanical means of expressing and implementing that philosophy. This philosophy of service need not, and indeed, must not, remain merely an abstraction but should be expressed in decisions and terms which will permit the planning of a serviceable machine operation at some future date.

The library profession if it could be questioned would, I think, exhibit a dichotomy in its thinking about the project. Some members would no doubt be firmly convinced that the project should deliver a compact little machine operation with all loose ends neatly tied up and ready to be plugged in. Others would probably feel that the project should attempt to answer the question as to whether mechanization is the new frontier for their profession and, if it is, what implications this has for their thinking, their actions and their philosophy. I feel the profession stands badly in need, not of a new unit or a plan which gives directions for hooking two units together in a workable system, but of a statement which can lift the thinking of its members above traditional routines to revitalized concepts of service. Too often today the approach to mechanization is an attempt to graft machine methods on to present practices. It seems inevitable that practices and even sacred cows will have to change to accommodate and incorporate automated procedures.

The UIC Library cannot expect to present the library world with a fait accompli machine operation, as a result of this project, but it can hope to point the way through revised routines, revitalized thinking and a semantic re-evaluation of traditional library methods, tools and service to the final future culmination--a successful machine operation.

Robert J. Adelsperger

EXPECTATIONS OF THE ULIS PROJECT

In terms of the UIC Library, it seems that the project should give us tangible results that could be implemented in the near future. It should also lay the groundwork for methods that might not be practical or feasible at present, but would of necessity be based on the systems developed now. Such features as the compilation of extensive bibliographic searches through the card catalog for example, might conceivably be an everyday function of the library a few decades hence. Looking at the present for now, I feel that we should see some practical applications in at least these fields:

Acquisitions department: If much of the work in acquiring
materials for the library could be mechanized, this
would hasten the ordering process considerably. Machine methods of determining whether or not we already have the item in question or whether it is already on order would save much time in checking
against the present records. Also, some means of
writing or printing the information once rather than
several times would greatly speed up the ordering
procedure and enable the requester to receive the desired material that much sooner. Also, some method
of notifying the person who requested the book as well
as others who are interested in that subject, should be
a by product of the ordering procedure.

Circulation department: Design a system whereby the patron
would have to do a minimum of writing and waiting.
It seems that students will possibly always be able to
figure out some means of "cheating the machine" or
at present, "pulling a fast one" on the circulation
clerk; but it should be possible to design something
that would greatly reduce if not limit entirely the opportunities for cheating. The system should be able
to distinguish between various types of materials and
various classes of borrowers, such as faculty, staff,

and students. Self-service would be the ideal method, it would seem.

Cataloging department: Make it possible to produce a book catalog and frequent supplements if this will ultimately be desired. This may eventually be designed to provide the necessary means for rapid bibliographic searches of the catalog for desired specific information. Any mechanical method of decreasing the time a book spends in the cataloging department should be investigated and utilized. Quality should continue to be of prime consideration in the mechanization of any of these processes as well as ease in finding and using for the library patron.

Methods in these areas as well as in others should be designed specifically for our library, but their planning should be broad enough so that the basic principles designed for UIC could be used in any similar situation with specific specifications left open for each individual institution to decide.

In all, the project should enable our library in particular to derive major benefits and, in turn, should give to other libraries definite plans and the "know-how" to put them or similar plans into effect in their institutions. Thus, it should benefit us directly and the rest of the country indirectly in leading the way to helping them set up similar programs in their libraries.

Marjorie Bengtson

WHAT I THINK THE ULIS PROJECT SHOULD ACCOMPLISH

When the project was first proposed I pictured the result as a book which would contain complete directions on how to analyze a whole library system and how to take the results of this analysis and compare them to the "ideal" library set forth in the book. Then it would only be a matter of changing the existing systems to the new ones listed to completely automate the library. We would have everything in the book showing an integrated library system; from work flow diagrams to the wiring of the boards of the tab equipment through the programs for a computer, if necessary. The whole idea would be that all of the investigative work would be done and as long as a library would be willing to accept our parameters they could adapt our systems to their library.

After the application for the grant was processed and we found we were to have $50,000, instead of the $100,000 we thought it would take to do the whole job, it was obvious that it was impractical to expect that the project be tackled on one half the amount really needed. When the emphasis was placed on cataloging, reference and some parts of acquisitions, this was a logical limitation. We should be able to go ahead on our own on most of acquisitions and circulation at a later date as these have already been done by others. I assume funds will be available from University sources to carry the program beyond the point where it will be left by the project.

At this point if we can keep enthusiasm for the project at a high pitch by coming up with some concrete results, such as a dissemination system with a clever twist like our book catalog with a permuted subject index, we should be able to tackle the next phase with little or no delay.

If we can't keep the staff at a high pitch, we will have spent an interesting year and $50,000 but little else.

Don S. Culbertson

IDEAS ON OUR PROJECT

We can consider what we do now to be the first stage in a continuing process in which machines and library routines and activities will interact upon each other. What we are doing now is to see what the present stage of machine technology (most especially computer and information storage types) can offer us for our present library routines and activities, and such modifications and projections of same as we can now reasonably expect to effect. ("Now" meaning, say, up to five years.) Presumably, new ideas and insights will come to us as we use present machines, and learn of future machines (or even suggest ideas for same). (This is what machine use will do for distant future mostly.)

Use of machines will enable us to do things we are doing now more quickly, efficiently, accurately and cheaply. (In general, that is: we may accept a certain amount of, say, inaccuracy in, say, circulation if it offers compensating advantages.) It will also, and perhaps more importantly, enable us to do things we can't do now at all, or can do in only a rudimentary way. (Dissemination, for example.)

Lloyd C. Engelbrecht

ULIS PROJECT: A STUDY

To show the possibilities of automation for library service that is

    a. better

    b. up to date

    c. quicker

    d. more complete

    e. more comprehensive

    f. less expensive

    g. auto-improving

h.   dissemination

i.   architecture;   housing the system

j.   standardization;   tie system in with worldwide or
     nationwide system

k.   individualization;   focus system to reject the irrele-
     vent so far as the individual user is concerned

l.   use most efficient method for each function, including
     electronic and gadget methods where indicated

Better cataloging means better author, title, subject and

entry description;   more sharply related to user needs, time-

saving for user;   quicker, same-day completion of technical

processes;   the entry work a sort of psychoanalysis of the

book, supplying in depth the perception of dimension and di-

rection in language concept and communication (dig that, boy!)

regardless of whether the data being processed are chapters

in books, whole books, or monographs in a series of books.

Less expensive is a relevent term;   for example, less

expensive steak may mean increased spending for steak and

greater consumption;   perhaps total spent will exceed what

was previously spent for all groceries together (and who can

say that this makes for a better or happier person?) but the

image that satisfies will be worshipped more intensely.

Better acquisitions: greater accuracy in selection to meet

needs;   immediate or running summaries of available funds &

commitments;   lacunae less;   accessioning time reduced.

Better circulation work: simpler & quick routines; books charged faster and returned to shelves faster after discharging.

Better reference work: awareness of frequently asked questions and hand/out aids to answering; reference service defined more clearly; (as dispensing assistance; when this means telling; when it means helping user help himself).

IMPROVED COMMUNICATION is the key; IMPROVED CATALOGING another word for the same; CATALOGING CONCEPT MEANS KEEPING RECORDS CLEARLY; to know what is in printed form, and to know how much and how good the library's holdings, is to know what to acquisition, what to offer the user, where to extract information reference-wise, etc.

AUTO-IMPROVING is a method of avoiding cultural crystallization; we need to be constantly improving our library methods so that we can meet needs in the best ways.

Carl Frommherz

WHAT I EXPECT THE ULIS PROJECT TO ACCOMPLISH

Librarians are eternally occupied with the need for more books, more space to put the books, and more staff to process the books. This seems to leave too little time for an equally essential problem: how to make the books useful and

meaningful to the users. I look to our Project to indicate
ways and means to bridging the gap between the Library and
the user.

There are certain practical problems that continually
bother the library administrator. One is exit control. Without it, far too many books are lost each year. We would
like to have each reader "searched" for contraband books by
some device. Another problem is shelf-reading. In an open
shelf library, the books are continually being disarranged by
the readers. Until the shelves are "read" again, any book
out of place is as good as lost. We would like a system
that will read the shelves frequently and indicate which books
are out of place. A device which could do this could perhaps
search for a book at the command of the reader and deliver
it to him at a service point. It could also inventory.

More and more libraries are confining their circulation
activities to a clerical staff, under the supervision of a good
professional. This would indicate that circulation activities
lend themselves to mechanization. We would like to see a
system which would handle the circulation of books with as
little human help as possible. Circulation assistants have a
notoriously high mortality rate, due probably to the pressures
of serving large numbers of readers continually.

Some sort of unit record that will follow throughout the book processing procedures and everywhere else in the library is needed. Without this, there is a needless duplication of work. This unit record could also be used for dissemination of information. Such a record is needed.

The cost of acquiring and cataloging books is assuming such proportions that library administrators are under fire from other university officials. Some universities report an average cataloging cost of $9.00. This is considerably more than the cost of the book and the vulnerability of the library is obvious. I hope the Project will indicate ways and means of cutting these costs to a minimum.

A university library stands or falls on its contribution to the main task of the university--teaching students. Our Project should envision a developing program that will integrate the library into the teaching program in a significant way. One facet of this integration is a first-hand knowledge of each professor's work. With such a knowledge, the library could be forewarned of demands to be made on its services, could make the professor aware of additional library resources in course planning, and could gear its services to make the optimum contribution to the teaching situation.

Without belaboring the word "image," I would like to hope that ways and means of improving the library image, especially in terms of achievement possibilities, can be developed. Perhaps release from clerical functions will enable the academic library staff to give more consideration to those elements necessary to create the proper image. More participation in faculty affairs and better training in public relations are part of this.

Above all, we want to develop a system that will be a far cry from the old custodial library that resented any intrusion. It must be a system that will live and grow with the society and institution of which it is a part. Every advantage must be taken of modern technology and psychology to help in doing this. Our Project must develop in this "ambiente."

Edward A. Heiliger

COMMENTS ON THE ULIS PROJECT

I expect the ULIS Project to determine whether or not it would be practical to mechanize the routine work of this particular library in the immediate future, and, if it would be practical, to recommend a suitable system. I am particularly concerned as to whether or not mechanization is economically feasible for a medium-sized library. A decision in favor of mechanization should be based on good indications that there would be either financial savings or more effective service (at a reasonable cost), or both, as a result of me-

chanization. Machines could certainly perform repetitive
work more quickly and accurately than could human beings,
but the cost of the machines plus the cost of the highly-
skilled people required to operate them may more than offset any saving in regular personnel--particularly when volume is relatively low.

The decisions which are made with regard to this library
will, of course, have significance for other libraries, even
those of different size and type, but I do not believe that
these broader implications will have great importance until
any system of mechanization which is recommended proves
itself definitely advantageous in actual operation in a specific
library situation.

Very specifically, a method of automatically reproducing
catalog cards would be most helpful.

Martha Kester

WHAT I HOPE THE INFORMATIONS SYSTEM PROJECT WILL ACCOMPLISH

1. Set up some kind of machine charging of books at the
    Circulation Desk. The use of a student and faculty ID
    card like a charge plate would require no writing on the
    part of the borrower, unless we wanted his signature, and
    would require very little supervision from the Circulations

Department staff.

2. Set up automatic typing of overdue notices.

3. Set up a system of notifying individual members of the faculty of the arrival of new books in their particular fields of interest. Make this as automatic as possible.

4. Prepare book catalogs to be placed in departmental of - fices. Author, title, and subject catalogs should be made, with monthly supplements, cumulated annually. If possible, it would be better to cumulate monthly.

5. Continue to maintain a card catalog in the Main Library.

6. Explore the possibility of establishing a unit record which would start in the Acquisitions Department, continue through the Catalog Department, and form the basis for whatever type of circulation charge records are kept. It would also form the basis for the book catalog.

Marie A. Rapp

ANY ONE FOR MECHANIZATION OF LIBRARIES?

I think the "Project" should adhere, so far as possible, closely to the aims which were submitted to the Council on Library Resources last summer. This was stated in some-what more specific language by Mr. Schultheiss and Mr. Cul-bertson when they returned to the library February 27 after spending two weeks at the General Electric plant in Bethesda.

As I understood from their report the main areas of investigation were to be library procedures in the fields of (1) cataloging, (2) dissemination of information, and (3) possibly acquisition and circulation.

To translate the aim of the project in another way, and in an over-used cliche, it should assist us in improving the fulfillment of university and library functions. The accomplishments of the project should indicate means of making fuller use of library resources at a reasonable cost. It should help us to improve our methods--we would hope in all departments. It should assist us in raising our standards of service, improving our controls, and making the best use of our physical lay-out. It should make coordination of all library and university services easier and better.

If at this time it seems unlikely that all of these areas can be investigated, and I think that this may be the case, then I would like to see one area fully studied. Since so much depends upon cataloging and the card catalog I would not be disappointed to see the remaining time of the project devoted exclusively to this one area.

To be more specific, I think the report should include the following general pattern about one or more of the areas mentioned in paragraph one. Here again keeping in mind improved methods, standards, controls and better physical lay-out.

(1) Philosophy to be followed now and in the foreseeable future. Both positive and negative features.

(2) Specific procedures for this library.

(3) Cost of these procedures.

(4) Practical advantages, opportunities, and risks. For an example, I think it wise to determine cost of printed catalogs, possible cost in several different forms; get faculty reaction to cost and use. (Or indicate specifically what, other than printed catalog, can be done in the area of dissemination of information.) What can we do which will improve circulation activities?

(5) For use in other libraries, what and how other university departments might use the same automatic machinery to reduce cost.

(6) Indicate how librarians in libraries with machine operations can do a better and more professional job.

In conclusion I will be disappointed to see only a theoretical report made of library procedures now, 25, 50, or 100 years hence or simply a theoretical report calling for further study and investigation. I will be pleased to know how we as librarians can take advantage of and develop leadership in the field of mechanization.

Giles B. Robertson

WHAT I EXPECT THE INFORMATION SYSTEMS PROJECT TO ACCOMPLISH

I expect the project to answer some general questions about the potential use of data processing methods and equipment in university libraries, as well as to give recommendations for use or non-use of machines in specific areas of our own library. The report should provide criteria for deciding costs of machine processing, and some indication as to the size of book collection, budget, and staff that a university library must attain before the use of machine systems can be justified. The evaluation and the recommendations must deal with not only the purely mechanical, clerical operations of acquisitions, bookkeeping, cataloging, circulation, and personnel records (the "Sears Roebuck operation"), which will expand very rapidly on our new campus but could still be developed as a purely human system without serious dislocation or breakdown if planned properly, but with some of the additional aspects of service that do not seem to be at all practiceable without mechanical assistance: the current dissemination of information to interested faculty and students, the preparation and distribution of catalogs, permuted lists or indices, the retrospective searching of cataloged and/or indexed literature, and the substitution of micro-storage for some categories of physical documents. The project report (and any articles published in the journal literature) should take the policy decisions arising from our own discussions of our philosophies of university library service, and using them for criteria for analysis and design, recommend which aspects of service should not be considered at all, which ones are feasible and which ones should be implemented first. The report should also outline specific procedures, programs, and equipment needed to carry out desirable applications.

Louis A. Schultheiss

REFERENCE QUESTIONS

1. Do you have any master plots of short stories?

2. I'm looking for the critical reception given the Glass Menagerie.

3. Where can I locate the American Pronouncing Dictionary? (Kenyon and Knotts)

4. Can a large dictionary be taken to the table?

5. How can I find a particular magazine in the library? (Current)

6. Do you have the Oxford Unabridged Dictionary?

7. Where is the O.E.D.?*

8. Did you receive the February 18 issue of Saturday Review?

9. Do you have any smaller dictionaries?

10. Can you tell me where the Webster's New World or Collegiate Dictionary is?

11. I want to know how the federal civil service compares with the university civil service, and what greater benefits the federal provides for its employees.

12. Adequacy of teachers' salaries in the U.S. to maintain a decent standard of living.

13. Information on techniques of fighting communism in the U.S.

14. Where do you keep reserve books?

15. Where is counter F?

*Oxford English Dictionary

16. Do we have a physical science syllabus?

17. Where can I find the New York Times films and information on ordering them?

18. Where are your books on sports?

19. Do you have these pamphlets? (She had a list of the national discussion question bibliography.)

20. How do you want students to come into the library to learn about writing term papers? They have not written any before.

21. Where is the O.E.D.?

22. List of accredited engineering schools.

23. Is there a list of term paper topics in the library?

24. Where is the O.E.D.?

25. Can you tell me about using microcards?

26. Where are the books on applied and theoretical mechanics?

27. Where is a dictionary? I have to look for some words for biology.

28. (Acquisitions asked:) Do you know what this Library of Congress order is supposed to be? Do you know if an order card was made?

29. Can you explain the visible index to me, and the use of the new serials titles?

30. Where is the World Almanac?

31. What happened to Chicago school teachers during the Depression?

32. Do you know if Mr. Mackin is in the library? We don't know what he looks like.

33. Do you have any materials on anthropology or civilization?

34. What is in reference books on the field of anthropology?

35. Would the place of publication be in New York? (Referring to a reference previously found for the student in the C.B.I.)

36. I looked in the card catalog for the book Take My Life by Eddie Cantor, but you didn't have it. I need biographical information (Questioning) -- no, I mean bibliographical information as I've already read it. (Do you know about when it appeared?) 1952, I believe. (It turned out to be 1957.)

37. I just checked the indexes and found some references. Do you have the magazines Coronet, etc.?

38. Good English-German dictionary.

39. What other periodicals deal with anthropology? (Than the two we have in anthropology.)

40. Is there any card file of microfilms?

41. Would like to look over the library's holdings in anthropology.

42. I'm looking for a one-act play. I know the title, but not the author. How do I find it?

43. I was looking for plays, but the card catalog gives information on how to produce plays. I want to find plays and a listing showing the number of people in the cast.

44. Where are the Spanish dictionaries translations. English-Spanish, Spanish-English.

45. Addresses of three British art schools.

46. Who is the person in charge of maps?

47. Are there any pamphlets on towns in Illinois?

48. Are there reference materials in anthropology? What other types of materials?

49. Where is the Library of International Relations located?

50. Suppose you are writing a term paper on Manolete, the bull-fighter, and have exhausted the card catalog, Reader's Guide, and encyclopedias. Where can I find more information about him?

51. I'm looking for an American Pronouncing Dictionary.

52. Where can I get the February Reader's Digest?

53. We want information about Decatur to plan a skating rink there.

54. Can you tell me if there's any way you can check out the Congressional Record?

55. How many Chambers of Commerce were there in the U.S. in 1858?

56. Is this the copyright date and publisher? (Student with copy of footnotes and bibliography form as recommended by the department.) And how do I enter an organization as an author?

57. Do you have anything on discrimination in Chicago?

58. Where can I locate an extended definition of Yankee, dorm and amateur?

MATHEMATICAL MODELS

BASIC MACHINE ASSUMPTIONS

1. <u>Tapes</u>

   15,000 alpha-numeric characters per second transfer rates.

   End of record gaps of .75"

   Character densities of 200/inch

   Forward speed of 75 inches/sec.

2. <u>Printing</u>

   120 print positions

   600 lines/minute

3. <u>Card Reading</u>

   400 cards/minute

4. <u>Card Punching</u>

   200 cards/minute

5. Simultaneous I/00

All combinations of tape manipulation, card reading and punching and printing should be capable of being overlapped.

PROCESS CALCULATIONS

Formula for finding the number of pages needed for printing 1000 titles.

The following formula was developed and table computed to aid the designer in making rapid calculations for various types of machine prepared catalogs.

The table shows the number of pages required to print 1000 titles where a title may contain 100, 200, 300 or 400 characters (CHACS/ENT); be printed with line densities (LINES/IN.) of 6, 8, 10 lines to the inch on two sizes of paper, 72 and 120 print positions (PRP/PG.).

PAGES REQUIRED TO PRINT 1000 TITLES

CHACS/ENT	100						200					
LINES/IN.	6		8		10		6		8		10	
PRP/PG.	72	120	72	120	72	120	72	120	72	120	72	120
PAGES OF PRINTING	56	28	42	21	34	17	77	46	56	36	46	28

CHACS/ENT	300						400					
LINES/IN.	6		8		10		6		8		10	
PRP/PG.	72	120	72	120	72	120	72	120	72	120	72	120
PAGES OF PRINTING	112	56	84	42	67	34	125	72	100	56	77	46

Number of Pages
per 1000 Titles

$$= \left[\frac{1000 \text{ Titles}}{\text{No. of Titles/ Page}} \right]$$

$$= \left\langle \frac{1000 \text{ Titles}}{\left(\dfrac{(9 \text{ In./Pg.}) \ (\text{No. of Lines/In.})}{\text{Total Lines/Entry}} \right)} \right\rangle$$

$$= \left[\left\langle \cfrac{1000 \text{ Titles}}{\cfrac{\left(\cfrac{(9 \text{ In/Pg.}) \ (\text{No. of Lines/In.})}{\left[\cfrac{\text{No. of Chacs/Title}}{\text{No. of Prp/Page}} \right] + 1} \right)}{\text{No. of Cols/Page}}} \right\rangle \right]$$

This table was computed using the following formula.

1) $y = [x]$ means   for some interger $\underline{a}$

$y = a + 1$ whenever

$a.o \langle x \langle\!\langle a.o + 1$

and

2) $y = \langle x \rangle$ means   for some integer $\underline{a}$

$y = a + 1$ whenever

$a.o \langle\!\langle x \langle a.5$

and $y = a + 1$ whenever

$a.5 \langle\!\langle x \langle a.o + 1$

Some examples are given to show how the formulas work.

$y = [2] = 2$ $\qquad\qquad$ $y = \langle 2 \rangle = 2$

$y = [2.14] = 3$ $\qquad\quad$ $y = \langle 2.14 \rangle = 2$

$y = [2.7] = 3$ $\qquad\quad$ $y = \langle 2.7 \rangle = 3$

$$y = \lfloor 3 \rfloor = 3 \qquad\qquad y = \langle 3 \rangle = 3$$

$$y = \lfloor 3.001 \rfloor = 4 \qquad\qquad y = \langle 3.001 \rangle = 3$$

Note that the addition of 1 in the formula for the total lines/ entry is to account for a space between titles.

EXAMPLE: Assume a 300 character title; 6 lines/inch; a

72 print position page, and one column per page.

Number of Pages   =

per 1000 Titles

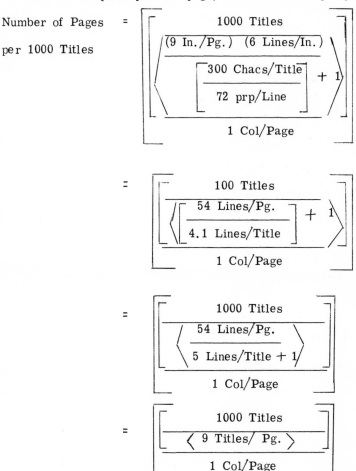

$$= \left[\frac{\left[\dfrac{1000 \text{ Titles}}{9 \text{ Titles/Pg.}}\right]}{1 \text{ Col/Page}}\right]$$

$$= \frac{\left[111.1 \text{ Pages/1000 Titles}\right]}{1 \text{ Col/Page}}$$

$$= \quad 112 \text{ Pages of Printing/1000 Titles.}$$

Formula for finding the computing cost to transfer N titles from tape to core

Another set of tables is given below which shows the cost of transferring 1000 titles from tape to the computer at five levels of machine rental ($100, $200, $300, $400 and $500/hour); three levels of titles per tape record (1, 5, 10) and two levels of tape speed and tape density (15 Kc, 60 Kc). The formula upon which the tables have been based is given below.

$ TO MOVE N TITLES

= (Hours To move N Titles) x ($/Hour)

= (No. of Records) x (Hrs. to Move 1 Record) x ($/Hour)

$$= \left[\frac{\text{No. of Titles Moved}}{\text{No. of Titles Per Record}}\right] \times$$

$$\left(\frac{\left\{\dfrac{(\text{No. of Chac./Title})\ (\text{No. of Titles/Record})}{(\text{No. of Chacs./In.})}\right\} = .75''}{\dfrac{(\text{Tape Speed; In./Sec.})}{(60\ \text{Secs./Min.})\quad(60\ \text{Min./Hr.})}}\right)$$

We take a small example. Assume a machine cost of $100/Hr.; ten titles/record; 300 characters/title; 200 characters to the inch; 75" per second for the tape speed; and we wish to move a block of 1000 titles.

$ TO MOVE 1000 TITLES:

$$\left[\frac{1000\ \text{Titles Moved}}{10\ \text{Titles/Rec.}}\right] \times$$

$$\left(\frac{\left\{\dfrac{(300\ \text{Chacs/Title})\ (10\ \text{Titles/Rec.})}{200\ \text{Chacs/In.}}\right\} + .75''}{\dfrac{75''/\text{Sec}}{3600\ \text{Secs./Hr.}}}\right)$$

$$= 100\ \text{Records} \times \left(\frac{\left\{\dfrac{3000\ \text{Chacs/Rec.}}{200\ \text{Chacs/Inc.}}\right\} + .75''}{\dfrac{75''/\text{Sec.}}{3600\ \text{Sec./Hr.}}}\right)\ \$100/\text{Hr.}$$

$$= 100\ \text{Recs.}\ \left(\frac{\dfrac{15.75''/\text{Record}}{75''/\text{Sec.}}}{3600\ \text{Secs./Hr.}}\right) \times (\$100/\text{Hr.})$$

$$= \left(\frac{\dfrac{1575''/\text{Record}}{75''/\text{Sec.}}}{3600 \text{ Secs.}/\text{Hr.}} \right) \quad x \quad \begin{array}{l} (\$100/ \\ \text{Hr.}) \end{array}$$

$$= \frac{21 \text{ Secs.}}{3600 \text{ Secs.}/\text{Hr.}} \quad x \quad \begin{array}{l} (\$100/ \\ \text{Hr.}) \end{array}$$

$$= \quad (.005833 \text{ Hrs.}) \text{ x } (\$100/\text{Hr.})$$

Cost to move 100 titles from memory to tape = $.5833.

COST TO TRANSFER 1000 TITLES WITH 100 CHARACTERS PER TITLE

Machine Rent/Hr.	Titles/Tape Rec.	Transfer Rate	Cost in $
$100	1	15	0.2355
$100	1	60	0.4628
$100	5	15	0.0868
$100	5	60	0.2407
$100	10	15	0.0683
$100	10	60	0.2129
$200	1	15	0.4712
$200	1	60	0.9259
$200	5	15	0.1736
$200	5	60	0.4815
$200	10	15	0.1367
$200	10	60	0.4259
$300	1	15	0.7068
$300	1	60	1.3889
$300	5	15	0.2604
$300	5	60	0.7222
$300	10	15	0.2050
$300	10	60	0.6389
$400	1	15	0.9424
$400	1	60	1.8517
$400	5	15	0.3472
$400	5	60	0.9629
$400	10	15	0.2733
$400	10	60	0.8518
$500	1	15	1.1781
$500	1	60	2.3149
$500	5	15	0.4340
$500	5	60	1.2038
$500	10	15	.3417
$500	10	60	1.0649

COST TO TRANSFER 1000 TITLES WITH 200 CHARACTERS PER TITLE

Machine Rent/Hr.	Titles/Tape Rec.	Transfer Rate	Cost in $
$100	1	15	0.2851
$100	1	60	0.6480
$100	5	15	0.1364
$100	5	60	0.4258
$100	10	15	0.1177
$100	10	60	0.3980
$200	1	15	0.5704
$200	1	60	1.2961
$200	5	15	0.2728
$200	5	60	0.8517
$200	10	15	0.2355
$200	10	60	0.7962
$300	1	15	0.8556
$300	1	60	1.9443
$300	5	15	0.4092
$300	5	60	1.2777
$300	10	15	0.3533
$300	10	60	1.1944
$400	1	15	1.1408
$400	1	60	2.5923
$400	5	15	0.5456
$400	5	60	1.7035
$400	10	15	0.4711
$400	10	60	1.5924
$500	1	15	1.4261
$500	1	60	3.2407
$500	5	15	0.6821
$500	5	60	2.1296
$500	10	15	0.5889
$500	10	60	1.9908

COST TO TRANSFER 1000 TITLES WITH 300 CHARACTERS PER TITLE

Machine Rent/Hr.	Titles/Tape Rec.	Transfer Rate 15 — Cost in $	Transfer Rate 60 — Cost in $
$100	1	0.3347	0.8331
$100	5	0.1859	0.6109
$100	10	0.1672	0.5832
$200	1	0.6694	1.6666
$200	5	0.3720	1.2221
$200	10	0.3344	1.1666
$300	1	1.0045	2.4999
$300	5	0.5580	1.8333
$300	10	0.5016	1.7499
$400	1	1.3392	3.3333
$400	5	0.7439	2.4442
$400	10	0.6688	2.3331
$500	1	1.6742	4.1667
$500	5	0.9300	3.0556
$500	10	.8361	2.9167

COST TO TRANSFER 1000 TITLES WITH 400 CHARACTERS PER TITLE

Machine Rent/Hr.	Titles/Tape Rec.	Transfer Rate 15 — Cost in $	Transfer Rate 60 — Cost in $
$100	1	0.3843	1.0182
$100	5	0.2355	0.7961
$100	10	0.2169	0.7683
$200	1	0.7688	2.0369
$200	5	0.4712	1.5924
$200	10	0.4338	1.5369
$300	1	1.1532	3.0555
$300	5	0.7068	2.3888
$300	10	0.6508	2.3055
$400	1	1.5375	4.0737
$400	5	0.9424	3.1849
$400	10	0.8677	3.0738
$500	1	1.9221	5.0927
$500	5	1.1781	3.9815
$500	10	1.0847	3.8427

Determination of Machine Rental Rate

Each of the lists and catalogs to be prepared by the machine were studied with respect to the time it takes to read information into the computer, the time it takes to transfer data from the computer to the tape and the time required for printing. Based on these calculations it became evident that the limiting characteristic would be the number of lines per minute the computer can print. It was originally thought that rather large machines would be required, but the analysis shows that most of the calculations can be done while the machine is printing and there is little reason to put the problem on the large machine.

From the programming point of view it is desirable to use a machine which handles variable field alphanumeric information in a facile manner.

The two main requirements, high printing speeds and ease of handling alphanumerics do not necessarily imply the use of a large machine and consequently a machine in the so-called middle price range was selected. The generic rate of $100 an hour is based on a study of average rental and purchase costs of such machines, (1) and is corroborated by the rate quoted by EDP service bureaus in the Chicago area.

The computations in each of the sections on COST are based on a computer whose minimum characteristics are specified below. These requirements are based on the machine's capability to handle the UIC work load.

BIBLIOGRAPHIC STRING ADDITION FREQUENCY

Assumptions:

1.) 1000 definitions will eventually be required. Such a list will cover the different types of authorship, bibliographic forms, and details of descriptive cataloging.

2.) 900 definitions can be accounted for on the initial survey.

3.) Let t be measured in weeks.

4.) Assume a rate, K, of less than or equal to 10%, where K is the percentage of remaining definitions to be found in a given week.

5.) A differential equation of the form

$$y' = -Ky$$

was assumed, where y is the number of changes to be made in week t. One would reasonably expect an exponential decay process.

Calculations:

1.) Solving 5). We have

$$y = ce^{-Kt}$$

2.) Let c = 1000 - 900 = 100; K = .10; t = 50 weeks.

$$y = 100e$$

$$y \cong 1 \text{ change.}$$

Acquisitions - Cost Calculations

Assumptions:

1. Page size: 11" x 14".

2. Page layout: 2 columns.

3. Lines per page: 54.

4. Characters per title: 300.

5. No. of titles per tape record: 10.

6. No. of titles per UNIT: 1000.

Data Supplied by U.I.C.:

1. Average processing time for a given piece of material is ten weeks.

2. The design load of 24,000 titles per year will be assumed as equivalent to 500 per week.

Calculations:

1. No. of pages required to print one UNIT: 56 pages.

2. Number of lines to be printed/UNIT.

   = (No. of pages/UNIT) x (No. of lines/page).

$=$ 56 pages x 54 lines/page

$=$ 3,024 lines/UNIT.

3. Time required to print one UNIT

$=$ $\dfrac{\text{(No. of lines/UNIT)}}{\text{(No. of lines/minute - printer speed)}}$

$=$ $\dfrac{3,024 \text{ lines/UNIT}}{600 \text{ lines/minute}}$

$=$ 5.04 minutes.

4. Estimated cost per year to print one UNIT/Issue

$=$ (Machine rental/hour) x $\dfrac{\text{(No. of min./UNIT)}}{\text{(No. of min./hour)}}$

$=$ ($100/hour) x $\dfrac{\text{(5.04 min./UNIT)}}{\text{(60 min./hour)}}$

$\cong$ $8 -9/UNIT/Issue.

5. Numbers of items to be printed per issue of the

PROCESSING INFORMATION LIST

$\Big\{$ $=$ Lower bound: $\left(\dfrac{\text{No. of Items}}{\text{Week}}\right)\left(\begin{array}{c}\text{No. of Weeks} \quad -1\\ \text{to Process}\end{array}\right)$

$=$ Upper bound: $\left(\dfrac{\text{No. of Items}}{\text{Week}}\right)\left(\begin{array}{c}\text{No. of Weeks} \quad +4\\ \text{to Process}\end{array}\right)$

$\Big\{$ $=$ L. B.: $\dfrac{\text{(500 Items)}}{\text{Week}}$ (10 Weeks - 1 Week)

$=$ U. B.: $\dfrac{\text{(500 Items)}}{\text{Week}}$ (10 Weeks + 4 Weeks)

$\left\{\begin{array}{l} = \text{ L. B.:   4500 Items} \\ \\ = \text{ U. B.:   7000 Items} \end{array}\right.$

6. Estimated Cost to print one issue of the PROCESSING

   INFORMATION LIST

   = (No. of UNITS/Issue)   (Cost to Print One UNIT)

   $= \left\{\begin{array}{l} \text{L.B.:   (4.5) (\$9.00)} \\ \text{U.B.:   (7.0) (\$9.00)} \end{array}\right.$

   $= \left\{\begin{array}{l} \text{L.B.:   \$40.50/Issue} \\ \text{U.B.:   \$63.00/Issue} \end{array}\right.$

7. Estimated cost per year to print one issue per week of

   the PROCESSING INFORMATION LIST

   = (No. of Weeks/Year) x (Cost/Issue)

   $= \left\{\begin{array}{l} \text{L.B.:   (52) (\$40.50)} \\ \text{U.B.:   (52) (\$63.00)} \end{array}\right.$

   $= \left\{\begin{array}{l} \text{L.B.:   \$2,106/year} \\ \text{U.B.:   \$3,276/year} \end{array}\right.$

CATALOGING:

Assumptions:

1. Cost of computer - printing one UNIT (UNIT = 1000

   Titles): $9.00

2. Cost of preparing an offset printed and bound catalog

   per UNIT = $57.16.

Bases for assumption as follows:

a. Computer cost/UNIT (18pp)   = $ 9.00

b. Offset press set-up costs:
   .50/pg   x   56pp.   =   28.00

c. Offset running: $.01/pg x 56pp x
   25 copies   =   14.00

d. Collation: $.0004/pg   x _56pp.   x
   25 copies   =   .56

e. Bindery: $.004/pg   x   56pp.   x
   25 copies   =   5.60
                                                    ‾‾‾‾‾‾
                                                    $57.16

5.   Estimated cost of preparing an offset-printed and bound

     POSH Index per UNIT = $18.48

     Bases for assumption as follows:

a. Computer cost/UNIT (18pp)   = $ 3.00

b. Offset press set-up costs:
   $.50/pg.   x   18 pp   =   9.00

c. Offset running: $.01   x   18 pp   x
   25 copies   =   4.50

d. Collation: $.0004/pg.   x   18pp   x
   25 copies   =   .18

e. Bindery: $.0004/pg   x   18 pp   x
   25 copies   =   1.80
                                                    ‾‾‾‾‾‾
                                                    $18.48

TOTAL HOLDINGS EDITION

Data Supplied by C.U.D.

1. Technical processing must be able to handle a load of
    24, 000 titles a year (2000 titles/month).

2. Each title will require five catalog cards (2.4 author-
    title and 2.6 subject heading) or its equivalent in book
    form.

3. In the new building it is assumed that one person will
    be filing in the central catalog and another person filing
    in the division libraries. The annual rate for these
    people is $4000/year. The supervision of these people
    and the revising of their filing will take half the time of
    one professional librarian at $3000/year. This gives a
    catalog maintenance cost of $11,000 a year.

4. Bound volumes of the book catalogs will be prepared in
    25 copies and copies of the catalogs produced directly
    from the machine will be made in 6 copies.

5. Offset printing, binding and collating cost are based on
    current rates in the Chicago area.

6. The present card catalog of 60,000 titles will be con-
    verted to machine readable form over a period of two
    years.

Calculations:

1. Cost of preparing Total Holding Edition (THE) is given

    by the following:

    $THE = (No. of UNITS in the Edition)
                (Cost of entering one item)

    $THE = (A   BM) C_1

    where A = is the number of UNITS appearing in the

                last edition of the THE

            B = the number of UNITS being added to the

                Monthly Edition each month

            M = the number of months since the last THE

            C_1 = the cost to enter one UNIT in the THE

MONTHLY EDITION

2. Cost of preparing the Monthly Edition (ME) over a peri-

    od is M months as given by:

    $ME = (No. of UNITS in MO. 1) x (Cost/UNIT)

            (No. of UNITS in Mo. 1 + Mo. 2) x
                (Cost/UNIT)

            (No. of UNITS in Mo. 1 + Mo. 2 + ...
                + Mo (M-1) x (Cost/ UNIT)

            $= \left\{ \dfrac{B}{2} \quad M \quad (M-1) \right\} C_2$

    where

    M is the number of Months since the last THE.   Note

    that we use (M-1) instead of M + 1 since we do not produce the last ME; all new entries plus all of the (M-1) ME data goes into the next edition of this THE.

B is the number of units being added to the MONTHLY EDITION each month

C_2 is the cost to enter one unit in the ME.

3. The equations appearing in 1) and 2) can be solved simultaneously to give the optimum interval of months (M) between successive publications of the THE

$$\$THE = (AC_1) + (BC_1) \quad M$$

$$\$ME = \quad +\left(\frac{BC_2}{2}\right) M \quad \left(\frac{BC_2}{2}\right) M^2$$

Solving for M gives

$$M^2 - \left(\frac{2C_1}{C_2} + 1\right) M - \frac{2AC_1}{BC_2} = O$$

Based on the assumptions we have, in terms of UNITS (= 1000 Titles)

$$C_1 = \$57.16$$

$$C_2 = \quad 9.00$$

$$A = \quad 60$$

$$B = \quad 2$$

Substituting, we get

$$M^2 - 14 M - 381 = 0$$

Solving we get

$$M = \frac{14 + \sqrt{196 + 1524}}{2}$$

$$\cong 28 \text{ months}$$

It must be kept in mind that M is the optimum interval
(in the sense of least cost) expressed in terms of months
that gives the lowest combination of production costs for
the THE and ME.

The values for M, multiplied by the number of titles
processed per month, is now added to the former value
of A to give a new value of A. The formula is solved
again to obtain the next interval which will be optimal
for the production of the next Total Holdings Edition.
This calculation has been carried out and we have:

$$M_1 = 28 \text{ months}$$

$$M_2 = 36 \text{ months}$$

$$M_3 = 42 \text{ months}$$

4. Estimated costs of producing book catalogs for a 5-year
span. The sum of M_1 and M_2 is a span of 64 months,
and the following calculation will be carried out on this
64-month base and later annualized.

The cost of producing the Monthly Edition is given by

$$\$ME = \left\{ \frac{B}{2} \ M \ (M-1) \right\} C_2$$

$$= \left\{ \frac{2}{2} \ M \ (M-1) \right\} \ \$9$$

$$= \ \$9 \ M \ (M-1)$$

Letting $M = M_1 = 28$ we get

$\$ME = \$9 \ (28) \ (27) = \$6804.$

Letting $M = M_2 = 36$ we get

$\$ME = \$9 \ (36) \ (35) = \$11340.$

For the Total Holdings Edition we have

$\$THE = (A \quad BM) \ C_2$

Letting $M = M_1 = 28$ we get

$\$THE = \left[60 + (2 \times 28) \right] \ \$57.16 = \$6631.$

Letting $M = M_2 = 36$ we get

$\$THE = \left[116 + (2 \times 36) \right] \ \$57.16 = \$10,746.$

Summing the costs for the Monthly Editions and Total Holdings Edition and annualizing we get an estimated cost of $6660/year.

The above cost of $6660 represents the equivalent of one card being filed in the card catalog. Since five cards are filed for every title, we have an estimated cost of $33,300 as the equivalent cost of book catalogs per year.

POSH INDEX

5. Estimated cost of production of the Permutation on Subject Heading Catalog.

    The formula expressing the intervals for the POSH index is the same as developed in 3:

$$M^2 - \left(\frac{2C_1 + 1}{C_2} \right) M - \frac{2AC_1}{BC_2} = 0$$

where the constants now have the values:

$$C_1 = \$18.50$$
$$C_2 = 3.00$$
$$B = 2$$
$$A = 60$$

Solving for M we get

$$M_1 = 26$$
$$M_2 = 33$$

Substituting these values in the formula for the Monthly Edition we get:

$POSH: M_1 = \$3 (26) (25) = \$1950

$POSH: M_2 = \$3 (33) (32) = \$3168

Solving for the bound edition we get

$POSH: TH = \$18.50 $\left[60 + (2 \times 26) \right]$ = \$2072

$POSH: TH = \$18.50 $\left[112 + (2 \times 33) \right]$ = \$3293

Summing the values for the MONTHLY and the TOTAL HOLDINGS for a POSH INDEX and annualizing we get \$2148.

6. Estimated costs using a combination of the full entry book catalog for authors-titles and the POSH Index for subject headings.

    Assuming 2.4 author entries per title we have:

    > Annual rate for authors: $6660 x 2.4 = $15,984.

    Assuming 2.6 subject heading entries per title we have:

    > Annual rate for subject headings:

    > $2148 x 2.6 = $5585.

    This yields a book catalog production cost = $21,569.

CIRCULATION

Daily Circulation List

Assumptions:

1. Page size: 11" x 14"

2. Page layout: 6 columns

3. Lines/pg: 57

4. Print positions/entry: 14 + blank for call number and

    > 3 + 2 blanks for date due,

    > equals 20 prp/entry.

5. Call number of length greater than 14 will occupy two lines of printing.

6. One UNIT: 100,000 entries.

7. It is assumed that the number of early returns equals the number of overdues.

8. The "date due" will be represented by a "day number."
    (For example, the day number 185 is the fourth of July.)

9. It is assumed that 100,000 circulation transactions per
    year is equivalent to 400 transactions per day.

10. Number of days in circulation cycle: 14 days.

Data Supplied by U.I.C.:

1. The Daily Circulation List will be produced Monday thru
    Friday although the library may eventually be open on
    Saturdays and Sundays.

2. The patron number identification will not be printed.

Calculations:

1. Number of entries/page

    = (No. of cols./pg.) x (No. of lines/pg.)

    = 6 x 57

    = 342 entries/page.

2. Number of entries/UNIT

    = (No. of transactions/UNIT) x
         (No. of days in circulation cycle).

    = (400) x (14)

    = 5600 entries.

3. Number of pages in the D.C.L. per day (5600 entries)

    = $\dfrac{\text{(No. of entries/UNIT)}}{\text{(No. of entries/page)}}$

    = $\dfrac{5600}{342}$

   = 17 pages.

4. Number of lines of printing/UNIT

   = (No. of lines/page) x (No. of pages)

   = (57) x (17)

   = 969 lines.

5. Time to print One UNIT

$$= \frac{\text{No. of lines of printing}}{\text{No. of lines/min. - printing speed}}$$

$$= \frac{969}{600}$$

   = 1.615 minutes.

6. Time to print DCL per year per UNIT

   = (No. of days/week) x (No. of weeks/year) x
        (No. of minutes to print One UNIT)

   = (5) (52) (1.615)

   = 420 minutes/year.

7. Cost to print the DCL/year

$$= (\text{Machine rental/hour}) \times \frac{(\text{No. of minutes to print/year})}{(\text{No. of min./hour})}$$

$$= \frac{(\$100) \times 420}{60}$$

   = \$700/year.

8.   Cost to handle C.U.D. estimated load/year

      = (No. of UNITS/year) x ($1 UNIT)

      = (4) ($ 700)

      = $2800/year.

SERIALS

Weekly Periodicals List

Assumptions:

1.   Page Size: 11" x 14".

2.   Page layout: 2 cols/page.

3.   Lines/page: 57.

4.   One UNIT = 1000 titles.

5.   Number of characters per title: 58.

6.   Number of titles per tape record: 20.

Data Supplied by U.I.C.:

1.   Number of pieces/serial: 10.

2.   Number of titles received/year: 6500.

Calculations:

1.   Number of items per page

      = (No. of lines/page) x (No. of cols/page)

      = 57 x 2

      = 114 items/page.

2. Number of pages required to print one UNIT

$$= \left[\frac{\text{(Number of items/UNIT)}}{\text{(Number of items per page)}} \right]$$

$$= \left[\frac{1000}{14} \right] = 9 \text{ pages.}$$

3. Number of lines to be printed per UNIT

= (No. of Pages) x (No. of Lines/Page)

= 9 x 57 = 513 Lines.

4. Number of cards received each week per UNIT

$$= \frac{\text{(No. of Titles per UNIT)} \times \text{(No. of Pieces per Title)}}{\text{(No. of weeks/year)}}$$

$$= \frac{1000 \times 10}{52} = \frac{10000}{52} = 193 \text{ Cards/Week.}$$

5. Number of cards punched per month for check-in card/ per UNIT

$$= \frac{\text{No. of Titles per UNIT} \times \text{No. of Pieces/Title}}{\text{No. of months/year}}$$

$$= \frac{1000 \times 10}{12} = 833 \text{ cards}$$

6. Number of seconds to transfer one UNIT from tape to memory

$$= \frac{\left(\frac{\text{No. of Titles/UNIT}}{\text{No. of Titles/Record}} \right)}{\text{(No. of Inches/Sec - Tape Speed)}} \times$$

$$\frac{\left\{ \frac{\left(\frac{\text{No. of Titles}}{\text{Record}} \right) \times \left(\frac{\text{No. of Chacs}}{\text{Title}} \right) + \left(\frac{\text{Length}}{\text{EOR Gap}} \right)}{\text{No. of Chacs/In.}} \right\}}{\text{(No. of Inches/Sec - Tape Speed)}}$$

$$= \frac{\dfrac{1000}{20} \times \left\{ \dfrac{(20 \times 58) + .75''}{200} \right\}}{75'' \text{ per second}}$$

$$= \frac{50 \times 6.55}{75''} \quad = \quad 4.37 \text{ seconds.}$$

7. Time to print one UNIT

    $$= \frac{\text{No. of Lines to Print one UNIT}}{\text{No. of Lines/Minute - Printer Speed}}$$

    $$= \frac{500}{600} \; \tilde{=} \; 1 \text{ Minute/UNIT.}$$

8. Time to print U.I.C. estimated load

    $= $ (No. of UNITS) x (Time to print one UNIT)

    $= $ 6.5 UNITS x 1 minute/UNIT = 6.5 min.

9. Estimated cost to print U.I.C. estimated load/week

    $= $ (Machine Rental/Hour) x
    $$\left(\frac{\text{Time to Print U.I.C. Load-in-mins.}}{\text{No. of minutes/hour}} \right)$$

    $$= (\$100/\text{hr.}) \quad \left(\frac{6.5 \text{ mins.}}{60 \text{ mins/hr.}} \right)$$

    $= $ \$11/week.

10. Estimated cost to process U.I.C. weekly periodical list

    per year

    $= $ (No. of weeks/year) (Estimated Cost to Print U.I.C.
    Est. load/wk.)

    $= $ (52 wks/yr.) (\$11/wk.) = \$572/yr.

SERIALS HOLDINGS LIST

1. Paper size: 11" x 14".

2. Page layout: 1 column/page.

3. Number of Lines/title: 1.

4. Number of titles/page: 80.

5. Page costs for offset printing at a volume of 1000 page: $10/page.

6. Computations will be carried out on the basis of 1 UNIT-1000 titles.

Data Supplied by U.I.C.:

   No. of titles received per year: 6500

Calculations:

1. Number of lines of printing/UNIT

   = (No. of Titles/UNIT) x (No. of Lines/Title)

   = 1000 x 1

   = 1000 Lines/UNIT.

2. Time required to print one UNIT

   = $\dfrac{\text{No. of Lines/UNIT}}{\text{Lines 1 min. - printing speed}}$

   = $\dfrac{1000 \text{ lines/UNIT}}{600 \text{ lines/min.}}$

   = 2 minutes/UNIT.

3.   Time to Print U.I.C. ANNUAL LIST OF SERIALS.

   = (No. of Estimates U.I.C. UNITS) x
        (Time to Print 1 UNIT)

   = (6.5 UNITS) x (2 minutes/UNIT)

   = 13 minutes.

4.   Estimated costs to print U.I.C. ANNUAL LIST OF

    SERIALS

   = ($100/Hr.) $\dfrac{13 \text{ Minutes}}{60 \text{ min./hr.}}$

   ≃ $22/year.

5.   Number of Pages to be Offset Printed per UNIT

   = $\dfrac{\text{No. of Lines/UNIT}}{\text{No. of Lines/Pg.}}$

   = $\dfrac{1000 \text{ lines/UNIT}}{80 \text{ lines/page}}$

   = 13 pages/UNIT.

6.   Estimated cost to offset print 1000 copies one UNIT

   = (No. of Pages/UNIT) x (Cost/Page)

   = (13 Pages/UNIT) ($10.00/page)

   = $130 per 1000 copies/UNIT.

7.   Estimated cost to offset print 1000 copies of the esti-

    mated U.I.C. Serials Load.

   = (No. of UNITS) x (Cost/UNIT)

   = 6.5 UNITS x $130/UNIT

   = $845 /year.

MULTIPLYING LIBRARY CATALOGS

The prohibitive cost of reproducing catalog cards and then filing these cards in another series of card trays has already been adequately covered in the literature, so primary emphasis was placed on using new techniques with the present records.

One suggestion which was made and then rejected for the UIC application was the Multiple Microfilm Catalog. This is not an original concept but it seems more efficient than previous suggestions along this line.

The Multiple Microfilm Catalog would work as follows: the present card catalog would be copied onto 16mm film using a high speed camera designed for microfilming checks and which operates at a maximum rate of 450 cards per minute. Considering 225 cpm as the effective operating rate, an operator would take 32.6 hours to film to 441,000 cards in the catalog of a 100,000 volume library. This would make a catalog of 32 reels of film using Recordak Lodestar film cartridges.

Catalog stations would be established anywhere in or around the library but for the sake of discussion seven, two on each floor of a three story building plus one in the reference department, were set up. The card catalog would be placed in the catalog department and would be closed to the public. Each catalog station would be supplied with a complete set of the 32 reels of film, one reader printer, and three readers.

Thirty days after the initial filming the catalog cards for that month would be filmed and a copy of that film placed at each station. The cards would be placed in a separate file. The next month the cards for that month would be cumulated with the first month's cards and then the new file filmed. This film would be placed at the catalog stations and the film for the previous month discarded. These cumulated filmings would continue for eleven months. One reel will hold a little less than 14,000 cards, or about the number of cards a $30,000.00 yearly expenditure for books would accumulate. On the twelfth month all the cards in the catalog supplement would be interfiled into the main catalog, the whole thing re-filmed, and a new edition of the catalog issued. The old edition of the film catalog would be discarded.

The costs of a program of this nature are as follows. The equipment named is not necessarily recommended and is not the only make which will do the job. Specific models are named so that prices can be listed. All figures are on the basis of 100,000 volumes and are listed as of February, 1961.

Film Processing Equipment -

Recordak Microfilmer - Reliant 500	$2695.00
Recordak Continuous Film Processor	4145.00
Photostat Contact Film Printer	1900.00
	$8740.00

Catalog Station Equipment -

Recordak Starlet Film Readers (3)	$1445.00
Thermo-Fax Model 100 Reader Printer (1) (Modified to accept Lodestar cartridges) *	750.00
Per station	$2205.00
Seven stations	$15,435.00
Total cost of equipment	$24,175.00

* Estimate (unmodifies the model 100 priced at $629.00)

Filming and Duplication -

Filming 100,000 volume catalog	$ 210.00
Seven copies of film at $144.00 each	1008.00
Monthly supplements at $5.00 per station per month	385.00
Total filming costs for the first year.	$1603.00

While a fairly high investment in equipment is indicated
the Film Processing Equipment could probably be leased or
shared with other departments in an institution. Figuring
conservatively that the microfilm readers would last ten
years it does not appear unreasonable then for seven extra
copies of the card catalog, kept current to within the last
thirty days, to cost slightly over $4000.00 per year or about
$575.00 per copy.

In addition to making more copies of the present catalog
available, a very interesting idea was proposed concerning
further exploitation of a bibliographic tool presently in most
libraries, the Library of Congress Catalog of Printed Cards,
Author List (National Union Catalog - Author List) and the
Library of Congress Catalog, Books: Subjects. Why should
a library attempt to reproduce their card catalog when they
already have a printed copy waiting for use? Copies of the
National Union Catalog are not expensive when compared to
the cost of reproducing a card catalog, so additional copies
could be placed in several areas of the library or at various locations around the campus. The holdings of the library could then be checked off in each of the copies so that
patrons would know which volumes were available in the local
collection. If titles cataloged by the local library did not
appear in the LC catalogs a copy of the catalog card could

be sent to LC for inclusion in the next supplement.   Location symbols might be included as they are in the National
Union Catalog 1952-1955 Imprints, although it is obvious that
if many libraries wished to be included the location symbols
would soon take more space than the entries, as they do in
the Union List of Serials.

The first question to be asked was,   "Who can afford to
go through several copies of the LC catalogs and check holdings?" A proposal was then advanced to create a list made
up of the LC card order numbers for each item acquired by
the library and to print this list in numerical order and keep
a copy near each set of the catalogs.   This way a patron
could note the LC card order number of an item in which he
was interested and then look in the list to see if that number appeared.   If the number was in the list he could then
look up the call number in the card catalog.

This system has a considerable amount of user frustra-
tion built into it.   The patron is exposed to the existence of
a good portion of the world's knowledge and might be unhappy
to discover the relatively small amount of this material available locally.   It is doubtful that a patron would be willing to
make extensive use of a triple table look-up procedure.   It
is also doubtful if he would be willing to look in at least
twelve places in the catalogs to find his references.   This

would include the main set (Author List) of 167 volumes, supplements of 42, 23, 26, 5, 5, and 5 volumes, plus the current receipts issues in paper covers and sets of 20, 22, and 3 volumes plus current receipts issues for the subject catalogs.

It is unfortunate that so many inherent difficulties surround this use of the LC catalogs in a library with a large number of general users.   Perhaps an application of this type could be made in a specialized situation.

BIBLIOGRAPHY

American Management Association. Changing dimensions of
    office equipment. New York, 1960.

--- Data processing today: a progress report. (AMA man-
    agement report, no. 46) New York, 1960.

--- Directory of consultant members - 1960. New York,
    1960.

--- Electronic data processing in industry; a case book of
    management experience. (Special report, no. 3) New
    York, 1955.

--- Electronics in action: the current practicality of elec-
    tronic data processing. (Special report, no. 22) New
    York, 1957.

--- Establishing an integrated data-processing system: a
    blueprint for a company program. (Special report, no.
    11) New York, 1956.

--- Keeping pace with automation. (Special report, no. 7)
    New York, 1956.

--- Leadership on the job. New York, 1957.

--- Men, machines and methods in the modern office. New
    York, 1958.

--- Organizing for effective systems planning and control.

(Special report, no. 12) New York, 1956.

--- Pioneering in electronic data processing: company experience with electronic computers. (Special report, no. 9) New York, 1956.

Andree, Richard V. Programming the IBM magnetic drum computer and data processing machine. New York, Holt, Rinehart, and Winston, 1958.

Bailey, Gerald B. and R. Presgrave. Basic motion time study. New York, McGraw-Hill, 1958.

Becker, Esther R. and Eugene F. Murphy. Office in transition. New York, Harper, 1957.

Beer, Stafford. Cybernetics and management. New York, Wiley, 1960.

Bell, David Arthur. Information theory, 2d ed. New York, Pitman, 1956.

Bell, James R. and Lynwood B. Steedman. Personnel problems in converting to automation. University, Alabama, University of Alabama Press, 1959.

Bell, William D. Management guide to electronic computers. New York, McGraw-Hill, 1957.

Booth, Andrew D. Progress in automation. Vol. 1. New York, Academic Press, 1960.

Bright, James R. Automation and management. Boston, Harvard Business School, 1958.

Broadbent, Donald E.   Perception and communication.   New
  York, Pergamon, 1958.

Burton, Alfred Joseph.   Electronic computers and their
  business applications.   New York, International Publications Service, 1960.

Canadian Conference for Computing and Data Processing.
  University of Toronto.   Proceedings.   Toronto, University of Toronto Press, 1958.

Canning, R. G.   Electronic data processing for business and
  industry.   New York, Wiley, 1956.

Canning, R. G.   Installing electronic data processing systems.   New York, Wiley, 1957.

Carroll, Phil.   How to chart data.   New York, McGraw-Hill,
  1960.

Casey, Robert S., and others.   Punched cards; their application to science and industry.   2d ed.   New York,
  Reinhold, 1958.

Conference of Eastern College Librarians.   Recruiting library personnel.   Automation in the library.   Report of
  the 41st Conference of Eastern College Librarians held
  at Columbia University, November 26, 1955.   (ACRL
  monographs, no. 17)   Chicago, Association of College
  and Reference Libraries, 1956.

Conference on the Practical Utilization of Recorded Knowl-
    edge - Present and Future, Western Reserve University,
    1956. Documentation in action. Edited by Jesse H.
    Shera, Allen Kent, and James W. Perry. New York,
    Reinhold, 1956.

Craig, Harold Farlow. Administering a conversion to elec-
    tronic accounting. Boston, Harvard University, Division
    of Research, 1955.

Dreher, Carl. Automation: what it is, how it works, who
    can use it. New York, Norton, 1957.

Einzig, Paul. The economic consequences of automation.
    New York, Norton, 1956.

Electronic Industries Association. Proceedings of the EIA
    Conference on Automation Systems for Business and
    Industry. Elizabeth, N.J., Engineering Publishers, 1958.

Eustis, William A. A primer to the automatic office. Con-
    tributions by Gilbert Dresser, William Alden, and Frank-
    lin Wyman, Jr. Westboro, Massachusetts, Automation
    Management, 1956.

Fairbanks, Ralph W. Successful office automation. Engle-
    wood Cliffs, N.J., Prentice-Hall, 1956.

Feinstein, Amiel. Foundations of information theory. New
    York, McGraw-Hill, 1958.

Flores, Ivan.   Computer logic: the functional design of digital computers.   Englewood Cliffs, N.J., Prentice-Hall,
  1960.

Fry (George) and Associates, Inc., Chicago.   Study of circulation control systems: public libraries, college and
  university libraries, special libraries.   (LTP publications, no.1)   Chicago, Library Technology Project of the
  American Library Association, 1961.

Geer, Helen Thornton.   Charging systems.   Chicago, American Library Association, 1955.

General Electric Company, Defense Systems Department,
  Information Systems Operation.   Improving information
  flow in a university library.   A final report prepared
  under contract with the University of Illinois, Chicago
  Undergraduate Division.   Washington, D.C., 1961.

Goodman, Leonard Landon.   Automation today and tomorrow.
  New York, Oxford University Press, 1958.

Gotlieb, C. C. and J. N. P. Hume.   High speed data processing.   New York, McGraw-Hill, 1958.

Grabbe, Eugene M., ed.   Automation in business and industry.   New York, Wiley, 1957.

Grabbe, Eugene M. and others.   Handbook of automation,
  computation, and control.   3 Vols.   New York, Wiley,
  1958-60.

Gregory, Robert H. and Richard L. Van Horn. Automatic
    data-processing systems. San Francisco, Wadsworth,
    1960.

Greniweski, H. Cybernetics without mathematics. New
    York, Pergamon, 1960.

Guilband, Georges T. What is cybernetics? New York,
    Criterion, 1959.

Hartkemeier, Harry P. Punch-card methods. Dubuque, Ia.,
    Brown, 1952.

Heyel, Carl. Organizing your job in management. New
    York, American Management Association, 1960.

International Conference on Scientific Information, Washing-
    ton, D.C., 1958. Proceedings. 2 Vols. Washington,
    National Academy of Sciences, National Research Coun-
    cil, 1959.

Ivall, T. E. Electronic computers. Principles and appli-
    cations. 2d ed. New York, Philosophical Library,
    1960.

Jacobson, Howard Boone and Joseph S. Roucek, eds. Auto-
    mation and society. New York, Philosophical Library,
    1959.

Jeenel, J. Programming for digital computers. New York,
    McGraw-Hill, 1959.

Jones, Gardner M. Electronics in business. Lansing,
Michigan, Bureau of Business and Economic Research,
Michigan State University, 1958.

Kellogg, M. Graham. Preparing the office manual. (Research study, no.36) New York, American Management
Association, 1959.

Kozmetsky, G. and P. Kircher. Electronic computers and
management control. New York, McGraw-Hill, 1956.

Laubach, Peter B. Company investigation of automatic data
processing. Boston, Harvard University. Division of
Research, 1957.

Lazzaro, V., ed. Systems and procedures: a handbook for
business and industry. Englewood Cliffs, N.J., Prentice-Hall, 1959.

Leveson, Joseph H., ed. Electronic business machines.
New York, Philosophical Library, 1960.

Levin, Howard S. Office work and automation. New York,
Wiley, 1956.

Los Angeles. University of Southern California. School of
Library Science. Modern trends in documentation; proceedings of a symposium held at the University of Southern California, April 1958. Edited by Martha Boaz,
London, New York, Pergamon, 1959.

McCormick, E. M. Digital computer primer. New York,
    McGraw-Hill, 1959.

McCracken, Daniel D. Digital computer programming. New
    York, Wiley, 1957.

McCracken, Daniel D. and others. Programming business
    computers. New York, Wiley, 1959.

McGaw, Howard F. Marginal punched cards in college and
    research libraries. Washington, Scarecrow Press, 1952.

Metcalfe, John Wallace. Information indexing and subject
    cataloging; alphabetical, classified; coordinate, mechan-
    ical. New York, Scarecrow Press, 1957.

Miller, Ben. Gaining acceptance for major methods changes.
    New York, American Management Association, 1960.

Milward, G. E. Organization and methods. New York,
    St. Martins Press, 1960.

Mundel, Marvin Everett. Motion and time study; principles
    and practice. New York, Prentice-Hall, 1950.

Mundel, Marvin Everett. Systematic motion and time study.
    New York, Prentice-Hall, 1947.

National Conference of Professors of Educational Adminis-
    tration. Automation: its meaning for educational admin-
    istration. New York, Teachers College, Columbia Uni-
    versity, 1957.

"The National Library of Medicine Index Mechanization Pro-
    ject," Bulletin of the Medical Library Association,
    49:1-96, January 1961, Part 2 of 2 parts.

Nett, Roger. An introduction to electronic data processing,
    by Roger Nett and Stanley A. Hetzler. Glencoe, Illinois,
    Free Press, 1959.

Parker, Ralph Halsted. Library applications of punched
    cards: a description of mechanical systems. Chicago,
    American Library Association, 1952.

Perry, James Whitney and Allen Kent. Documentation and
    information retrieval; an introduction to basic principles
    and cost analysis. Cleveland, Western Reserve Univer-
    sity, 1957.

Perry, James Whitney, Allen Kent, and Madeline M. Berry.
    Machine literature searching. With a foreword by Jesse
    H. Shera. Cleveland, Western Reserve University, 1956.

Perry, James Whitney and Allen Kent, eds. Tools for ma-
    chine literature searching: semantic code dictionary,
    equipment, procedures. With the semantic code diction-
    ary under the general editorship of John L. Melton.
    (Library science and documentation; a series of texts
    and monographs, vol.1) New York, Interscience Pub-
    lishers, 1958.

Pollock, Frederick. Automation. New York, Praeger, 1958.

Postley, John A. Computers and people. New York, McGraw-Hill, 1960.

The Punched card data processing annual. Vol. 1- . Detroit, Michigan, Gille Associates, 1959- .

Ragazzini, John R. and Gene Franklin. Sampled-data control systems. New York, McGraw-Hill, 1958.

Robichand, B. Selecting, planning, and managing office space. New York, McGraw-Hill, 1958.

Ross, H. John. How to make a procedure manual. 4th ed. Miami, Florida, Office Research Institute, 1958.

Ross, H. John. Integrated data processing for every office. Miami, Florida, Office Research Institute, 1957.

Shiskin, Julius. Electronic computers and business indicators. (Occasional paper 57) New York, National Bureau of Economic Research, 1957.

Schultz, George P. and Thomas L. Whisler. Management organization and the computer. (A publication of Graduate School of Business, The University of Chicago, Third series) Glencoe, Illinois, Free Press, 1960.

Smith, J. Sandford. Management approach to electronic digital computers. (Essential Books) New York, Oxford University Press, 1957.

Symposium on Information Storage and Retrieval Theory,
Systems and Devices, Washington, D.C., 1958   Infor-
mation storage and retrieval theory, systems and de-
vices.   Edited by Mortimer Taube and Harold Wooster.
(Columbia University studies in library science, no.10)
New York, Columbia University Press, 1958.

United Nations Educational, Scientific and Cultural Organization.   Proceedings of the UNESCO International Conference, 15-20 June 1959.   Paris, UNESCO, 1959.

U.S. Congress.   Senate.   Committee on Government Operations.   Documentation, indexing, and retrieval of scientific information.   86th Congress, 2d Session, Washington, D.C., Government Printing Office, 1960.

U.S. Department of the Navy.   Navy Management Office.
Source data automation guide.   Washington, Navy Management Office, March, 1961.

U.S. National Science Foundation.   Current research and
development in scientific documentation, No. 8-
Washington, Govt. Print. Off., May 1961-

Weeks, Robert P., ed.   Machines and the man: a source
book on automation.   New York, Appleton-Century-
Crofts, 1961.

Western Reserve University, Cleveland. School of Library
    Science. Information retrieval and machine translation.
    Based on the International Conference for Standards on
    a Common Language for Machine Searching and Trans-
    lating, sponsored by Western Reserve University and
    Rand Development Corporation, held in Cleveland, Ohio,
    September 6-12, 1959. Editor: Allen Kent. 2 parts.
    (Advances in documentation and library science, vol.3)
    New York, Interscience Publishers, 1960.

Western Reserve University, Cleveland. School of Library
    Science. Information systems in documentation. Based
    on the symposium on systems for information retrieval,
    held at Western Reserve University, Cleveland, Ohio,
    in April 1957 under the auspices of the School of Li-
    brary Science of Western Reserve University and its
    Center for Documentation and Communications Research.
    Editors: J. H. Shera, A. Kent, and J. W. Perry. (Ad-
    vances in documentation and library science, vol.2)

Western Reserve University, Cleveland. School of Library
    Science. Progress report in chemical literature re-
    trieval. Based on symposia of the Division of Chemical
    Literature, American Chemical Society, held in Minne-
    apolis, Minnesota, September 1955 and in Dallas, Texas,

April 1956. Editors: Gilbert W. Peakes, Allen Kent, and James W. Perry. (Advances in documentation and library science, vol.1) New York, Interscience Publishers, 1957.

Wilkes, M. V. and others. Preparation of programs for electronic digital computer. 2d ed. Reading, Massachusetts, Addison-Wesley, 1957.

Wrubel, Marshal H. Primer of programming for digital computers. New York, McGraw-Hill, 1959.

Wylie, H. L., ed. Office management handbook. New York, Ronald Press, 1958.

AN ANNOTATED BIBLIOGRAPHY OF READINGS
ON LIBRARY MECHANIZATION

American Management Association.   The impact of computers on office management.   New York, AMA, 1954.

Dwells on planning that had to be done before computers were added to offices and the results of their careful work after the equipment was put into operation.

Babat, G.   Informarium [an imaginary report from the beginning of the 3rd millennium.] Library Association Record, January 1960.

Interesting possibilities on where automation could end (in hundreds of years).   Fun.   (Maybe we're closer than he thinks.)

Bacon, F. R. et al.   Application of a telereference system to divisional library card catalogs.   Final report. 1958.

While possibly a good example of "or" action and statistical analysis applied to libraries this seems to be based upon a shallow idea which has been explored from the wrong (cost only) direction.   The telereference system uses television and a card turner for remote catalog usage.

Ball, Howard R.   Document retriever introduced by BUSHIPS.

Bureau of Ships Journal 9:9-11, December 1960.

High speed multi-output electronic document storage

machine uses microfilm as a storage medium and can

send 4320 sq. in. of material per minute.

Bello, Francis.   How to cope with information.   Fortune

62:160-7+, September 1960.

Covers information retrieval systems from the stand-

point of history.   Types, firms working in the field,

government agencies who have them, effectiveness to

date and future.   Excellent general information.

Birnbaum, Henry.   General Information Manual.   IBM

circulation control at Brooklyn College Library.   IBM

Corporation 1960.   32p.

Explains in some detail the circulation procedures used

at Brooklyn College using the IBM No. 24 card punch,

No. 82 sorter and a No. 85 collator.   This transaction

card system with a loan file.   Overdues and end of

semester notices are still done by hand.

Blodgett, C. C.   Distribution of cataloging tasks.   Library

Journal 81:881-2, April 15, 1956.

Discusses the division of work between professionals

and non-professionals in the catalog department.

Brownson, Helen L. Research on handling scientific infor-

 mation. Science 132:1922-31, December 1960.

 A general article covering current research in the field.

 Taken from the Current Research book by the NSF.

 States the problems pretty well.

Bush, V. As we may think. Atlantic Monthly 176:101-8,

 July 1945.

 An analysis of the strides taken in communication during

 World War II and estimates upon the direction they could

 go with proper management. Very accurate predictions.

Cavender, T. P. Time and motion techniques related to

 costs of expanding the card catalog. Library Resources

 & Technical Services 1:104-8, Spring 1957.

 Not much time and motion study here. Article is story

 of how they shifted their 1900 drawer catalog in 1-1/2

 working days.

Contract awarded for experimental electronic library equip-

 ment. Library Journal 84:1421, May 1, 1959.

 Note concerning $200,000 grant given AVCO for devel-

 opment of a micro-storage and retrieval machine. They

 said project should take a year.

Contract with Thompson-Ramo-Wooldridge Incorporated for

 research in machine indexing. New indexing pattern for

 nuclear science abstracts. American Documentation

11:120-7, April 1960.

Details a method of using IBM punch-card equipment and photography to print N.S.A. indexes. Something to come back to.

Dewey, H. Punched card catalogs - theory and technique. American Documentation 10:36-50, January 1959. Excellent basic discussion of all steps necessary for the production of a book catalog using IBM cards. Many examples of catalogs already done.

Donley, A. M. Jr. Library ecology and electronics. American Documentation 8:300-5, October 1957. "Blue sky" speculations on possible regional information centers led by one in New England (his home). States that machines would be useful but nothing more helpful.

Dubester, H. J. Catalog - a finding list? College & Research Libraries 18:107-11+, March 1957. General discussion concerning the function of the catalog (finding list vs. reference tool) and what changes could be made in rule revision to better realize reference department objectives.

Dyke, H. G. Figure-of-merit ordering system for a search output. American Documentation 10:85-6, January 1959. Clever system of giving weight to the depth to which a researcher is willing to go in searching the literature.

Might be useful if this ever gets to the machine stage.

Eaton, Thelma. What price revision? Illinois Libraries
42:297-305, May 1960.

Covers cost and desirability of following, blindly or no,
changes in the editions of cataloging tools (DC Classifi-
cation-Sears-etc.) with the required catalog revision.

Electronic Data Processing. Subject bibliography of periodical literature, 1959. New York, Lybrand, Ross Bros.
& Montgomery, 1960.

This is a bibliography of 1959 articles only and is arranged by subject (Multiple). Some interesting and little
known items in the 75 titles checked. General (for us)
but good.

Field, O. T. Experiment in catalog reform. College & Research Libraries 17:414-19+ , September 1956.

Air University's catalog reform consisted of dividing
their catalog (author and title-subject), removing 43,000
subject guide cards (!) and reducing their see also's.
No mechanizations involved except stamping subject headings on (instead of typing).

Flow charting helps to visualize, analyze in office layout
study. Navy management review 5:10-1, September 1960.

Covers flow charting relating to work flow through an
office with aim to reorganize the flow of work so effi-

ciency is increased. Warns that reorganization of work
cannot be attempted without being able to make physical
changes.

Francisco, F. L. Use of the Uniterm coordinate indexing
system in a large industrial concern. Special Libraries
47:117-23, March 1956.

Lists the problems and successes GE has had with a
coordinate index using posted numbers. Says that in
2 years of use they have gotten no false coordinations.

Garfield, E. Preparation of printed indexes by automatic
punched-card techniques. American Documentation 6:
68-76, April 1955.

Describes production of Current Medical Literature, an
author, subject, item list, produced from IBM punch-
cards. Nothing very exciting but does emphasize the
careful planning necessary for good results.

General Electric Company, Computer Department. An electronic information system for the Library of Congress.
Phoenix, Arizona, General Electric Company, 1959.

Presents an analysis of operations in the Library of
Congress which may be applicable to EDP and requests
a bid from LC to do the work. Divisions particularly
apt to derive good from this application is Card Division

Sales Operations, Legislative Reference Service, Central
charge file and Inquiry stations.

Gibson, R. W. and others.   Prepare your own catalog cards.
Special Libraries 46: 428-33, December 1955.

He says Battelle Institute prints catalog cards with 15%
reduction by Xerox for 1-1/4 cents each vs. 2-1/2 cents
for LC cards.   They are printed in sheets of 8 cards.
Preparation of card material is by typing from process
forms done by the cataloger.

Grubb, C.   How to reduce cataloging costs.   American
Documentation 5:146-54, August 1954.

This article debates the use of various reproduction
methods when LC cards are unavailable or will come
too late.   Discusses multilith, mimeograph and xerog-
raphy vs. typing.   Mentions a catalog process form.

Gull, C. D.   Posting for the Uniterm system of coordinate
indexing.   American Documentation 7:9-21, January 1956.
Shows eight different ways to set up cards for a coordinate index.

Hasting, E. R.   Use of serial shelving numbers in the National Library of Medicine.   Library Resources & Technical Services 3:62-3, Winter 1959.

Illustrates a system of Cutter-like numbers homemade

and expanded to fit the large number of similar titles in
the N. L. of M.   Not adequately explained.

Hensel, E.   Card catalog reproduction.   Journal of Cataloging & Classification 12:209-10, October 1956.
Details the use, operation, volume done, costs and problems of two different libraries for each of three methods
of card reproduction-addressograph-multilith-mimeograph
and one combination method, Xerox and multilith.

Higgins, C. L.   Reference work and recodification.   Journal
of Cataloging & Classification 11:181-5, October 1955.
Reference requirements of the card catalog and an im-
passioned (for a librarian) plea for the status quo.

IBM punched-card accounting is adapted to make scholarly
indexes.   Publishers' Weekly 170:2150-2, November 5,
1956.
Use of IBM tab equipment to sort, alphabetize, etc. pre-
punched cards.   Result: We have a concordance, a
dictionary, a word frequency list, a latin "word-endings"
list, etc.

Jackson, J. B. S.   Loose-leaf printed catalog.   Library
Association Record 57:470-3, December 1955.
Gives reasons for and method of producing a loose leaf,
classified printed (multilithed) catalog for many small
and widely scattered "branch" libraries.   One printed

card is furnished with each book for an author file if
wanted by the branch.   Main has a full author, title,
subject card catalog also.

Johnson, N. W.   Automated catalog card reproduction.
Library Journal 85: 725-6, February 15, 1960.
Discusses the automatic production of sets of catalog
cards using a Friden Flexowriter driven by 2 tape
readers.

Jones, Gardner M.   Electronics in business 1958.   Bureau
of Business and Economic Research.   Michigan State,
Lansing, Michigan.
Covers the EDPM available, the pitfalls surrounding
their use, the value of the system, analysis preceeding
the selection, and the changes in accounting methods and
training needed to cope with these machines.

Keller, A. H.   Flexoline record of serial holdings.   Library
Journal 75:722, April 15, 1950.
News of a punched card drive of a card-a-type for Flexoline entries of serials records for LC.   Collator will
sort, kick out, and interfile entries.

Kingery, R. E.   New library technology.   Library Journal
84:1387-91, May 1, 1959.
Lists new inventions and research likely to aid in automating the library of the future. No blue-sky this.

Loftus, H. E. and A. Kent. Automation in the library; an annotated bibliography. American Documentation 7:110-26, April 1956.

Lubetzky, S. Function of the catalog. College & Research Libraries 17:213-15, May 1956.
Basic statements on the value and purpose of the card catalog. Very good.

Luckett, G. R. Partial library automation with the Flexowriter automatic writing machine. Library Resources & Technical Services 1:207-10, Fall 1957.
Extols the virtues of the Flexowriter in printing catalog cards and doing other jobs around the library. Sounds good.

Luhn, H. P. The Automatic Creation of Literature Abstracts, IBM (Reprint of IBM Journal of research & development 2: April 1958).
Discusses auto indexing and abstracting with use of word frequency and linear position.

Luhn, H.P. The automatic derivation of information retrieval encodements from machine-readable texts. IBM Corporation, Advanced Systems Development Division, 1959.
Discusses briefly problems involved in a common machine language and points out that artificial languages

have the same disadvantages of natural languages. Advocates the use of the keyword-in-context system (KWIC Index) made from either titles or abstracts.

Luhn, H. P. A business intelligence system. Reprinted from IBM Journal of research and development 2:314-9, October 1958.

Explains an automatic system to disseminate information to "action points" of an organization using auto abstracting and auto encoding of documents and the creating of interest profiles for each of the "action points."

Luhn, H. P. Keyword-in-context Index for technical literature. IBM Corporation, Advanced Systems Development Division, 1959.

Explains the criteria used in the selection of titles or abstracts that will be meaningful in a KWIC Index. Also explains in detail the derivation of the bibliographic notation and how to avoid duplication of notation when indexes are cumulated. Contains samples of the KWIC Index and a bibliography both machine produced.

Luhn, H. P. A statistical approach to mechanized encoding and searching of literary information. Reprinted from IBM Journal of research and development, 1:309-17, October 1957.

Uses statistical probability to set up an auto-encoding of

documents with the use of a dictionary of "notions" made up from sample documents and used to later encode the whole gamut of documents in the field of the "dictionary." Points out why present subject approach is inadequate.

MacQuarrie, Mrs. C. O. IBM book catalog. Library Journal 82:603-4, March 1, 1957.

Discusses the problems of organization incurred when they printed a book catalog (or really several catalogs) for their branches. Branch librarians report enthusiasm from staff and patrons alike. Costs of this project not listed.

Maierson, Alvin T. and W. W. Howell. Application of Standard business machine punched-card equipment to metallurgical literature references. American Documentation 4:3-13, Winter 1953.

Explains operation of Western Reserve's project to coordinate index, through use of punched card (IBM) equipment, the ASM Review of Metal Literature. This is the beginning of one of the three systems being proposed for information retrieval today.

Marien, Ray. How to make a paper mountain. Data Processing 2:21, June 1960.

Explains how the efforts of data processing equipment can be wasted by assigning tasks that can be done cheaper and easier by hand.

Melcher, D.   Primer in machine information storage and
retrieval.   Library Journal 85:909-12, March 1, 1960.
Mr. Melcher mentions many marvelous machines.
Meaning: machines mightn't mean much.

Merryman, J. H.   (pseud.)   Tactics and terminology in
information retrieval: a summary of recent work.
College & Research Libraries 19:33-7, January 1958.
Mr. Merryman is obviously related by blood (probably
drawn) to Stephen Potter, although he will not admit it.
Explains, carefully, Chadwick's Law.

Mooers, Calvin N.   Zatocoding applied to mechanical organ-
ization of knowledge.   American Documentation 2:20-32,
Winter 1951.
Covers basic concepts of coding including a list of
"principles" which must apply to any coding system.
Shows how these principles apply in the use of the
Zator cards (a one field marginal punch card).

Mount, E.   Increasing usefulness of card catalogs.   Special
Libraries 48:467, December 1957.
Ideas (little gimmicks) for improving use of catalog
cards.   The only one which seems of potential use is a
colored plastic jacket for reference books rather than
the term "ref" typed on cards to denote location.

Myers, J. E. Automation and what it is and what it is not. Special Libraries 46: 308-13, September 1955.

Examines automation from the point of view of management. States that many jobs will have to be redistributed but more jobs will have to be created building and servicing the machines than will be lost by their use. Contains a good definition of automation.

National Science Foundation. Current research and development in scientific documentation. No. 7. National Science Foundation. Office of Science Information Service, November 1960.

Lists many research projects. Ones of interest are: 1.14, p. 15, 2.4, 2.10, 2.16, 2.20, 2.30, 2.31, 2.32, 2.43, 2.44, 4.1, 4.4, 4.5, 4.10, 4.11, 5.38.

Penalosa, F. Card catalog: a failure in communication. College & Research Libraries 17:483-5, November 1956.

Excellent discussion of the supposed functions of the card catalog vs. what is really used by the patron. Promotes the consideration of 2 catalogs--one for the library staff and bibliographers and one for the public (with annotations prepared by the public service staff).

Perry, James W. Information analysis for machine searching. American Documentation 1:133-139, Summer 1950.

Discusses the language of machines and which factors

can and cannot be converted to "machine talk." Covers
basic concepts only and is applicable to any type of
machine.

Perry, J. W. and others. Machine literature searching:
Machine language: factors underlying its design and
development. American Documentation 6:242-54, October
1955.
Part 10 of a series. Discusses factors to be taken into
account when considering the underlying basis of machine
literature searching (purpose - symbolism - language).

Perry, James W. Superimposed punching of numerical
codes on hand-sorted punch cards. American Documentation 2:205-212, Fall 1951.
Using E-Z Sort cards, Mr. Perry has a system for
punching up to 6 different 5-digit numbers in the edges
of a 4 field marginal punch card. Unwanted cards are
reduced by punching paired sums between rows 1 & 2;
digits row 1 & edge.

Pile, C. Production of bulletin and catalogue entries.
Library Association Record 61:190, August 1959.
Lists experience gained in the production of catalog
cards and lists for the "bulletin" (?) by using multilith.

Plankeel, F. H. Automation in documentation. American
Documentation 11:128-34, April 1960.

Discusses a theoretical scheme for automating a coordinate index. Seems pretty impractical but should probably be considered when the time comes as, like the boy who threw rocks at sea-gulls, we should leave no tern unstoned.

Planning office buildings for automation. Architectural Record 128:220-9, September 1960.

Actually 3 articles concerned with the general problems of EDP architecture. Floor loading, electrical circuits, air conditioning requirement, spacial needs, and how these problems were met in two recent installations are covered.

Poage, S. T. Work sampling in library administration. Library Quarterly 30:213-18, July 1960.

Tells how to do work sampling in the library. Includes formulae for figuring results.

Posner, F. A. Practical side of card reproduction. Illinois Libraries 38:283-7, November 1956.

Lists spirit duplicated, mimeographed, multilithed, photographed and punch-card catalog cards. Information neither recent nor extensive.

Programming: a new profession for you! UNIVAC educational series, No.2. In vocational pamphlet file under Electronic Data Processing.

Shows how computers are programmed starting with
analysis, flow charting (both word and symbolic), coding.
Very basic.

Randall, G. E. Practicality of coordinate indexing. College
& Research Libraries 15:419-20, October 1954.
Mr. Randall states that coordinate indexes and/or UNI-
TERM might save as much as 10% (vs. a claimed 200%
to 300%) space saving, take longer to file, generate too
much noise, etc. in comparison with a standard card
catalog and that, because of these drawbacks, are not
worth the effort involved.

Rather, J. C. Tradition-bound demands on the catalog.
Journal of Cataloging & Classification 11:175-80, October
1955.
A somewhat tedious rehash of the literature (since 1900)
on the use of the card catalog.

Reilly, W. J. Jr. How to avoid those "gadgets." Navy
Management Review 5:10-12, July 1960.
Gives some basic criteria in the selection of machines
for office work. Tells how to tell if you need additional
or new equipment.

Richmond, P. A. A divided catalog then what? American
Documentation 7:315-19, October 1956.
Discusses the problems of catalogs which might be

alleviated by the division of the catalog. While little
argument concerns either the author or title list, the
subject catalog, machine production of it, preliminary
public subject index, Uniterm index are fully discussed.

Ross, H. J. Integrated data processing for every office.
1958. Office Research Institute, Miami, Florida. 80p.
An excellent plea for the adoption of an integrated paper-
work system for every office. Makes the point that
most EDP savings are the result of improved systems
and not the result of the addition of the hardware. 10
points for reducing clerical costs are very pointed.

Shachtman, B. E. Cataloging statistics and standards.
Journal of Cataloging & Classification 12:157-65, July
1956.
The part of this article which may be of value to librarians is that concerning what cataloging department
statistics may be kept (and by whom) which may be
meaningful. Includes a chart of cataloging department
statistics kept by one library and suggestions for possible additions.

Shera, J. H. Effect of machine methods on the organization
of knowledge. American Documentation 3:15-20, Winter
1952.
Thoughts on the eventual reorganization of knowledge

from our present book classification to a knowledge classification and the personnel requirements of librarians for this work.

Simmons, J. R. M. New developments in industrial control. Punched Card Annual of Machine Accounting & Data Processing, v. 6.

Compares data processing and electronic computing by function and intended use. Gives criteria for need of each.

Shera, J. H. New tools for easing the burden of historical research. American Documentation 10:274-7, October 1959.

Excellent general statement on the possible applications and limitations of machines to literature searching. Advises careful inspection of each new item with an open mind for new ideas but a healthy scepticism for proven application.

Spalding, C.S. Keeping serials cataloging costs in check. Library Resources & Technical Services 1:13-20, Winter 1957.

Catchy title but article only discusses the three ways of handling serials (early title, latest title, multiple entry) and a few points on cataloging serials. No decisions made.

Taube, M. and I. S. Washtel. The logical structure of coordinate indexing. American Documentation 4:67-8,
September 1953.

Mathematical basis for combining unit terms in coordinate indexing. Based on Boolian algebra.

Taube, M. Reply to article by Randall, G. E. (College &
Research Libraries 15:417-19, October 1954). College
& Research Libraries 15:419-20, October 1954.

Refutes (or at least, attempts to refute) Mr. Randall's
statements that coordinate indexes and UNITERM are
not worth the effort involved.

Taube, M. and others. Storage and retrieval of information
by means of the association of ideas. American Documentation 6:1-18, January 1955.

Discusses problems concerned with the storage and retrieval of information through the association of ideas.
This is primarily concerned with the logic of this approach.

Taube, M., C. D. Gull and I. S. Wachtel. Unit terms in
coordinate indexing. American Documentation 3:213-18,
Fall 1952.

Explains the Taube system of information retrieval
through the coordinate index based on unit terms derived
from the text of the document being indexed.

Taylor, A. J. Book catalogues: their varieties and uses.
Newberry library, Chicago, Illinois, 1957.
Gives historical backgrounds into printers, publishers,
collectors, booksellers, and library catalogs (book catalogs only). Very interesting but hardly "our cup of
tea."

Vertanes, Charles A. AUTOMATION raps at the door of
the library catalog. Special Libraries 52:237-42, May-
June 1961.
Tells how the Long Island Lighting Company, Hicksville,
New York library printed a book catalog in March 1960
after months of work using a 407 and cards. They distribute about 100 copies throughout the company.

Vickery, Brian C. Some comments on mechanical selection.
American Documentation 2:102-107, Spring 1951.
Mr. Vickery takes a long look at just what machine
methods are reported to do vs. what they are really
capable of doing. Pricks some balloons. End of article contains notes on coding.

Voight, M. J. Trend toward mechanization in libraries.
Library Trends 5:193-205, October 1956.
States (usually quoting Shaw) that we are not to look to
mechanization as the be all of the future of librarianship
but that some interesting things are in store.

Waldo, W. H.   Routine report writing by computer.   American Documentation 9:28-31, January 1958.

Techniques on assembling information and writing a highly technical (limited to chemistry) report from it. Report has all aspects of a finding list (which is its purpose).

Weaver, Warren.   The mathematics of communication. Scientific American 181:11-15, July 1949.

Gives the basic facts dealing with the concept of entropy and information.   This new science (statistics and semantics) is now called cybernetics.

Warren, J. P. and W. M. Barnard.   Cataloging statistics: report on an experiment.   Library Resources & Technical Services 1:67-81, Spring 1957.

A brief relatively meaningless collection of statistics with no conclusions drawn, except the obvious one that libraries do not keep the same statistics the same way.

Weed, K. K.   Tool for management evaluation of library services.   Special Libraries 48:378-82, October 1957.

Advocates the use standard work measurement techniques in a library situation.   Claims that efficiency can be increased and costs reduced when applying these principles.

Wise, Carl S. and Perry, James W.   Multiple coding and
    the rapid selector. American Documentation 1:76-83,
    Spring 1950.
    Coding, using a four field keysort card, up to 16-4
    letter terms. This system uses the rapid selector (an
    optical-electronic device for scanning code on film) to
    pick up the abstract entry.
Woodruff, Mrs. E. L.   Work measurement applied to li-
    braries. Special Libraries 48:139-44, April 1957.
    Outlines the portions of work measurement technique
    which can be applied to library study. Includes sam-
    ples of forms.

INDEX

A

Acme Visible Records, Incorporated, 160

acquisitions
cost analysis, 100-102
flow chart explanations, 84-87
flow charts, 197-213
proposed system, 127-138

Alanar Book Processing, 47-48
work needed in spite of, 48

Alden Electronic and Impulse Recording Equipment Company, 185

American Book Publishing Record see BPR

American Chemical Society, 36, 125

American Library Association, 192

American Library Association, Library Technology project, 8

analytic cards, 95

Annual Periodicals Holdings List see Serials Holdings List

annual reports, 67

aperture card, 182

AVCO Corporation, 182

B

Ball, Howard R., 177

Bell Technical Laboratories, Inc., 36

"bibliographical quotient," 16

"bibliographic string," 122-124, 318-319

bibliography
annotated, 336-388
general, 343-355

binary coding, 176, 179

Birnbaum, Henry, 4

block purchase of books, 87

book, function of, 106

book catalog see catalog

book funds, 84-85, 131

book selection, 49

BPR, 37, 44

Bro-Dart Industries, Inc. see Alanar Book Processing

Brooklyn College, New York, 4

Date Due

Due	Returned	Due	Returned